10632147

Global Interactions in the Early Modern Age, 1400–1800

Global Interactions in the Early Modern Age, 1400–1800, is an inter-disciplinary introduction to cross-cultural encounters in the early modern age (1400–1800) and their influences on the development of world societies. In the aftermath of Mongol expansion across Eurasia, the unprecedented rise of imperial states in the early modern period set in motion interactions between people from around the world. These included new commercial networks, large-scale migration streams, global biological exchanges, and transfers of knowledge across oceans and continents. These in turn wove together the major regions of the world. In an age of extensive cultural, political, military, and economic contact, a host of individuals, companies, tribes, states, and empires were in competition. Yet they also cooperated with one another, leading ultimately to the integration of global space.

Charles H. Parker is Professor of History at St. Louis University. He has published extensively on the religious and cultural history of early modern Europe, with a focus on the Low Countries. His books include *Faith on the Margins: Catholics and Catholicism in the Dutch Golden Age* (2008); *The Reformation of Community: Social Welfare and Calvinist Charity in Holland, 1572–1620* (1998, paperback 2006); and a co-edited volume, *From the Middle Ages to Modernity: Individual and Community in the Early Modern World* (2008). His articles and essays have appeared in the *Journal of World History*, the *Sixteenth Century Journal*, the *Journal of Ecclesiastical History*, the *Journal of Religious History*, and the *Journal of Early Modern History*.

CAMBRIDGE ESSENTIAL HISTORIES

Series Editor

Donald Critchlow, St. Louis University

Cambridge Essential Histories is devoted to introducing critical events, periods, or individuals in history to students. Volumes in this series emphasize narrative as a means of familiarizing students with historical analysis. In this series, leading scholars focus on topics in European, American, Asian, Latin American, Middle Eastern, African, and world history through thesis-driven, concise volumes designed for survey and upper-division undergraduate history courses. The books contain an introduction that acquaints readers with the historical event and reveals the book's thesis; narrative chapters that cover the chronology of the event or problem; and a concluding summary that provides the historical interpretation and analysis.

Titles in the Series

John Earl Haynes and Harvey Klehr, *Early Cold War Spies: The Espionage Trials that Shaped American Politics*

James H. Hutson, *Church and State in America: The First Two Centuries*

Maury Klein, *The Genesis of Industrial America, 1870–1920*

John Lauritz Larson, *The Market Revolution in America: Liberty, Ambition, and the Eclipse of the Common Good*

Global Interactions in the Early Modern Age, 1400–1800

CHARLES H. PARKER

St. Louis University

CAMBRIDGE
UNIVERSITY PRESS

CAMBRIDGE UNIVERSITY PRESS
Cambridge, New York, Melbourne, Madrid, Cape Town,
Singapore, São Paulo, Delhi, Mexico City

Cambridge University Press
32 Avenue of the Americas, New York, NY 10013-2473, USA

www.cambridge.org
Information on this title: www.cambridge.org/9780521688673

© Charles H. Parker 2010

This publication is in copyright. Subject to statutory exception
and to the provisions of relevant collective licensing agreements,
no reproduction of any part may take place without the written
permission of Cambridge University Press.

First published 2010
Reprinted 2012 (twice)

A catalog record for this publication is available from the British Library.

Library of Congress Cataloging in Publication Data

Parker, Charles H., 1958–
Global interactions in the early modern age / Charles H. Parker.
   p.   cm. – (Cambridge essential histories)
Includes bibliographical references and index.
ISBN 978-0-521-86866-2 (hbk.) – ISBN 978-0-521-68867-3 (pbk.)
1. Social history – 16th century.   2. Social history – 17th century.
3. Social history – Medieval, 500–1500.   4. Acculturation – History.
5. Culture and globalization – History.   6. International cooperation – History.
7. World politics – To 1900.   8. International relations – History.
9. Europe – Relations – Asia.   10. Asia – Relations – Europe.   I. Title.   II. Series.
HN13.P37   2010
303.48′20903 – dc22   2010005436

ISBN 978-0-521-86866-2 Hardback
ISBN 978-0-521-68867-3 Paperback

Cambridge University Press has no responsibility for the persistence or accuracy of URLs
for external or third-party Internet Web sites referred to in this publication and does not
guarantee that any content on such Web sites is, or will remain, accurate or appropriate.

In memory of Hugh and Joan McGruer

Contents

Maps

Acknowledgments

A number of people have gained my deep gratitude for their contributions to the making of this book. It is a genuine pleasure to acknowledge them publicly in this format. Don Critchlow, the series editor, first approached me about submitting a proposal to the Cambridge Essential Histories in January 2005. Through the long and winding road to publication, Don provided me with valuable criticism of the manuscript and offered sagacious advice on the review and production processes. Lewis Bateman, senior acquisitions editor at the Press, encouraged me as the project unfolded and displayed patience with me at critical junctures. I am very grateful to Don and Lew for their support; it was a privilege to work with them. Thanks also to David Cox of Cox Cartographic Ltd. for producing the maps.

The Provost's Office at St. Louis University granted me a Summer Research Award in 2006 to travel to Minneapolis to use the James Ford Bell Library at the University of Minnesota. Many thanks to the selection committee and to the curator of the Bell Library, Marguerite Ragnow, for her assistance during my stay.

John Carroll, George Ndege, and James Tracy read the entire manuscript, sometimes more than once, giving me the candid scholarly critique one needs in writing a book. They have made this a better book than it otherwise would have been. Likewise, three anonymous reviewers for Cambridge University Press forced me to rethink basic assumptions about early modern history and pushed me to make the book more global in scope. Others have read portions of the manuscript or listened to my quandaries and offered timely suggestions. These include Toby Benis, Phil Gavitt, Christine Johnson, Georgia Johnston, Sherry Lindquist, Matthew Mancini, Colleen McCluskey, Elisabeth Perry, Judith Pollmann, Allyson Poska, Paul Shore, Annie Smart, Penny Weiss, and Hayrettin Yucesoy. All of these friends and colleagues have my abiding appreciation for their willingness to share their time and their learning with me.

My family listened with forbearance to stories about such things as red seal ships, teeth-breaking rituals, and Mongol military tactics. I am grateful to my wife Jean, my son Drew, and my parents Charles and Dolores Parker for their affection and support. This book is dedicated to the memory of my parents-in-law, Hugh and Joan McGruer, who, despite their misgivings about my academic pursuits, took me in as part of their family.

Global Interactions in the Early Modern Age, 1400–1800

Introduction

The Global Integration of Space

Traditionally, historians have presented the 1400s and 1500s as the "age of discovery," when Europeans began to explore, encounter, and exploit territories in Asia, Africa, and America. Yet research over the past twenty-five years has made it increasingly clear that this age of discovery was rooted in extensive contact among peoples across Eurasia (the land mass comprising Europe and Asia) long before Vasco Da Gama landed off the Malabar coast of India in 1498. No episode better illustrates the extent of these intercontinental connections than a fairly well-known anecdote from the initial encounter between Portuguese and Indian officials in Calicut. According to the story, Da Gama prepared to make contact with native peoples shortly after dropping anchor offshore. Apparently he harbored some apprehension about how a foreign Portuguese mariner might be received, so Da Gama selected a convict on board, João Nunez, to go ashore first to see what would happen. Much to the relief of Nunez, and the surprise of Da Gama, local officials recognized him as someone from Iberia (on the western coast of Europe), perhaps even as Portuguese, and took him to two north Africans who were conversant in Castilian and Genoese, languages in Spain and Italy.

The recognition of Nunez as an Iberian, as well as the presence of Africans familiar with two European languages in India, highlight the cosmopolitan character of Asian commercial centers and the prevalence of long-distance travel long before the period of European expansion. The hundred-year period from roughly 1250 to 1350 was a relatively peaceful one across Asia, so adventurers and missionaries from various parts of Europe, most famously Marco Polo from Venice and William Rubruck, a Franciscan priest from Flanders, traveled as far as Beijing (also known as Peking) and Karakorum (in present-day Mongolia), respectively. Europeans were not the only ones venturing into strange lands, since Arab, Indian, Chinese, Persian, and Turkish peoples joined travelers like Ibn Battuta (a well-known Moroccan explorer) on the Silk Roads; on the Muslim Hajj, the obligatory pilgrimage to Mecca; and on ships in the Indian Ocean. As a result, Indians and Africans in Calicut had already discovered European peoples before Vasco Da Gama arrived at the end of the fifteenth century.

Just as the 1400s and 1500s were not exactly the paramount age of European discovery (at least of Asia), they were also not simply the era of European expansion throughout the world. To be sure, Spanish, Portuguese, Dutch, English, French, German, Swedish, and Danish officers carved out overseas outposts and colonies from the 1400s to the 1700s. But these European countries were by no means the only empire builders, for a number of Asian states established political control over much more vast tracts of land during this time. Three expansive and prosperous Muslim empires rose, sprawling across north Africa, eastern Europe, and western and central Asia all the way from Anatolia (present-day Turkey) to the Ganges River basin (today Bangladesh). The Ottoman, Safavid, and Mughal Empires all emerged in the 1400s and 1500s, promoting the revival of Islam; the intermingling of Arab, Turkish, and Persian cultures; and the expansion of regional and long-distance trade networks across these immense territories.

On the eastern end of the continent, a vigorous dynasty arose in China; in the mid-1300s, it was the most powerful empire in the world. The Ming (1368–1644) and later the Qing (1644–1911) dynasties rebuilt the economic infrastructure in east Asia and expanded broadly across central Asia into Mongolia, Turkestan, and Tibet. In the extreme north, Russian emperors created an immense north Asian empire, spanning the frozen tundra of Siberia all the way to the Pacific Ocean. The subjugation of Siberia and the exploitation of its vast resources enabled emperors to construct a highly centralized state that made it a forceful presence in Asian and European geopolitical affairs. This empire brought Russian merchants into contact with English, Dutch, Turkish, Iranian, Armenian, Indian, and Chinese traders. Indeed, this was a time of global expansion.

This unprecedented empire building across Eurasia inaugurated a new era in world history characterized by cross-cultural interaction among peoples from around the globe. Historians refer to this age, extending from roughly around 1400 to 1800, as the early modern period. Though peoples from Africa, Asia, and Europe had engaged one another intermittently since ancient times, early modern cross-cultural exchange was distinctive in its worldwide scale and its ongoing regularity. Global interactions in the early modern period also had far-reaching ramifications, leading to foundational shifts in economic structures and political power relations on every continent.

Early modern interaction was distinctive, also standing out from later, modern patterns that emerged in the 1800s with the advent of industrialization. The Industrial Revolution equipped western nations with the technical capacities that enabled a handful of European countries, and later Japan and the United States, to dominate world affairs in the nineteenth and twentieth centuries. In this age of imperialism, these powers heavy-handedly imposed direct colonial rule or introduced a more veiled political control over almost all the surface area of the globe. Despite all of the violent subjugation that occurred in early modern times, no region stood at the apex of world dominion.

This book illustrates the unique character of cross-cultural encounters in the early modern age and their influences on the development of world societies. The emergence of powerful empires around the world set in motion processes of exchange that reached across all continents except Antarctica. Empire building in this period established four central forms of interaction: new commercial exchange networks, large-scale migration streams, worldwide biological exchanges, and transfers of knowledge across oceans and continents. This was a period in world history characterized by intense cultural, political, military, and economic contact, yet all this interaction was not the story of one region dominating all the rest. Rather a host of individuals, companies, tribes, states, and empires clashed and competed – but also cooperated with one another – bringing regions of the world into sustained contact and leading ultimately to the integration of global space.

Global Empire Building

Why did so many empires develop throughout Eurasia in the 1400s and 1500s?

Even though a host of immediate factors specific to particular regions contributed to the development of these empires, from a long-term perspective the episode that linked them all was the rise and fall of the Mongols in the 1200s and 1300s. During this time, this nomadic people from western Mongolia under the charismatic leadership of Chinggis Khan (Genghis Khan), conquered and subjugated vast regions of Asia. The Mongol empire in its heyday in the late 1200s stretched all the way from the Mediterranean Sea to the Sea of Japan. To the north, one branch of the Mongols, the Golden Horde, controlled Russia by reducing it to a vassal state. This was the largest empire in world history, comprising one third of the land area of the globe.

Mongols were fierce fighters, showing no mercy to those who resisted their demands, and brilliant tacticians, coordinating complex battlefield maneuvers. The secret to their success, however, lay in their unsurpassed horsemanship. Bred for speed, stamina, and sturdiness, Mongolian horses could cover a hundred miles in a day. On a long campaign, a Mongol warrior could subsist for over a week on the milk from a mare and the blood of his mount, obtained by cutting open a vein in the steed's neck and stitching it together after use. Opposing armies across Eurasia proved no match for the dexterity and the aggressiveness of Mongol forces. After conquering a defiant city, warriors laid waste to it, taking away women and children, and slaughtering all the men. Despite this brutality, once Mongol hordes had conquered a region, they promoted trade, diplomacy, and travel. Mongol rulers from China to Persia encouraged travel and welcomed foreign merchants, emissaries, and even missionaries, thus opening cities across Asia to international exchange.

When the empires established by Chinggis Khan and his successors began to break apart in the mid- to late 1300s, a powerful Turkish leader, Timurlane, invaded and wreaked havoc on Mongol territories from the Black Sea to the Indus River. Thus, the broad region including eastern Anatolia, Persia, Afghanistan, Armenia, Azerbaijan, and Uzbeck, fell under the control of Timurid dynasties, so named for

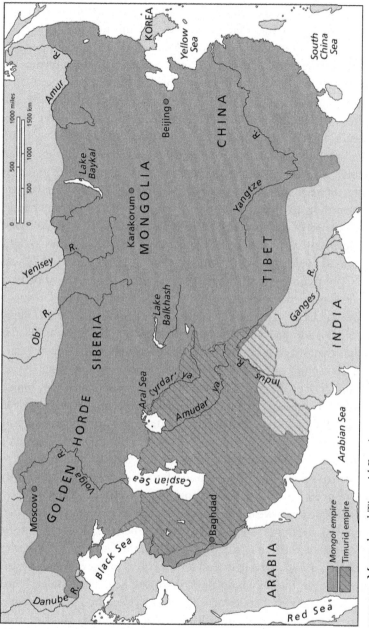

MAP 1.1. Mongol and Timurid Empires

5

Timurlane and his descendants. Just as the spread of Mongol empires bred all sorts of interaction, the decline of Timurid empires exerted a powerful pull on expansion-minded Asian dynasties.

How did these Mongol and Timurid empires play such a pivotal role in the emergence of Eurasian states, which eventually produced a new pattern of global exchange in the early modern period? The Muslim empires (Ottoman, Safavid, and Mughal) that came to power in central and south Asia grew directly in response to weak Mongol-Timurid regimes. Mongol incursions in central Asia pushed the Ottomans into Anatolia where they found a home on the borders of the Byzantine empire, a Greek and Christian realm centered at Constantinople. After the demise of the Mongols in the 1300s, Ottoman sultans expanded at the expense of Byzantine and Mongol-Timurid territories. Likewise, the decentralized character of the Timurid dynasty in Iran enabled the Safavid dynasty, a Shi'ite Muslim clan in Ajerbaijan, to rally warriors to take control of the region. The Ottoman and Safavid regimes, therefore, formed successor states to Mongol-Timurid rule.

The Mughals, however, represented the continuation of a Mongol-Timurid kingdom, since Timurlane conquered Delhi in 1398. The Mughal dynasty that conquered large portions of India in the early sixteenth century came from Mongol and Timurid ethnic stock. Babur, the founder of the Mughal Empire, claimed descent from both Chinggis Khan and Timurlane, and thus regarded northern India as part of his heritage. Babur distributed the top military and administrative posts to Mongols and Timurids who accompanied him in India. "Mughal," which means Mongol, denotes this nomadic warrior lineage.

The expansion of both Russia and China across northern and central Asia, respectively, also resulted from the presence of Mongol power and its subsequent weakening in the 1400s and 1500s. Russian tsars (emperors) saw opportunities for conquest when the Mongol territories broke apart in the late 1400s. In the 1230s, the Golden Horde pushed into Russia and decisively defeated the princes of Kiev, the most powerful figures in the region north of the Black Sea. The Golden Horde made Russia a vassal state for well over two hundred years, exacting tribute from princes and cities. Russian lords regularly trekked to the Horde's headquarters in Saray, bearing all sorts of goods to their overlords. Should Russian leaders fail to meet these obligations, the Horde would exact revenge by raping, pillaging, and terrorizing local peoples.

After the Golden Horde went into decline in the 1400s, the Grand Prince of Moscow declared independence in 1480. As the Mongol states crumbled, Tatars (Mongol and Turkic peoples some of whom had belonged to the Golden Horde) came to rule over a patchwork of territories to the east in Kazan, western Siberia, and Kazakhstan. Russian tsars in the 1500s seized the opportunity to enlarge their holdings in the east at the expense of these Tatar territories.

After throwing off Mongol rule in 1368, the Ming dynasty in China turned its attention to the west, where Mongols and other groups posed a threat to Chinese society. The Chinese state extended the Great Wall of China in the north, negotiated with tribal leaders, and eventually embarked on a long campaign to subdue its enemies. This struggle against Mongol tribes led to the Chinese conquest of central Asia in the 1600s and 1700s. By the close of the early modern period, the Qing dynasty controlled an imperial expanse that extended across Mongolia, Manchuria, Turkestan, and Tibet. The move toward the central Asian plain was an important factor in the growth of Chinese hegemony from the South China Sea to the Himalayas. As a result of imperial expansion into the central Asian land mass, China did not pursue an empire in southeast Asia or the Indian Ocean. The government in fact turned away from maritime Asia, seeking to limit contacts between Chinese merchants on the southern coasts and foreign traders.

On the far western end of Eurasia, Europe too felt the impact of Mongol empires. Mongol rulers encouraged travel and trade, giving a variety of Europeans the opportunity to encounter the wonders of Asian lands. Many travelers composed accounts of their experiences, and these narratives found a ready market among urban elites, aristocrats, and churchmen. Merchants, missionaries and diplomats such as Marco Polo, Giovanni di Piano Carpini, Odoric of Pordenone, William Rubruck, and John of Marignolli wrote about the places they visited, which circulated widely across Europe.

In many instances, the tales told by travel accounts were tall ones, and we should not regard them as faithful reports of facts. *The Travels of Sir John de Mandeville*, for example, describes monsters in Egypt who have the torso of a man, but the abdomen and legs of a goat. And on islands in southeast Asia, different peoples have either ears that hang to their knees, or small holes for mouths, or no heads, or horse feet, or possess both female and male sexual organs. Some scholars doubt that the most famous account, *The Travels of Marco Polo*, describes the Venetian merchant's actual experiences, but instead reflects his awareness of the profit in a good story. Polo's account also came with tales of dog-faced men and all sorts of exotic women. Regardless, *The Travels of Marco Polo* attracted wide popularity, firing the imagination of merchants, missionaries, princes, and popes. These embellished travel narratives exerted a powerful pull on Europeans' imaginations and propelled them on a quest to find more efficient routes to the lands of the great Khan. In fact, Christopher Columbus had in his possession a copy of *The Travels of Marco Polo* when he ventured out into the Atlantic in 1492.

Thus, the appearance of the Mongol and Timurid empires from the 1200s to the 1400s made central Asia the epicenter of a dynamic movement of peoples that rippled across Eurasia. The rise and fall of this great empire prompted four critical Eurasian developments: the establishment of extensive Muslim empires from the Mediterranean Sea to the Ganges River basin; the Russian conquest of Siberia to the Pacific Ocean; the inland, western push of the Ming and Qing dynasties; and the European voyages of exploration. These four events fueled the exchanges that integrated the civilizations of the world in time and space.

Before embarking on the journey of exploration into this fascinating period, it is important to consider several concepts and problems that have figured into the study of the early modern period. For even though the story of global interaction might seem like a fairly straightforward affair, scholars disagree on a range of issues that influence general interpretations about the period.

Problems and Possibilities in Early Modern World History

Analyzing societies from a genuinely global framework presents a number of difficulties for scholars. The professional study of history developed first in Europe and the United States from the mid-1800s to the early 1900s, a time when Europe dominated world affairs and when an aggressive nationalism gripped western nations. It is not surprising, then, that history books and articles, written by European and American historians, either explicitly portrayed western culture as the highest expression of human achievement or tacitly assumed the superiority of western values. In addition, histories cast Europeans and Americans as forward-moving, dynamic agents of change, whereas non-western societies were passive and nonchanging, always responding to western incursions and initiatives. Until the last forty years or so, a fairly brief period in the development of historical research, these assumptions underlay much of western scholarship. As a result, western institutions and value systems became the standard models by which scholars evaluated the rest of the world. Historians became absorbed with questions associated with the rise of the West and the attendant failure of African and Asian societies to industrialize and develop democratic forms of government. Despite a wide variety of perspectives, most explanations emphasized that European (and by extension North American) culture was exceptional in important ways. Whether more disciplined, more industrious, more inventive, more acquisitive, or simply more predatory, Europeans had something that other peoples did not possess.

Beginning in the 1960s, a number of scholars began to contest the notion of European exceptionalism. This occurred as history departments around the world started to increase the number of their faculty significantly, offer graduate programs in a wide variety of non-European regions, and stress the utility of social science disciplines, especially sociology and anthropology. Consequently, academically trained historians in non-western fields began to expose the depth of "Eurocentric" assumptions about the past and to challenge them. For example, Marshall Hodgson, a historian of Islam at the University of Chicago, disputed the idea that Europeans possessed any superior cultural disposition, but argued that most achievements attributed to Europe actually originated much earlier in the eastern hemisphere. He pointed out that most historical accounts at the time (he wrote in the 1950s and 1960s) glossed over the cultural achievements of Asian societies and the extent to which they influenced European history. Rather, traditional historical writing presented world history as a narrative about the inevitable rise of western civilization over Asia, Africa, and America, whose insularity bound them to outmoded patterns of thought. Further, Hodgson argued that studying civilizations, whether western or eastern (i.e. Asia), in isolation from one another unavoidably laid stress on essential, unique traits of that society at the expense of all others who were categorically different and foreign.

A conviction that informs newer methods today is the need to study peoples and societies from around the world in relation to one another. This global perspective has helped us move past short-sighted interpretations that treat civilizations as self-contained categories. One method that scholars have used to ground their analyses in the values of diverse cultures is comparative study of similar patterns in different parts of the world. For example, Victor Lieberman has compared parallel political, institutional, and economic developments at various ends of Eurasia: Japan, Burma, Siam, Vietnam, France, and Russia. Having identified striking resemblances in territorial consolidation, political integration, and military innovation, Lieberman observes that "commercial, communications, and patronage circuits" across Eurasia were leading to "more sustained interaction" among different peoples. Intense research in non-western areas has complemented long-range comparative studies and has shown that economic vitality in east Asia paralleled European levels and illustrated that "urban and commercial vigor, trends toward political absolutism, emphases on orthodox, textual religions" were just as much a feature of Asian societies as they were European ones. Anthony Reid in particular has drawn attention to the economic and political dynamism throughout southeast Asia from 1450 to 1630.

Another fruitful strategy for pursuing a more balanced global approach has come from scholars who focus on points of contact between different societies. Jerry Bentley has championed the study of cross-cultural processes, like trade, mass migration, and imperial expansion, to understand the development of societies across space and time. From this perspective, the external interaction of groups, such as the Portuguese and Kongolese, the Chinese and Japanese, or the Indian and Arab, plays a vital role in the internal changes that take place in a society. In a period of intense exchange, the examination of the interconnections between peoples offers a means to relate local developments to global movements.

It is from this vantage point of contact and interconnection that the idea of an early modern world makes the most sense. The "early modern" periodization comes directly out of European history, as scholars over the past thirty years have used this terminology to refer to the era from the Renaissance to the Industrial Revolution. Since the late 1980s or early 1990s, historians have also applied "early modern" to other parts of the world for the period from roughly 1400 to 1800. It has become commonplace, for example, to substitute "early modern China" for "Ming and Qing China" or "early modern India" for "Mughal India." Despite its European pedigree, this periodization does not impute western characteristics across the globe or make Eurocentric judgments about non-western lands. In fact, "early modern" implies just the opposite. For when applied to world history, the term connotes a set of global processes, described by the historian John Richards, as the creation of global sea passages, the emergence of a world economy, the growth of centralized states, the rise of world populations, the intensification of agriculture, and the spread of new technology. Thus, "early modern" provides a comprehensive framework to study world history from the aftermath of the Mongol-Timurid empires to industrialization.

This present study takes the early modern world as its focus and leans heavily on recent research that has pointed the way to more evenhanded, objective approaches. *Global Interactions in the Early Modern Age, 1400–1800* considers early modern peoples on their own terms rather than from modern perspectives, realizing that all societies actively made choices in keeping with their own priorities, which connected global processes to local circumstances. The central argument running through *Global Interactions* is that the extraordinary rise of powerful empires inaugurated a series of sustained interactions that brought societies around the world into interdependent relationships. With these perspectives in mind, the following six chapters examine the most wide-reaching forms of interaction that grew out of early modern empire building in Europe and Asia: long-distance trade, migration, biological exchange, and globalization of knowledge. From there, the concluding chapter discusses the effects of these exchanges on the various regions of the world.

Works Consulted

Bentley, Jerry H. "Cross Cultural Interaction and Periodization in World History," *American Historical Review* 101(1996), 749–770.

———. "Early Modern Europe and the Early Modern World," in Charles H. Parker and Jerry H. Bentley eds. *Between the Middle Ages and Modernity: Individual and Community in the Early Modern World.* Lanham, Md.: Rowman & Littlefield Publishers, 2007, 13–32.

Blaut, J. M. *The Colonizer's Model of the World: Geographical Diffusionism and Eurocentric History*. New York: Guilford Press, 1993.

Coleman, E. C. *The Travels of Sir John Mandeville*. Stroud: Nonsuch, 2006.

Darwin, John. *After Tamerlane: The Global History of Empire since 1945*. New York: Bloomsbury Press, 2008.

Dunn, Ross E. *The Adventures of Ibn Battuta: A Muslim Traveler of the 14th Century*. Berkeley: University of California Press, 2005.

Frank, Andrew Gunder. *ReOrient: Global Economy in the Asian Age*. Berkeley: University of California Press, 1998.

Goldstone, Jack A. "Whose Measure of Reality?" *American Historical Review* 105(2000), 501–508.

Hodgson, Marshall G. S. *Rethinking World History: Essays on Europe, Islam, and World History*. Cambridge: Cambridge University Press, 1993.

Larner, John. *Marco Polo and the Discovery of the World*. New Haven, Conn.: Yale University Press, 1999.

Lieberman, Victor. "Introduction," and "Transcending East-West Dichotomies: State and Culture Formation in Six Ostensibly Disparate Areas," in Victor Lieberman ed. *Beyond Binary Histories: Reimagining Eurasia to c. 1830*. Ann Arbor: University of Michigan Press, 1999, 1–18, 19–102.

Mancall, Peter C. ed. *Travel Narratives from the Age of Discovery: An Anthology*. Oxford: Oxford University Press, 2006.

Phillips, Seymour. "The Outer World of the European Middle Ages," in Stuart B. Schwartz ed. *Implicit Understandings: Observing, Reporting, and Reflecting on the Encounters between Europeans and Other Peoples in the Early Modern Era*. Cambridge: Cambridge University Press, 1994, 23–63.

Ravenstein, E. G. ed. *A Journal of the First Voyage of Vasco Da Gama, 1497–1499*. New York: Burt Franklin Publishers, 1963.

Richards, John F. "Early Modern India and World History," *Journal of World History* 8(1997), 197–209.

Silva, Chandra Richard de. "Beyond the Cape: The Portuguese Encounter with the People of South Asia," in Stuart B. Schwartz ed. *Implicit Understandings: Observing, Reporting, and Reflecting on the Encounters between Europeans and Other Peoples in the Early Modern Era*. Cambridge: Cambridge University Press, 1994, 295–322.

Wood, Frances. *Did Marco Polo Go to China?* Boulder, Colo.: Westview Press, 1996.

I

European States and Overseas Empires

In 1684, Philippe Couplet, a Jesuit missionary, gained an audience with the French king, Louis XIV, at his court in Versailles to ask for financial support for the Christian mission to China. To illustrate the potential of the Chinese mission, Couplet introduced Louis to Shen Fuzong, a youthful convert to Christianity preparing for the priesthood. Shen, whose baptized name was Michael Alphonse, demonstrated the use of chopsticks to the enchanted king. The gifts stoked Louis's interest in Chinese culture and his admiration for the renowned Kangxi emperor. Shortly thereafter, the French king authorized a delegation of Jesuit scientists for service in the imperial court, spawning a rich cultural exchange between France and China that has lasted into modern times.

For Europe's most powerful monarch, the Qing dynasty under the Kangxi emperor (r. 1661–1722) represented an ideal political order. The emperor wielded absolute power and enjoyed divine blessing; he employed an army of civil servants to govern his dominions; he possessed authority over a vast domain stretching from the eastern coastline to Outer Mongolia and Tibet; and he resided in a magnificent palace that exuded majestic order and power. In many respects, Louis's reign (1643–1715) also embodied these characteristics, though on a less grand scale. Casting himself in the image of Apollo (the Greek god of light and sun), Louis promoted himself as the Sun King and he professed to rule by divine right; he dominated Europe and pushed France's borders to their farthest point; and he too presided over an elaborate court life at Versailles that reflected his prestige and authority. The Kangxi emperor and the Sun King, on opposite ends of Eurasia, were cut from the same cloth.

Though Louis and Kangxi might have been the most powerful political figures in their own parts of the world, they were not alone in wielding absolute authority. For the late 1600s and early 1700s witnessed the rise of mighty monarchs in other parts of the world, such as the Russian tsar, Peter the Great (r. 1682–1725), and the Mughal emperor, Aurangezeb (r. 1658–1707). These and other rulers in Asia, Europe, and Africa directed governments that were becoming increasingly centralized and bureaucratic, possessing sole authority to administer laws and collect revenues in their realms. This centralization of political authority marked an important shift away from an earlier era in which royal power was offset by warring aristocrats, tribesmen, and warlords.

A number of these centralized governments launched empires that functioned as the primary agents of the economic, cultural, and biological interactions across the early modern world. Powerful states led by royal executive figures – kings, sultans, shahs, or emperors – determined policy, provided patronage, unleashed military force, and enforced legal codes, which enabled merchants, migrants, and missionaries to seek their fortunes in foreign lands. At the same time, the growth in trade, exploitation of resources, expansion of migration, and spread of religious ideas also advanced the interests of the states that directed extensive empires around the world.

Several major imperial states in particular drove the processes of interaction in the world: European overseas colonial dominions, Muslim regimes (Ottoman, Safavid, and Mughal) in western Asia and northern Africa, China and its Asian territories, and Russia and its grand stretch across eastern Europe and Siberia. Other important empires also existed, namely the Inca in Peru and the Aztec (Mexican) in Central America, while several smaller regimes flourished in Africa: the Caliphate of Sokota, and the Bugunda, Oyo, Asante, and Rozwi Empires. These states were important; however, they did not foster the kind of global cross-cultural interactions and engagements that the Eurasian empires did. Since our purpose is to understand worldwide exchange, it is useful to focus attention on the Eurasian regimes. This chapter will discuss the development of maritime European empires, and the next chapter will examine the large territorial empires of Asia.

The Formation of States in Europe

European overseas empires grew out of a remarkable expansion of state power from the 1400s to the 1700s. The growth of powerful sovereign states stemmed from two developments that occurred throughout Europe. First, in a time of endemic war and religious strife, monarchs and governmental ministers managed to subdue the two longstanding impediments to royal authority, the church and the nobility. Second, major innovations in the construction of armies and navies put powerful weapons at the disposal of European states.

Bitter theological disputes in the Reformation between Catholics and Protestants turned into warfare that lasted almost a century, from the 1560s to the 1640s. Bloody wars took place in France, Germany, England, central Europe, and the Netherlands. The most gruesome episode, known as the St. Bartholomew's Day Massacre, happened in France in August 1572. On the order of King Charles IX, French soldiers murdered Protestant leaders in Paris at night as they slept. When Catholic Parisians learned what was going on, they joined in the blood sport, beating, shooting, hanging, and drowning their Protestant neighbors. Violence spread out from Paris into the countryside, as thousands perished.

By the time the blood had dried across Europe in the mid-1600s, the breach between Protestants and Catholics was permanent. Territorial churches emerged with close links between political and ecclesiastical authorities. The typical arrangement was for the ruler of a state to determine the religion for the realm (either Catholic or a Protestant variety), and the laws of the state required, or strongly encouraged, all subjects to practice that religion. This pattern allowed the ruler in each country to exercise considerable authority over the church and its clergy. Rulers gained the right either to make or approve all appointments to important ecclesiastical offices and demanded political allegiance from church leaders.

At the same time, royal governments also greatly restricted the traditional independence of the aristocracy. Noble factions initiated or enthusiastically participated in religious civil wars in many parts of Europe. Monarchs had always schemed to subdue fractious nobles, but in the second half of the 1600s, this royal agenda gained broad support from populations weary of civil unrest. Royal officers like

Cardinal Richelieu (1585–1642) in France and Count-Duke of Olivares in Spain (1587–1645) cracked down on nobles who raised their own armies, created streamlined bureaucracies, and displayed little tolerance for disloyalty. Richelieu dispatched royal armies to destroy the castles of independent-minded nobles who defied the king. In most cases though, nobles were not suppressed as much as they were coaxed into line. Nobles enjoyed a wide range of social and economic privileges, including tax exemptions, and served in various capacities for king, queen, or emperor. In return, they surrendered political independence.

The ability to field and deploy effective military forces gave states undisputed power at home and offered great advantages overseas. The leading European states – England, the Netherlands, France, Prussia, Spain, and Austria – underwent a transformation in military capacity, referred to by many scholars as the "military revolution." While historians debate the timing and the scope of these changes, it is clear that enhancements in fortifications, firepower, and troop size provided armies and navies far more lethal capability than what had been present in medieval warfare. The construction of more formidable defensive fortifications, notably the star shape design and low thick walls of the "trace italienne," made the quest for more powerful weaponry necessary. Consequently, military technicians utilized improved metallurgy to produce increasingly larger cannons and more effective muskets. Shipbuilders applied this technology, outfitting ships with dozens of high-caliber cannons. Governments recruited huge numbers of men to infantry and artillery service, drilling them for untold hours to instill battlefield discipline and obedience to commanding officers. Armies in the early 1600s numbered in the hundreds of thousands. The size of the Spanish army at this time was approximately 150,000 troops, while Louis XIV of France fielded an army of 395,000 in 1696 and 650,000 in 1713. Many of these developments came out of previous advances in the late middle ages, yet they came together in a comprehensive way to support a sprawling military industrial complex.

The expansion of military capability required an enormous amount of capital to pay for the ships, forts, guns, training complexes, hospitals, and soldiers. Raising revenue at this scale through taxation and debt financing, as well as collecting, accounting, and disbursing the funds, entailed the building of a sizable bureaucracy. For example,

Spain spent four million florins in wars against France in the 1550s and expended nine million florins per year fighting against the Dutch (the Netherlands), English, and French in the 1590s. Thus, by the end of the 1600s, state structures that equipped governments with vast revenues, large administrative staffs, and powerful armies had emerged in Europe.

From a broad Eurasian perspective, state formation in Europe had a distinctive character. There emerged a cluster of independent powers that competed and fought with one another, rather than a single overarching regime as was the case in China, Russia, Anatolia, Iran, and India. The clustering of states fostered conflict, as European powers since the middle ages regularly clashed over territory and access to trade. In 1204, for example, the powerful city-state of Venice redirected crusader forces called by the pope to assault Constantinople, a chief commercial rival of the Italian city. The Venetians convinced the crusaders to attack Constantinople rather than Muslim armies in Palestine. Transported by Venetian ships, the crusaders sacked Constantinople, thereby giving Venice control over trade in the Mediterranean. Thus, war for the sake of commerce had a long history among the constellation of competing states in Europe. As Europeans ventured overseas in search of trade and land, this warrior ethos made it natural for merchants and mariners to wage war against one another and indigenous peoples. Competition among European states made them effective and aggressive at empire building overseas.

Competition among countries compelled governments to ally with an assortment of economic elites – merchants, commercial firms, lending institutions, and investors – to finance directives and policies. This alliance between business and government formed an essential characteristic of overseas colonial and commercial operations. A range of economic theorists, such as Jean Baptiste Colbert (1619–1653) in France and Thomas Mun (1571–1641) in England, known later as mercantilists, advocated developing the productive capacities of overseas colonies to support a country's economic growth. Mercantilists contended that states should take the leading role in managing commercial activity by establishing policies to maximize exports while minimizing imports. From a mercantilist perspective, the sole purpose of commerce was to expand national wealth, measured by the amount of gold and silver bullion in the government's treasury.

As countries established trading posts and colonies in Asia, Africa, and America, governments pursued mercantilist policies aimed at controlling commerce in the interests of the home country. The English Parliament, for example, passed Navigation Acts in the 1650s and 1660s that prohibited colonial merchants from doing business with non-English parties. Mercantilism illustrates the central role states played in promoting trade and building maritime empires. State building, imperial expansion, and overseas commercial ventures reinforced one another, as economic elites joined forces with monarchs, ministers of state, and legislative bodies in undertaking colonial ventures.

Maritime Empires in Asia

European empire building took root in two major ocean basins, the Indian and Atlantic. Along the extraordinarily diverse coastlines of the Indian Ocean, Portuguese and Spanish mariners set up fortified trading posts in the 1500s; the Dutch, English, and French followed suit in the 1600s and 1700s. Denmark also established several outposts in India from the 1620s onward. The basic purpose behind all European imperial enterprises in Asia and the African east coast was to control as much of the lucrative trade in spices and luxury items as possible. In the Atlantic, by contrast, European powers pursued a land-based strategy devoted to extracting riches from the earth and producing highly profitable commodity crops, such as sugar, cotton, and tobacco. Spain and Portugal established bases in the Caribbean and Central and South America in the 1500s; northern Europeans began to appear in the 1600s primarily in the Caribbean and North America. In addition, Portugal, the Netherlands, France, Spain, England, Denmark, and Sweden set up sites on the western coast of Africa largely for procuring slaves. In time, the American colonies became home to millions of European settlers and African slaves.

Unlike Asian empires, European imperial endeavors occurred a remarkable distance from their homelands. Atlantic crossings to America took several months, and voyages from England to India averaged around eight months, requiring at least eighteen months to complete a circuit of communication between homeland and colony. The distance between Amsterdam and Batavia (today Jakarta), the Dutch East India Company headquarters in Asia, extended 13,500 nautical miles.

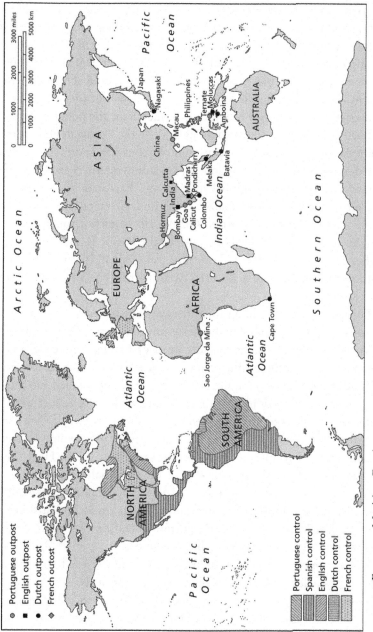

Legend (point markers):
- Portuguese outpost
- English outpost
- Dutch outpost
- French outost

Legend (control areas):
- Portuguese control
- Spanish control
- English control
- Dutch control
- French control

Scale:
0 1000 2000 3000 miles
0 1000 2000 3000 4000 5000 km

Map labels:

Arctic Ocean

EUROPE

ASIA

Japan
Nagasaki
Macau
China
Philippines
Ternate
Moluccas
Amboina
Batavia
Melaka
Colombo
Pondicherry
Madras
Calcutta
India
Calicut
Goa
Bombay
Hormuz

AUSTRALIA

Pacific Ocean

Indian Ocean

AFRICA

Sao Jorge da Mina

Cape Town

Southern Ocean

Atlantic Ocean

NORTH AMERICA

SOUTH AMERICA

Pacific Ocean

Atlantic Ocean

MAP 1.1. European Maritime Empires

In order to conduct trade and maintain communication on a regular basis, as well as to carry out naval operations, European countries and merchant companies constructed and launched an enormous number of ships into the Atlantic and Indian Oceans. The Dutch East India Company, for example, kept more than one hundred ships in operation in Asian waters in the mid-1600s. By the end of the century, the Netherlands boasted over four thousand merchant and military ships in service. Thousands of ships from England, Spain, Portugal, France, the Netherlands, and other European countries connected ports around the world in the early modern period. As a result, westerners served as the primary transmitters of global interaction. The Spanish, for example, introduced American maize (corn) and sweet potatoes to Asia in the 1500s. Europeans carried Old World strains of smallpox and measles to America in the 1500s and to the Pacific islands (Oceania) in the1700s. And, European slave ships transported Africans and their cultures to a new world across the Atlantic from the 1500s well into the 1800s.

European empire building got underway long before Da Gama came ashore in Calicut in 1498. On the westernmost end of the Eurasian land mass, Portuguese mariners had dreamed of finding a much quicker all-water route to the trading centers in Asia since the 1300s. Portugal's advantageous geography and barren landscape added incentive to maritime exploration. Out of crusading zeal, King João (John) I and his sons attacked and captured the Muslim port city of Ceuta on the Moroccan coast in 1415. After the conquest, John's youngest son, Infante Dom Henrique (more famously known as Prince Henry the Navigator), learned about the riches of the trans-Saharan gold trade. Henry subsequently became consumed with tapping into African gold, as well finding a more efficient route to Asian spices and striking a blow against Muslim empires. He promoted maritime navigation into the Atlantic and exploration of the African coast.

In their forays out into the Atlantic, the Portuguese had to overcome several obstacles in order to make their way down the African coast and around its southern tip. Through trial and error, shipbuilding specialists working for the Portuguese crown were able to construct a vessel that could withstand the powerful currents of the Atlantic and to sail against the wind, critical to navigating the fixed wind pattern in the Atlantic. Unlike wind patterns in the Indian Ocean, which reverse course seasonally, the winds in the Atlantic always move in the same direction. Consequently, sailors had to be able to sail against the wind to return home. The caravel, produced around the mid 1400s, was a light (seventy feet long, weighing between fifty and one hundred tons) and swift vessel that brought together many technological components from ship construction in the Mediterranean and in Asia. Caravels combined square-rigged sails with lateen (triangular) ones, allowing mariners to navigate against the wind, and utilized a stern-post rudder, providing greater steering precision. To orient sailing vessels beyond sight of land, mariners required navigational equipment, such as the compass, astrolabe, sextant, back staff, and cross staff that Europeans adopted from Arab, Persian, and Chinese technology. Finally, wherever Portuguese ships went, technicians mapped the earth's surface, observed wind patterns, and recorded sea currents, which enabled them to amass a body of practical navigational information. This knowledge of earth, wind, and sea proved indispensable in charting navigable routes and returning home safely.

After rounding the African cape and making their way into the Indian Ocean, Da Gama and his successors moved quickly to try to wrest the spice trade away from all rivals. In 1499, Da Gama claimed the entire Indian Ocean for the king of Portugal, after discovering that Asian powers considered the seas outside of any political jurisdiction. King Manoel (Manuel) I also proclaimed himself "Lord of the conquest, navigation, and commerce of Ethiopia, Arabia, Persia, and India."[1] The papacy had already sanctioned Portuguese empire building and Christianizing in Asia in the Treaty of Tordesillas (1494). In this treaty, Pope Alexander VI divided the newly discovered lands between Spain and Portugal, decreeing a north–south border three hundred leagues west of the Cape Verde Islands in the Atlantic Ocean. In an attempt to prevent conflict between the Christian powers, Tordesillas allotted the Portuguese all lands east of the boundary and Spain all lands lying west.

Portuguese commanders used military power to enforce their imperial claims. In the first half of the sixteenth century, commanders blasted away at coastal towns to bring strategic areas under Portuguese control. The able and ruthless governor, Afonso de Albuquerque, established the foundation for operations in Asia by capturing Goa (India) in 1510, Melaka (also Malacca in Malaya, today Malaysia) in

1511, and Hormuz (Persian Gulf) in 1515. In some instances, the display of military force had little to do with imperial strategy. In 1502, for example, Vasco Da Gama's crew sank a ship off the coast of India filled with Muslim pilgrims returning from Mecca and watched the passengers drown because the Portuguese considered them commercial rivals and religious infidels. Since caravels were the only vessels at the time in the Indian Ocean armed with cannons, Portuguese commanders enjoyed a decided military advantage in the early 1500s. They required all ships in the Indian Ocean to purchase a passport (*cartaz*) permitting them to travel to specific destinations with their particular cargo, though enforcement was quite uneven.

The Portuguese empire was a state-run enterprise, known as the *Estado da India* (the state of India), and administered through a viceroy in Goa. The *Estado* established fortified trading centers at key sites on the trade routes along the ocean's coastlines. During the 1500s, over fifty factories (as they were called) stretched from Kilwa and Mombasa on the east African coast to Melaka on the Malay peninsula. Other factories included Nagasaki in Japan, Macau in China, and Goa, Cochin (Kochi), and Diu in India. The only European competition the Portuguese encountered was from Spain, after Miguel López de Legazpi secured the Philippines for his king in 1565, which set in motion a long process of colonizing the islands.

By the end of the 1500s, the *Estado* had successfully incorporated Portuguese merchants and officials into the port city trade of the Indian Ocean. The *Estado* enjoyed uneven success, however, in monopolizing the spice trade. Resistance and adjustments by local merchants along various trade routes undermined Portuguese ability to maintain a monopoly. Egyptian and Ottoman competitors bedeviled the *Estado* at the western end of the Indian Ocean; merchants in India took action to sidestep Portuguese controls; and the sultan of Aceh (Sumatra) mounted a major challenge in the east.

Nonetheless, the Portuguese retained a presence in the Indian Ocean throughout this period, though by the 1600s the *Estado da India* was undergoing serious contraction. The greatest nemesis to the Portuguese proved to be Dutch competitors who strung together a number of important military victories in the first half of the 1600s that drove the *Estado* out of Indonesia and many areas of India. With such keen military competition, the Portuguese crown increasingly turned its imperial investments to Brazil and its other Atlantic operations.

The Dutch displacement of the Portuguese marked an important turning point in empire and trading relations in the Indian Ocean. The *Estado* had incorporated itself as an important player in maritime trade in the region, but, despite their best efforts, Portuguese commanders really controlled very little land in Indian, Malayan, or other Asian territories. Northern European powers, such as the Dutch, came to exercise far greater control not only over commerce but also over spice production in specific regions of maritime Asia. By the 1660s, the Netherlands dominated the production and trade of cloves and nutmeg in the Molucca Spice Islands from Batavia, the center of Dutch operations. In the 1700s, the English and French held sway over areas in India from Madras and Calcutta.

Dutch ships entered the Indian Ocean in 1595, almost one hundred years after Da Gama's voyage, when Cornelis de Houtman sailed to the island of Java, landing in June 1596, and arriving back in the Netherlands in February 1597. In many respects, the voyage was a fiasco, as de Houtman alienated Indonesian merchants, two-thirds of the 249 crewmen died from scurvy and other diseases, and the expedition barely made any profit. Yet the promise of profits from the spice trade heartened investors in Amsterdam, and so they commissioned ships to seek out Asian sources for spices. Competing among themselves, these merchants made little headway against the might of the Portuguese fleet. To counter Portuguese naval power and to eliminate competition from within the Netherlands, the Dutch government in 1602 formed the East India Company, known as the VOC (Vereenige Oost-Indische Compagnie), and granted it exclusive rights to conduct trade in Asia. The Dutch government also gave the VOC the authority to wage war, to negotiate with local political leaders, and to construct fortifications. The Dutch enmity against the Portuguese extended beyond commercial competition in the Indian Ocean. Between 1580 and 1640, Portugal fell under Spanish rule, against whom the Dutch were fighting a war of independence in the Netherlands. Thus, a blow against the *Estado* was indirectly a blow against Spain.

The Dutch were able to control production and trade in Indonesia and east Asia far more effectively than the Portuguese for two basic reasons. First, the VOC functioned with ruthless economic efficiency because highly capable administrators served as governors of the company. Governed by a board of seventeen directors, the VOC was a private, joint-stock company that raised capital by selling shares publicly. Governor-generals, such as Jan Pieterszoon Coen and Antonio van Diemen, placed company profits above all other considerations and guarded against internal corruption. Second, the Dutch were successful in controlling trade in east Asia because of their unflinching use of military force to maintain a monopoly of trade. Eager to unseat the Portuguese, the directors of the VOC invested heavily in naval firepower and employed naval commanders in the service of the company. During the 1600s and 1700s, company shipyards in Amsterdam constructed 1,600 ships for service in Asian waters.

By virtue of this significant naval presence, the VOC staked claims to trading sites, negotiated exclusive deals with local political authorities, and simply imposed their will on trade and production on the base of its operations, the Spice Islands of Indonesia. For example, Jan Pieterszoon Coen, an officer in the VOC, led a punitive expedition against the inhabitants of the Banda Islands in 1621 on trumped-up charges that they had violated commercial agreements. Helped by Japanese mercenaries, Coen and his military forces committed wholesale massacre against the population, beheading leaders, and placing their heads on bamboo poles. The VOC occupied the Banda Islands, enslaved the remaining people, and imported other slaves to work on nutmeg plantations. When other Indonesian producers did not comply with the treaties the VOC forced on them, Dutch forces responded almost as ruthlessly as Coen did in Banda. The VOC attacked Makassar in the 1660s, cutting down clove trees and burning villages. Like the Portuguese, Dutch fleets did not allow ships to pass that did not carry purchased permission forms. By the late 1600s, the primary Dutch holdings in Asia included Java, the Moluccas, and other islands of Indonesia, Melaka, Sri Lanka (at the time called Ceylon), and the Cape Town colony of South Africa, utilized as a way station for Dutch ships between the Netherlands and Asia.

The VOC faced much stiffer competition in the late 1600s as English and French mercantile companies made headway in south Asia. The Dutch had driven the English out of various sites in Indonesia and harassed the French in India. The failure of the English to secure a foothold in Indonesia ironically turned out well for England, which centered its operations in India. Indian products, especially calicoes and cottons, acquired a much more durable market than spices, which began to reach a saturation point at the end of the 1600s. The rising costs of controlling spice production cut deeply into VOC profits, at a time when English naval power was ascending. By the early 1700s, the Netherlands ceded dominance in Europe and Asia to England and France; less than a century later the VOC closed its doors. The Dutch government would, however, maintain a colonial grip on Indonesia, as the Dutch East Indies, until 1949.

English merchants first sailed into the Indian Ocean in 1591, and French counterparts followed a few years later. England gained a foothold in south Asia in 1608, when a crew set up a trading operation in Surat on the northwestern coast of India; soon thereafter crews from the young English East India Company constructed factories on the Coromandel coast. At the time, India was not a single state, but a region ruled by Mughal emperors in the north and many regional chieftains in the south.

A board of directors in London governed the English East India Company, a joint-stock company commissioned by Queen Elizabeth I in 1600. Local administrators in factories throughout Asia actually handled the daily regulation of company policies. The English company played a formative role in the development of English dominions until the mid-1800s. French commercial ventures, by comparison, fared less successfully. Jean Baptiste Colbert, finance minister to Louis XIV, organized the French East India Company (Compagnie Francaise des Indes Orientales) in 1664. He failed to generate support in French business circles, so it remained a royal enterprise, though an underfunded one that underwent several reorganizations. Its ultimate demise came at the end of the 1700s.

In competition with the Dutch, the English and French made the most of fortified settlements in India. Unlike the Portuguese and Dutch who often tried to blast their way into markets, English and French directors negotiated arrangements with Mughal officials and also sought protection in alliances with local Indian governors who fell outside the Mughal Empire. Initially, the most active factories for the English company were in the Indian state of Gujarat (including Surat), though after the 1650s the center of activity shifted to the Coromandel coast and Bengal. Factors at Gujarat, Coromandel, and Bengal formed the most significant English colonization in Asia in the 1600s and became the basis of a colonial empire that began to emerge in the 1750s. The French company had a much more checkered history. Embroiled in financial scandals in France, a reorganized French Indies Company carved out sites in Mauritius off the coast of east Africa, Mahé on the Malabar coast, Pondicherry on the Coromandel coast, as well as a handful of other factories in India. Denmark also organized a mercantile organization in India with a post in Serampore, just north of Calcutta.

English and French East India Companies also explored and set up colonies in Australia, New Zealand, and islands of the Pacific (Oceania) in the 1700s. Dutch mariners had already visited Australia, New Zealand, Tasmania, and other areas in the 1600s, but the VOC's interest remained focused on spices in Indonesia. The English captain James Cook became the most accomplished explorer of Oceania, traveling to Australia, Hawaii, and Tahiti, among other places. Louis-Antoine de Bougainville visited Tahiti on behalf of France in 1768. The English established an initial colony at New South Wales in Australia in 1788 and settled several outposts in New Zealand primarily to launch whaling expeditions. Over the course of the late 1700s and early 1800s, the English and French established an imperial presence throughout Oceania.

A critical transition from a trading post arrangement to a colonial empire occurred in English factories in the mid 1700s. The weakening of Mughal authority over much of India and the intensification of competition with the French Indies Company resulted in outright English conquest in 1757. As the Mughal regime began to unravel, French and English merchants sought to manipulate regional political affairs for their own economic benefit, which escalated into military hostilities. The regional tensions between the imperial powers comprised one theatre in a global struggle for empire in North America, the Caribbean, and Europe. In south Asia, fighting between France, England, and their Indian allies engulfed the region in the 1750s and 1760s. The key battle occurred when English forces under Robert Clive defeated the local governor (Nawab) at the Battle of Plassey, north of Calcutta. This victory, along with the subsequent conquests across India, enabled England to oust the French as a political force in south Asia by the end of the Seven Years' War in 1763.

Maritime Empires in the Atlantic

At the same time that European powers were launching commercial empires in the Indian Ocean basin, they were also carving out land-based colonial regimes throughout the Atlantic world. Just as the Iberian countries were the first European powers in the Indian Ocean, they also led the way into the Atlantic. Infante Dom Henrique launched the initial Portuguese expeditions that took explorers to islands in the north Atlantic and down the coast of Africa. Mariners came ashore at their first discoveries on the Madeira Islands and Azores between 1418 and 1431. In a matter of years, officers set up naval stations for further expeditions, and planters set up plantations on the uninhabited islands.

While Portuguese explorers were making their way south along the western coast of Africa in the 1400s, they made contact with local rulers and set up factories at several locations. The most significant were located on the Gulf of Guinea (Ghana), in the Kongo, and nearby Ndongo. In 1469, Fernão Gomes landed on the Gulf of Guinea, and later in 1469 the Portuguese constructed the first European outpost south of the Sahara at Elmina to gain an entrée into the gold trade and to purchase slaves. Though the Portuguese lost Elmina to the Dutch in 1637, it became the primary center of the slave trade on the Guinea coast during the early modern period. Shortly after making contact at Elmina, the explorer Diogo Cão arrived in the Kongo in 1483 and struck up an alliance with the king, Nzinga a Nkuwu. Later, this and other Kongolese monarchs and their nobles converted to Christianity, allowing the spread of Portuguese language and customs into the region. In time, a number of Portuguese married Kongolese women and resided permanently in the Kongo; their children formed an important merchant class that negotiated commercial deals between Kongolese and Portuguese merchants. Initially, this alliance benefited Kongolese monarchs as well, enabling them to enhance their authority over confederated territories.

By the late 1500s, however, the Kongolese proved unable and unwilling to meet the Portuguese demand for slaves, so Europeans moved into Ndongo and other nearby areas, setting up trading settlements at Loango to the north and Luanda, an island just off the coast. Competition from these sites and Portuguese duplicity led to the collapse of Kongo and Ndongo at the end of the 1600s. During this struggle, Portuguese officers established a permanent colony to the south, known as Angola.

Other European states and trading companies set up posts on the west coast of Africa beginning in the 1500s. Spain, England, France, the Netherlands, Sweden, and Denmark all constructed sites where they traded for slaves and a range of goods. The Dutch East India Company organized a site in Cape Town, on the southern tip, in 1652 as a resupply station for crews on the Asia circuit. It developed into a European settler colony in Africa, as thousands of migrants put down homesteads in the 1700s. Aside from Angola and Cape Town, European parties were not able to break past their coastal establishments into the interior until the late 1800s. African coastal societies in most cases wielded formidable military capability that kept European intruders at bay along the continental perimeter. The lack of immunity to the disease environment, especially to malaria, also took a toll on soldiers, merchants, missionaries, officials, and portage animals who managed to venture inland. After European manufacturers developed rapid-fire guns to kill more effectively and quinine to combat malaria, the so-called scramble for Africa got underway at the end of the nineteenth century.

The Spanish monarchs, Ferdinand and Isabella, consented to sponsor Spain's first voyage to Asia under the leadership of an experienced Genoese mariner, Christopher Columbus. The uniqueness of this voyage in 1492 lay in Columbus's proposal to sail west across the Atlantic, rather than around Africa, to reach Asia. Like most well-read navigators, Columbus believed the world was spherical, so sailing west to get east made sense. What he had not counted on was a continental landmass lying between Europe and Asia and a globe eight thousand nautical miles larger than he estimated.

After Columbus dropped anchor off the coast of Hispaniola (present-day Dominican Republic) in October 1492, Spanish explorers, merchants, and crown officials focused their energies on the Caribbean for twenty years. In the first few years after the maiden voyage, Spanish authorities mistakenly thought Columbus had accomplished his aim of reaching Asia. He dubbed the Arawak (also known as Taino) natives as "Indians," described the region as the "Indies," searched for the court of the Chinese emperor, and tried to locate trading centers in the Indian Ocean.

When it became clear that these lands were nowhere near Asia, Spanish officials took a different imperial strategy: control land and labor. The colonists experimented with sugar production on the Caribbean islands, coercing Arawaks into agricultural labor. Not keen on working for Spanish planters, many Arawaks resisted or fled, provoking bloody massacres of the indigenous peoples. Farming sugarcane required intensive labor and, as the indigenous population began to die at the hands of Spanish oppression and European diseases, plantation owners faced chronic production problems. The discoveries of gold and silver on the mainland in 1519, however, quickly diverted Spanish attention away from the Caribbean. The Caribbean islands would not get much European attention again until the mid-1600s, when Spanish, English, French, Dutch, Swedish, and Danish planters turned almost all of the islands into sugar plantations.

The conquest of the extensive empires in Central and South America in the early 1500s confirmed the Spanish land-based economic strategy. Hearing fabulous stories of gold, Hernán Cortés set out from Cuba in 1519 with a small band of soldiers for Mexico. They landed on the coast at Vera Cruz, proceeded inland for seven months to Tenochtitlan (present-day Mexico City), and subdued the Aztec (Mexican) Empire by 1522. The Spanish conquest became possible only because of the alliance Cortés struck with the neighboring Tlaxcaltecans, implacable foes of the Aztecs. Eight years later, Francisco Pizarro took an even smaller force and managed to capitalize on internal rivalry and civil war within the Inca Empire, centered in Peru. The collapse of the Inca Empire resulted in no small part from a civil war between two contenders for the Inca throne, Atahualpa and Huáscar, which Pizarro and his men happened to step into. When both rivals were killed, Huáscar by Atahualpa's forces and Atahualpa by Pizarro's, the Spanish seized the opportunity of confusion and division to insert themselves atop the regime. Tenochtitlan, renamed Mexico City, and Lima (Peru) developed into the two centers of the largest European territorial empire in the early modern world in the early 1500s.

Though the Spanish had conquered the two most extensive empires in America, the conquerors had little idea about the expanse of this new hemisphere. Thus, in search of gold, fertile land, and a passage to Asia, Spanish explorers fanned out from the hubs of initial conquest. Between 1513 and 1540, figures such as Ponce de Leon, Vasco

Nuñez de Balboa, Hernán de Soto, Francisco Vásquez de Coronado, and others traveled across, mapped, and claimed for Spain most of Central America and the southern portion of North America from Florida to California. Discovery proceeded apace on the sea as well. In Ferdinand Magellan's round-the-world voyage from 1519 to 1521, his ships followed the contours of the eastern and western coasts of South America, sailing around the southern tip of the continent through a strait that bears his name. Consequently, over the course of the 1500s the Spanish developed a much clearer geographical picture of their American empire. It comprised almost all of South America (except for Brazil and Guiana), all of Central America, and large stretches of North America.

As quickly as they possibly could, Spanish conquistadors staked out claims to large tracts of land and began to extract wealth from it. Acting in the mode of European aristocrats, the new landowners imposed labor demands on the native residents as was common in agricultural regions in Iberia. The labor requirements in the Americas, known as the encomienda system, reduced native peoples to a level of bondage that was only a step above slavery. Spanish landholders mandated that the people who lived in areas under their control provide the labor for mining operations and agricultural estates, known as haciendas. The grueling physical demands of the work and the virulence of Spanish diseases had a devastating affect on the American peoples.

The ruthlessness with which conquistadors, soldiers, and other opportunists appropriated the land and exploited the people moved the Spanish king, Charles V (r. 1519–1556), to institute an effective government in the American empire. The Spanish government not only wanted to check the rapacious exploitation by private individuals, but it also intended to secure its control over newly discovered lands, rich with natural resources. Consequently, Charles appointed Antonio de Mendoza as the first viceroy over what authorities now referred to as New Spain, which extended from the southern region of what is today the United States to Panama and Venezuela, including the Caribbean islands. Seven years later, Charles created the viceroyalty of Peru that comprised all Spanish lands to the south of New Spain. The viceroys, as the name implies, possessed monarchical power over their American jurisdictions, yet answered to the king and the Council of the Indies, a governing board in Spain responsible for all overseas territories. The vastness of the empire made it necessary to create smaller administrative districts, called audencias that governed provinces and cities within their realms. Though this administrative structure had its origins in Mendoza's appointment in 1535, it was not until the 1570s that a governing apparatus became fully formed. Despite the attempt to impose greater control, the distance between Iberia and the Americas greatly limited Spanish authorities' ability to control affairs in the empire.

Portuguese colonization of Brazil began in 1500, when the navigator Pedro Álvares Cabral came ashore after sighting land in the western Atlantic en route to India. Cabral had taken a more southwesterly course out into the Atlantic than previous mariners, and ocean currents pushed him close to the South American shoreline. Like the Spanish, the Portuguese established an extensive land-based empire in Brazil. Originally the Portuguese conceived of Brazil as not much more than a way station for maritime traffic to Asia. Traders also set up temporary settlements to extract and export Brazilwood, for which Cabral named the land, yet by the 1530s permanent settlers came in search of land to develop sugar plantations. The cultivation of sugarcane on large agricultural estates became a driving force in Brazil, owing to strong demand in Europe. By 1600, Brazil was the most prolific sugar producer in the world.

The northern European countries – England, the Netherlands, France, Sweden, and Denmark – trailed the Iberian powers in the Americas, just as they did in Africa and Asia. The major European colonizers, France, England, and the Netherlands, did not get underway in earnest until the early 1600s, over one hundred years after Columbus set foot on Hispaniola. One reason for the later start by northern Europeans involves the influence of geography. Due to their location in the northern hemisphere, England and the Netherlands developed as maritime regions oriented toward the North and Baltic Seas. Since the 1500s, English and Dutch mariners competed with one another and with German, Polish, and Scandinavian companies for trading opportunities. England launched its Muscovy Company in 1555 to cultivate commercial relations with Russian merchants.

Stories of enormous American wealth and continued interest in an all-water route to the east, aroused the interests of merchants and rulers in the early 1500s. Operating on Columbus's principle, French and English explorers tried to locate a northwest passage that would lead them to Asia. John Cabot sailed on behalf of England in 1496 and 1498, landing in his second voyage on the coast of Canada around Labrador and Newfoundland. In the 1530s and 1540s, Jacques Cartier explored the St. Lawrence River valley for Francis I of France. Efforts to establish permanent settlements, however, proved unsuccessful until the early 1600s when Samuel Champlain founded the first French colonies in Port Royal (Nova Scotia) in 1604 and Quebec in 1608; John Smith and several explorers planted the initial English settlement in Jamestown in 1607. Several years later, the Dutch set up their only colony in North America in 1623 at Manhattan. The Dutch experiment proved short-lived as the English took it from them in a brief naval war in 1664 and renamed the colony New York.

The character of French and English ventures in North America varied considerably. For the first one hundred years, the French enterprise resembled the European mercantile empires in Asia, as merchants, missionaries, and military officers constructed small, fortified settlements at key sites to engage in trade with local peoples and, in the case of the priests, to spread Roman Catholic Christianity. Explorers, such as Champlain, originally set up settlements along the St. Lawrence River, and beginning in the 1670s, a second generation of voyagers, such as Fr. Jacques Marquette and Robert de LaSalle, reconnoitered the Great Lakes region and sailed all the way down the Mississippi River to the Gulf of Mexico. The French kings Louis XIII (1601–1643) and Louis XIV (1638–1715) claimed the vast, uncharted territory from Newfoundland to the Gulf of Mexico and the Appalachian to the Rocky Mountains. Like English and other European voyagers, French explorers still held out hope in the 1600s of discovering a direct northwest passage through North America to China. In 1634, Jean Nicolet (1598–1642) made his way from Quebec to the eastern shore of Lake Michigan. Convinced that China lay just to the west of this great body of water, Nicolet dressed himself in Chinese robes to put his best foot forward and set sail. To his dismay and perhaps embarrassment, Nicolet discovered what is today Green Bay, Wisconsin.

Relatively few Frenchmen, and far fewer French women, embarked on a new life in New France. For most of its history, New France functioned largely as a commercial empire to acquire fur from American tribes, and merchant companies discouraged migration out of a concern that settlers would encroach upon their trade. Major wars with the Iroquois, who conducted devastating campaigns against the Hurons and their French allies, also dampened enthusiasm for frontier settlement. Consequently, the French population of New France totaled only 7,200 in 1672.

The turning point for New France occurred in 1663 when Louis XIV placed the empire under direct royal control. Louis's capable minister, Colbert, supervised the reorganization of France's North American empire. Colbert provided for stronger central government in New France by dividing it into provinces ruled by a governor, responsible for military and Indian affairs, and a civil administrator (intendant) with charge over the enforcement of law and administration of finances. The original provinces consisted of Montreal, Quebec, and Trois Rivières (between Montreal and Quebec on the St. Lawrence River). Under a stable government, New France began to attract settlers at the end of the seventeenth century, motivated by land grants from the colonial administration. By the mid-eighteenth century, the population reached a high of more than 55,000.

English empire building in the Americas differed markedly from that of the French and its other European rivals. From the founding of the first permanent settlement in Jamestown in 1607 to the outbreak of the American Revolution in 1775, more than 700,000 migrants from Great Britain came to the Americas. This volume far surpassed the numbers of migrants from France (51,000), Spain (437,000), and Portugal (100,000). Most English migrants settled in colonies scattered along the Atlantic seaboard largely to claim, clear, and cultivate land, though some went to labor in plantations established by English planters in the Caribbean. Not only did many thousands more English take the Atlantic voyage than migrants from other lands, but they also came from all ranks of society. English colonists were not just soldiers, merchants, missionaries, and colonial administrators but men and women from the lower levels of society who sought economic opportunity and religious freedom. Since a large majority of the settlers were too poor to pay for the transatlantic voyage, they came as indentured servants contracted to work as laborers for their patron for anywhere between four and seven years. Other migrants, particularly in the Plymouth and Maryland colonies, fled in order to practice their Christian faith outside of the prescribed boundaries of the Church of England. Consequently, the English empire in North America consisted of settler colonies centered around farming and characterized by relatively dense European settlement.

After several failed attempts to plant colonies, the English finally achieved a permanent toehold with the Jamestown colony in Virginia in 1607. The colonists there struggled mightily in the first several years and would have starved without the benevolence of Powhatan tribes. In the ensuing years, merchant companies of the English crown started a number of new colonies, including Plymouth (1620), Salem (1626), Boston (1630), and Providence (1636). The colonies were reorganized several times so that by the late eighteenth century, thirteen fairly extensive settlements dotted the Atlantic seaboard. Unlike the other European empires, the English colonies remained independent from one another, though subject to the monarchy and to Parliament. Appointed by the charter holder of the colony (either a merchant company or the king), a governor ruled the colonies.

The quest by the European maritime powers to consolidate their control over lands they laid claim to led to increasing conflict on the high seas and in colonial territories in the 1700s. Empire building around the world was encased in much violence with indigenous peoples and between colonial powers. Powerful governments amassed large armies to expand their realms in Europe and to advance their colonial ambitions overseas. In America, English, French, and Spanish forces, along with native allies, seized opportunities to raid one another regularly during the 1700s. Yet their imperial ambitions in Asia and America came to a head in the Seven Years' War.

In North America, English settlers and French migrants, largely fur traders, had been on a collision course in the Ohio territory since the early 1700s. English grants for colonial charters on the Atlantic seaboard did not specify any western boundaries, and the heavy flow of immigration pushed settlements into the Ohio River valley. French exploration, beginning with Robert de La Salle in the 1670s, and immigration from France picked up considerably after Colbert took control of the North American settlements. In addition to these overlapping claims, another contributing factor in the run-up to war was the political alliances of several powerful American tribes. In general, the French enjoyed a more collaborative relationship with American peoples, despite fierce hostilities with the Iroquois, because most French migrants did not establish homesteads for farming. French colonialists primarily occupied themselves trading with native Americans for furs. English settlers, in contrast, transformed the landscape for agriculture, thereby driving out wild game that formed an important part of the American diet. Consequently, the English attracted more hostility from American tribes than the French did.

The French and Indian Wars, as the Seven Years' War was known in North America, brought to a head the ongoing commercial and geopolitical rivalry between France and England. Native nations also sought to use the war to their advantage: the Iroquois remained neutral until it was clear that the momentum had turned in favor of the English. At that time, they joined the English side. The Creeks in the southeast continued a policy of neutrality throughout this conflict, though the Cherokees reversed themselves and fought against the English in the Carolinas. The Iroquois eventually allied with the Ottawans and the English in order to control fur supplies and routes in the western Great Lakes. The French found common cause with the Ottawa and Creek nations, to defend against English incursions. The Creek confederation employed the same strategy, setting English, French, and Spanish in opposition to one another. And the English relied consistently on sympathetic Cherokee neutrality in their efforts against Spanish and French forces.

The 1763 Treaty of Paris concluded the Seven Years' War, confirming English colonial dominance in North America and India. The English, as discussed earlier, expelled the French from India and gained control over all of North American colonial possessions east of the Mississippi River. France retained two lucrative sugar-producing islands, Martinique and Guadeloupe, in the Caribbean and compensated Spain for its alliance by ceding New Orleans and the Louisiana territory west of the Mississippi River. The clear winner in the war for empire was England, though within twenty years it would lose the thirteen North American colonies to a successful campaign for independence. Despite this loss, the English were well positioned through control of trade and territory in India, the Caribbean, and Canada to become the world's most developed imperial power at the onset of the modern age.

The fighting, the French loss in this war, and the success of the American Revolution in 1783 all combined to usher in a new era characterized by native American decline and by the ascent of a new

Anglo-American nation. The Iroquois and the Cherokee sustained heavy losses and extensive property destruction. France's ouster from North America undermined the autonomy of native nations, since they could no longer play one colonial power against the other. As the American colonies gained independence from England, the new American government pursued a ruthless policy of westward expansion at the expense of what became known as Indian territory.

Originating in a project to find a shorter route to Asia, empire building in America shifted quickly to a quest for land, precious metals, and other valued resources. A variety of individuals – conquistadors, merchants, mariners, entrepreneurs, and adventurers – joined forces with their respective European states to stake claims all across America. From a European perspective, the assertion of state sovereignty over a region gave claimants legitimacy to set up colonies or trading stations on behalf of parties in the home countries. These declarations flew in the face of the sovereign rights over lands of native American societies, though Europeans generally did not recognize (or they chose to ignore) the inviolability of indigenous authority over physical borders and natural resources. So in many areas, colonists and colonial troops conquered or pushed aside American states and tribal societies.

Yet, European empire building in America did not proceed straight-forwardly as an inevitable conquest of one group of people over another. Europeans simply did not have the demographic wherewithal or the technological capacity to conquer most native American societies. Rather, it was the direct involvement of American nations and tribes, divided in their own self-interests, that enabled European settlers to found and maintain a permanent presence.

Europeans as Vectors

European states established overseas empires and, as the primary agents of maritime travel, they served as the chief vectors that brought peoples, goods, pathogens, and cultures together in the early modern world. The Portuguese launched this process in the 1400s, as mariners in the employ of the royal dynasty learned to navigate the Atlantic, ultimately taking merchants, sailors, soldiers, missionaries, and colonial officers across the Indian Ocean as far as Macau, China. Once the news got out that the Atlantic could be navigated, Spain, the Netherlands,

England, France, Denmark, and Sweden pursued profit and power in Africa, America, and Asia. These maritime empires facilitated the exchange of ideas, technologies, goods, plants, animals, and pathogens that set world history on a new course.

Works Consulted

Bentley, Jerry H., and Ziegler, Herbert F. *Traditions and Encounters: A Global Perspective on the Past*, vol. 2 *From 1500 to the Present*. 2nd ed. New York: McGraw Hill, 2003.

Boxer, C. R. *The Dutch Seaborne Empire, 1600–1800*. Hammondsworth: Penguin, 1973.

Brook, Timothy. *The Confusions of Pleasure: Commerce and Culture in Ming China*. Berkeley: University of California Press, 1998.

Burkholder, Mark A., and Johnson, Lyman L. *Colonial Latin America*. 2nd ed. Oxford: Oxford University Press, 1994.

Chaudhuri, K. N. *The English East India Company: The Study of an Early Joint Stock Company, 1600–1640*. London: F. Cass, 1965.

Ehret, Christopher. *The Civilizations of Africa: A History to 1800*. Charlottesville, Va.: University of Virginia Press, 2002.

Furber, Holden. *Rival Empires of Trade in the Orient, 1600–1800*. Minneapolis: University of Minnesota Press, 1976.

Games, Alison. "Migrations and Frontiers," in Toyin Falola and Kevin D. Roberts eds. *The Atlantic World, 1450–2000*. Bloomington: Indiana University Press, 2008, 48–66.

Heath, Byron. *Discovering the Great South Land*. Dural, New South Wales: Rosenberg Publishing, 2005.

Horn, James. "English Diaspora," in P. J. Marshall ed. *The Oxford History of the English Empire*, vol. 2 *The Eighteenth Century*. Oxford: Oxford University Press, 1998, 28–52.

Lenman, Bruce. "Colonial Wars and Imperial Instability, 1688–1793," in P. J. Marshall ed. *The Oxford History of the English Empire*, vol. 2 *The Eighteenth Century*. Oxford: Oxford University Press, 1998, 151–168.

Mancall, Peter C. ed. *Travel Narratives from the Age of Discovery: An Anthology*. Oxford: Oxford University Press, 2006.

Marshall, P. J. "The English in Asia: Trade to Dominion, 1700–1765," in P. J. Marshall ed. *The Oxford History of the English Empire*, vol. 2 *The Eighteenth Century*. Oxford: Oxford University Press, 1998, 487–507.

———. "The English in Asia to 1700," in Nicholas Canny ed. *The Oxford History of the English Empire*, vol. 1 *The Origins of Empire*. Oxford: Oxford University Press, 1998, 264–285.

Mungello, D. E. *The Great Encounter of China and the West, 1500–1800*. 2nd ed. Lanham, Md.: Rowman & Littlefield Publishers, 2005.

Nash, Gary B. *Red, White, and Black: The Peoples of Early North America.* 3rd ed. New York: Prentice-Hall, 1992.

Oliver, Roland, and Atmore, Anthony. *Medieval Africa, 1250–1800.* Cambridge: Cambridge University Press, 2001.

Parker, Geoffrey. *The Military Revolution: Military Innovation and the Rise of the West, 1500–1800.* Cambridge: Cambridge University Press, 1988.

Pearson, M. N. "Merchants and States," in James D. Tracy ed. *The Political Economy of Merchant Empires.* Cambridge: Cambridge University Press, 1991, 41–116.

_____. *The New Cambridge History of India.* vol. 1 *The Portuguese in India.* Cambridge: Cambridge University Press, 1987.

Pomeranz, Kenneth, and Topik, Steven. *The World That Trade Created: Society, Culture, and the World Economy, 1400 to the Present.* Armonk, N.Y.: M. E. Sharpe, 2006.

Russell, Peter. *Prince Henry 'the Navigator': A Life.* New Haven, Conn.: Yale University Press, 2000.

Spalding, Karen. "The Crises and Transformations of Invaded Societies: The Andean Area (1500–1580)," in Frank Salomon and Stuart B. Schwartz eds. *The Cambridge History of the Native Peoples of the Americas*, vol. 3, pt. 1 *South America*, Cambridge: Cambridge University Press, 1999.

Subrahmanyam, Sanjay. *The Career and Legend of Vasco Da Gama.* Cambridge: Cambridge University Press, 1997.

_____. *The Portuguese in Asia, 1500–1700: A Political and Economic History.* New York: Longman, 1993.

Vink, Marcus P. M. "Between Profit and Power: The Dutch East India Company and Institutional Early Modernities in the "Age of Mercantilism," in Charles Parker and Jerry Bentley eds. *Between the Middle Ages and Modernity: Individual and Community in the Early Modern World.* Lanham, Md.: Rowman & Littlefield Publishers, 2007, 285–306.

Vries, Jan de, and Woude, Ad van der. *The First Modern Economy: Success, Failure, and Perseverance of the Dutch Economy, 1500–1815.* Cambridge: Cambridge University Press, 1997.

Zoltvany, Yves F. ed. *The French Tradition in America.* Columbia: The University of South Carolina Press, 1969.

2

Asian States and Territorial Empires

Matteo Ricci, an Italian Jesuit missionary to China in the late 1500s, remarked on the highly exalted status of the Ming emperor, "The King is observed with more Rites than any other in the World. None speaks to him but his Eunuchs, and those which live in the Palace, Sons and Daughters. None of the Magistrates without the Palace . . . speak to the King but by Petition, and those with so many forms of veneration."[1] Though no Asian monarch possessed the resources of the Chinese emperor, Ricci's depiction could also have applied to the courts of the great Ottoman, Safavid, and Mughal rulers or the Russian tsar in the 1600s. While a handful of European countries were erecting governmental structures and launching overseas empires, powerful states in Asia were also consolidating their political authority and expanding enormously across the continent. Just as empire building in Europe was predicated on state power, political centralization also became major features of Asian states in the early modern period.

The power vacuum left by the faltering Mongol-Timurid Empires afforded ambitious dynasties – Ming and Qing in China, Romanov in Russia, Ottoman in Anatolia, Safavid in Iran, and Mughal in India – opportunities to acquire power over rival families and to rule their realms absolutely. Other regions that did not launch large empires also developed powerful, stable states. On the Korean peninsula, a military commander Yi Song-gye (1335–1408) ousted the ruling dynasty in 1392 and established the Choson dynasty, which lasted until the twentieth century. Yi Song-gye's successors developed a centralized state and cultivated a prosperous agricultural society. The dynasty withstood invasions by Japan at the end of the 1500s and China in the 1600s. Afterward the Choson dynasty pursued an isolationist stance that has earned Korea the nickname of "the Hermit Kingdom." Outside of mainland Asia, the Tokugawa regime (1603–1867) internally established complete control over Japan. In all of these territories, the efficient extraction of revenue not only supported the royal house, but more importantly it also outfitted enormous armies that utilized cutting-edge techniques and technologies.

Nevertheless, the imperial states of Asia formed the most important agents in promoting global interaction across Eurasia. The Ming and Qing states expanded into Tibet, Mongolia, Yunnan, and Guizhou; Cossacks (independent peoples in the northern areas of the Black and Caspian Seas) in the pay of the Romanovs forged through Siberia to the Pacific Ocean; the Ottomans conquered lands from Iraq to Austria and Asia Minor to Qatar. The Safavid dynasty controlled Iran, and Mughal emperors ruled over almost all of India.

Ming and Qing China

Long before Ming emperors came to power – as far back as 206 B.C.E. when the Han dynasty emerged – China had experienced a long history of centralized rule. Though dynasties came and went over this long period of time and though factional struggles figured significantly in China's political history, nevertheless a centralized state remained an integral feature of Chinese society. In the early modern period, the Ming and especially the Qing dynasties were exceptionally stable, authoritative governments directed by many ambitious and capable rulers. These emperors appropriated traditional political theory and built upon long-established bureaucratic structures that enabled these dynasties to extend their imperial reach across central Asia. In so doing, they fostered cross-cultural exchange across central and southeast Asia.

Early modern Chinese conceptions of empire were rooted in the hierarchical conception of China as the "Middle Kingdom" with the emperor ruling as the "Son of Heaven." According to this worldview, the emperor reigned as the intermediary between the divine realm of the heavens and the earthly orbit of human existence. Chinese theory held

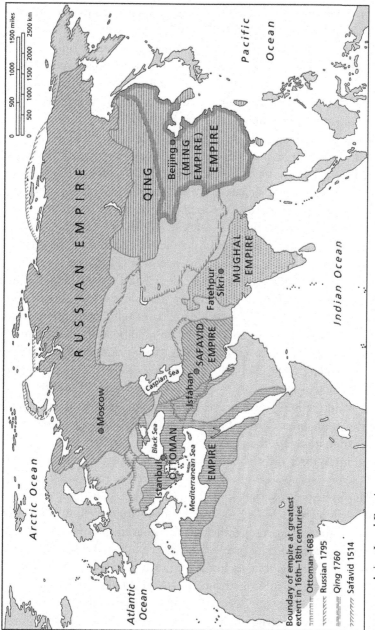

MAP 2.1. Asian Land Empires

that the Middle Kingdom represented the highest and most hallowed civilization in the world. Non-Chinese peoples who lived under Chinese military authority and who paid regular tribute to the emperor comprised an intermediate-favored category. A minimal favored status was accorded to peoples who lived outside Chinese control and only offered tribute irregularly. Finally, those in remote regions and who paid no tribute were contemptible barbarians.

The Chinese intellectual tradition that came to be known as Confucianism anchored this theoretical rationale for imperial rule and served as the philosophical foundation for all aspects of Chinese governance. Since the Han dynasty, an extensive bureaucracy of Confucian scholars (called mandarins by foreigners) administered all the practical functions of government, except for military affairs. Civil servants regulated agricultural production, commercial activity, construction of public works and transportation systems, storage of grain reserves for emergencies, and administration of civil and criminal law. Unique in world history before the modern era, the Chinese civil service operated on a merit system, in which candidates (all male) competed for positions based on their performance on qualifying written examinations on the Confucian classical texts. The idea behind this system was to produce well-schooled administrators to carry out the responsibilities of government in a wise, competent manner and to act in the best interests of society. The examinations were grueling affairs. Boys, whose parents aspired for sons in the civil service, prepared for the examinations from a young age, and the examinations themselves lasted up to three days. The few who were successful took important and prestigious positions in the Chinese bureaucracy.

This system of examination and civil service had three significant ramifications for Chinese society. First, governing elites owed their positions to a meritocracy rather than aristocratic privilege or political patronage, ensuring a capable civil service and reducing the risk of corruption. Throughout its history, the Chinese government did not have to depend on subsidies from aristocratic bodies (i.e., Parliaments) as European kings did. Second, Chinese society inherited the most wide-ranging state structure in the early modern period, a government responsible for a vast array of services and controls. Third, Confucian tradition developed into the guiding philosophical system in Chinese culture. Confucian thought exercised a most powerful influence in

Chinese elite culture – much like Christianity in Europe and Islam in Arabia.

The durability of the Chinese bureaucracy enabled the government to weather the periods of political turmoil, even the collapse of the Ming dynasty in the mid-1600s. Since the 1550s, self-indulgent and lackluster emperors reigned in China; they ignored large-scale piracy at sea and devastating famines throughout the land. Later, pressure from widespread internal rebellions allowed Manchurian forces to conquer Beijing in 1644 and proclaim a new dynasty (the Qing). Building on gains in the Ming era, the Qing dynasty emerged as an expansive, powerful regime intent on broadening the territorial reach of the Middle Kingdom. The centralized Chinese state under both the Ming and Qing dynasties amassed an enormous empire that stretched into Tibet and east Turkestan in the early modern period.

Though China established a large land-based empire, the direction of Chinese empire building, however, did not become clarified until the mid-1400s. During the early Ming period, many influential court officials promoted an overseas empire in the Indian Ocean basin. A recent book by Gavin Menzies has even claimed that Chinese mariners discovered and explored far-flung regions of the world, including Australia, New Zealand, Antarctica, and America in the 1420s. His intriguing thesis is based on meager evidence; thus, historians have not accepted his interpretation. What we do know is that the Chinese embarked on a series of seven massive naval expeditions in the early 1400s under the eunuch, Zheng He (1371–1433).

Shortly after his accession, the Yongle emperor (r. 1402–1424) embarked on an ambitious shipbuilding program at the Nanjing (also Nanking) shipyards and appointed Zheng He as admiral of the imperial fleet. From 1405 to 1433, the Chinese treasure fleet conducted its voyages with hundreds of ships and thousands of sailors, soldiers, officials, and merchants in the China Sea and Indian Ocean; the maiden voyage in 1405 employed 255 ships staffed by 28,000 men. Over 400 feet in length and 180 feet in width, the treasure ships were the largest maritime vessels constructed, and they tripled the size of Portuguese caravels. In these expeditions, the Chinese called on ports throughout the Indian Ocean, including Melaka, Sumatra, Calicut, Hormuz, Aden, and Mogadishu on the east African coast. Zheng He successfully established a tribute system whereby rulers in lands along the coastlines offered gifts and duties to the emperor and recognized his political authority over them.

This maritime and mercantile orientation came to an end in the 1430s because of political opposition and financial costs. Chinese merchants had to contend with the growing menace of piracy, especially from Japanese bandits, in southern coastal waters. For Confucian mandarins, who held contempt for trade and for foreigners anyway, the problem of piracy only confirmed their inclination to pull away from the sea and from maritime trade. Confucian thought extolled the virtues of the soil, enshrining agriculture as the most noble of occupations. According to a Confucian worldview, trade was at best a necessary evil to be regulated. As a result, mandarins attempted to limit the polluting effects of any foreign mercantile presence in China.

The voyages of the treasure fleet also created a drain on the imperial treasury, at a time when the Xuande emperor (r. 1425–1435) was waging expensive military campaigns in Mongolia and Vietnam, as well as financing the newly constructed capital city of Beijing. Overseas expeditions ended in 1433, and by midcentury naval technology languished, as treasure ships rotted in the Nanjing shipyards. Private traders continued to operate in coastal ports and even engaged in maritime trade, though they did so under increasing scrutiny and suspicion. In 1656, China outlawed all overseas trade; the imperial edict stating not even "one plank drifting into the sea." The Chinese government was never able to eliminate maritime commerce, though it devoted a great deal of attention to regulating trade in ports on the southern Chinese coast.

Another force had historically pulled Chinese dynasties to the lands north and west: powerful nomadic societies in Mongolia, Manchuria, and the central Asian plain. Nomadic Mongol and Turkish groups frequently attacked frontier regions in the north and west, if they could not obtain the trading advantages they desired. Built from northern defense works dating from the third century B.C.E., but mainly during the Ming dynasty, the Great Wall stands as a permanent monument to the hostility between the Chinese and steppe peoples. The Ming and Qing dynasties possessed an absorbing preoccupation with central Asia and therefore constructed Beijing as a window on the northern frontier.

On the Asian mainland, the early modern Chinese empire developed in two theatres of operation. The region of initial concern was the south, as the Qing rulers faced local resistance to centralized rule and antagonism from enclaves of Ming loyalists. For the first forty years of their reign, Manchu emperors only ruled Manchuria (their home-land) and northern China from Beijing to Nanjing directly. The Qing had ceded large territories, known as feudatories, in southern China to three generals who had defected from the Ming side and promised loyalty to the new regime. Even though the generals pledged loyalty in principle, in reality they governed these feudatories as independent rulers. In 1673, uncertainty over the political fate of the territories came to a head when Kangxi decided to take an aggressive line against the feudatories. A ten-year military struggle, known as the Revolt of the Three Feudatories, ensued, pitting imperial forces against Ming loyalists and other rebels. Fierce fighting and bloody reprisals char-acterized the struggle, though by 1681, Kangxi had routed his foes throughout southern China and Taiwan. Eventually, Hunan, Guang-dong, Fujian, Sichuan, Shaanxi, and Taiwan (Formosa) came under the authority of the Son of Heaven.

The second theatre of Chinese empire building lay on the west-ern frontier. After the Kangxi emperor had defeated the independent feudatories in the south, he took measures to fortify the western fron-tier against restive Mongol khans and to counter the Russian push into northern Manchuria, especially in the fertile Amur River basin. For almost one hundred years, the Qing dynasty engaged Mongol groups in Tibet and Turkestan through trade, diplomacy, and war. From the Chinese imperial perspective, harmony reigned when nomadic peoples, many of whom fell under the tributary jurisdiction of the emperor, subordinated themselves completely to the Son of Heaven and lived in peace among their neighboring tribes. Though Qing emperors justified intervention in central Asian affairs from this heavenly mandate, prac-tical geopolitical interests in the region were also at stake. The court wanted to stabilize its borders, keep the Russians at bay, and utilize regions in Tibet and Turkestan for the resettlement of peoples from overpopulated areas in China.

The most problematic peoples, from the Chinese viewpoint, were the Zunghar Mongols who inhabited western Tibet. With little regard for the semidivine claims of Qing emperors, Zunghar tribesmen sought to maintain their independence and to pursue their own geopolitical and economic courses of action. The Zunghars were fiercely indepen-dent, which sometimes meant that they raided other peoples who came under the protection of the Qing emperor. On several occasions in the early 1700s, Chinese forces marched into Tibet in order to carry out a campaign of "righteous extermination." By 1730, China had established control over Kokonor and, for a short time, the region around Khobdo in Mongolia. The Zunghars at this interval proved too resilient for extermination. After an interlude of peaceful trading relations in the 1740s and 1750s, infighting among Zunghar tribal leaders led to instability and raiding that spilled over into other areas. The Qianlong emperor decided the time had come to extinguish the Zunghar people and in 1750 ordered 50,000 troops into Tibet. These forces attacked the Zunghars fiercely and embarked on a pogrom of extermination. The Chinese also went after other tribes, such as the Khoja Mongols, who had given support to the Zunghars. By 1765, China had crushed its enemies and stood as the dominating colonial power over an enormous region comprising Tibet, Gansu, Kokonor (Qinghai), Mongolia, and Turkestan (present-day Xinjiang).

In order to consolidate Chinese sovereignty over these western frontier areas, the Qing state pursued a policy of mass migration from the late seventeenth through the eighteenth centuries. Chinese migration into Tibet and Turkestan is discussed extensively in Chapter 4, though it is worth noting here that migration served as a tool of empire building for the Chinese government. Hundreds of thousands of peasants relocated in these areas and transformed the pastoral grasslands and forests into farmland to support military garrisons. Civilian and military officials worked to enforce imperial law and promote the universal rule of the Son of Heaven in the newly conquered regions. So by the early nineteenth century, China had carved out a massive land-based empire in response to geopolitical concerns in central Asia. As a result, China developed into one of the most extensive colonial powers in the world and the most influential cultural force in central, southeast, and east Asia.

Romanov Russia

Lying along the edges of eastern Europe and northwestern Asia, Muscovy formed the core region around which Russia developed in the early modern period. Muscovy, and Russia, underwent a remarkable transformation from a backwoods territory under the thumb of

Mongol overlords in the 1400s to the hub of a massive land empire by the 1700s. Because of Muscovy's unique location, its expansion into a state and an empire incorporated both European and Asian features. The development of a central government paralleled European patterns of state formation, yet the rise of the empire most closely resembled China's model of imperial conquest.

As rulers of Muscovy, the grand princes of Moscow constructed a territorial regime from the ground up, for the area contained little more than a few scattered villages in the middle ages. Muscovite princes expanded their holdings, beginning in the 1300s, through strategic marriages, diplomatic alliances, and battlefield conquests. Princes considered this expansion a duty that they referred to as the "gathering of the Russian lands," signifying their identity with the Rus peoples of the region. And, in 1480 the grand prince of Moscow, Ivan III, renounced the payment of tribute to the Mongol khan of the Golden Horde, thus declaring Russia's independence from Muslim rule.

Territorial expansion accelerated under Ivan III's successor, Ivan IV (1533–1584), also appropriately known as Ivan the Terrible for his horribly cruel methods of dealing with his enemies (and sometimes friends and family) and for his psychotic personal traits. He threw sexual orgies at court and relished gruesome executions, including impalement and disembowelment. In an outburst of rage in 1581, he killed his son and successor Ivan Ivanovich by striking him on the head with a staff. As an imperialist, he expanded into neighboring Novgorod, Lithuania, Ryazan, Astrakhan, and Kazan. Ivan also waged war against the landed nobility of Russia, the boyars, though his motives for doing so remain unclear. It is possible that he was attempting to augment royal authority or was even beginning to construct a centralized state, since Ivan's councilors instituted a number of administrative reforms and sought to inquire into the conditions of the common people. But the more likely case is that Ivan's campaign of terror grew out of his absorbing paranoia against enemies, both real and imagined.

In 1565, he created an elite squadron of servants, the oprichniki, whose loyalty lay only with the tsar and who took possession of the confiscated estates of resistant boyars. Dressed in black and displaying the symbols of a dog's head and a brush (to bark, bite, and sweep the tsar's enemies), the oprichniki developed into Ivan's personal dragoons. They scoured the countryside, mounting campaigns of terror against boyars and other "traitors." In some cases, the oprichniki brutally tortured their victims by skinning them alive and boiling them in front of family and neighbors. For reasons that are unclear, Ivan disbanded the oprichniki in 1572.

Ivan IV's harsh, heavy-handed reign produced a backlash against centralized state authority in Russia. At his death in 1584, aggrieved boyars and other forces at court vying for power went at one another in a "Time of Troubles" that engulfed Russia from 1598 to 1613. As civil war broke out, neighboring Sweden and Poland took the opportunity to invade; thus, the Russian state fragmented during the Time of Troubles. When the fighting came to an end, Mikhail Romanov, from an important boyar dynasty, ascended to the throne. Ruling until the communist revolution of 1917, the Romanovs established one of the most absolutist monarchical regimes in the early modern period.

Political centralization represented one of the primary themes in Russian history in the 1600s and 1700s. During this period, tsars and their ministers adopted a number of practices that effectively merged the interests of boyar nobles and the monarchy with the needs of a powerful state. Unlike the violent antagonism of Ivan IV, the aristocracy and monarchy found ways to collaborate to produce a large and formidable army and to establish control of the middle class and peasantry. A chief component of this structure was the reshaping of the boyar nobility into a body to serve the state, rather than defend its own separate territorial and political interests. In 1722, Tsar Peter I (the Great, r. 1682–1725) adopted a Table of Ranks that established a system of rewards for nobles who entered government service either as civil officials or military officers. This policy transformed the territorial aristocracy into a service nobility with allegiance to the state and became essential to the development of a centralized regime. Though some representative institutions existed, the policies of Peter I rendered them moribund.

The peasantry and middle class paid the price for the convenient collaboration of nobility and monarchy. The tax burden fell primarily on non-elites, especially the peasantry. The tsars rewarded the boyars for their service by placing the peasants at the complete disposal of the nobility. In the mid-1600s, Tsar Alexis I imposed greater restrictions on Russian serfs. Subject to their noble landlords, Russian peasants labored under a host of financial and labor obligations as well as legal constraints, including such requirements as working on the lord's domain, obtaining permission to travel or marry, and paying all sorts of fees. Russian peasants remained serfs until serfdom was abolished in 1861.

The high-water mark of state building occurred during the reign of Peter I, Russia's most capable and ambitious tsar. His driving aspiration was to refashion Russia into an advanced nation in the western European mold, and to make the country a dominant player in the region from the Baltic to the Balkans. After touring the Netherlands, Germany, and England in 1697 and 1698, Peter became convinced of Russia's need to adopt western practices to become competitive with the rising power of European nations. He promoted travel to Europe, welcomed European visitors to Russia, pushed educational and military reforms, and compelled Russians to dress in western styles. Peter even issued a law prohibiting boyars from wearing long beards as was their custom. More importantly, he constructed the city of St. Petersburg as a "window to the west" to serve as a model to Russians of a modern European city. The program of westernization, sponsored initially by Peter I, never embraced any policy or reform that might undermine the emperor's grip on political power. Catherine II (the Great, r. 1762–1796) was the strongest advocate of westernization, but even she reiterated the obligations of the nobility and urban classes in the Charter of the Nobility and Charter of the Towns. Though she abolished torture and the death penalty, the tsarina returned to a more autocratic style after a major rebellion threatened her reign in 1773. Emelian Pugachev led an uprising of Cossacks and peasants demanding land and political rights, but the insurrection was put down with great bloodshed.

In keeping with their absolutist agenda, Russian tsars in the 1700s took an assertive approach to the acquisition of land. Since the days of Ivan IV, Russia had expanded west into Ukraine and competed with Poland and Lithuania for territory. In the mid-1600s, Russia had wrested control of a large portion of Ukraine from Poland. Peter I continued this westward thrust, joining with several allies in a major military struggle with Sweden and its allies in the Great Northern War (1700–1721). Russia's victory in this war achieved his imperial goals of mastering the Baltic. Later in the century, Catherine II allied with Austria and Prussia to partition Poland and Lithuania on three separate occasions, the last occurring in 1795. This division of these two countries enabled Catherine to incorporate large tracts of Poland and Lithuania into Russia.

Within eastern Europe, Russia championed the cause of ethnic Slavs, many of whom were members of the Orthodox Church and who lived under Muslim Ottoman rule. As Ottoman power began to wane in the region in the 1700s, Russia pushed into new areas, taking control of the northern Black Sea district and establishing closer relations with Slavic peoples of the Orthodox faith throughout the Balkans. By the beginning of the 1800s, Russia's empire to the west shadowed over eastern Europe from the Baltic to the Balkans, a matter of serious concern to European governments.

Despite gains in the west, Russia's great imperial conquest in the early modern period lay to the east in Asia. The colonization and exploitation of northern Asia greatly aided state building, and at the same time, the centralized Romanov government made such imperial conquest possible. The original point of departure for empire building in Asia came with the conquest of the Kazan Khanate in 1552, enabling Ivan IV to establish a presence in the rich steppe region between the Urals and the Volga River. From there, Ivan consolidated his gains and expanded eastward as Cossacks waged war on the Siberian Tatar Khanate at the end of the 1500s. The Cossack campaigns struck a severe blow to various Tatar clans that had bedeviled the Muscovite heartland for centuries. The Tatars had often raided into Moscow and Novgorod, plundering property, enslaving people, and generally wreaking all sorts of havoc. In fact, the Tatar groups captured and sold over 10,000 Russians a year at slave markets in the Crimean, making it the second largest slaving reservoir in the world, behind Africa, in the 1500s. It would take tsars two hundred years to defeat these groups totally, especially the Crimean Tatars in present-day Ukraine. Nevertheless, with these victories and the ruthless suppression of local peoples, tsars took effective control of the region at the end of the sixteenth century and launched Russia's imperial quest over Siberia.

The particular evolution of empire left in place three well-defined regions. The western zone, extending from the Urals to the Yenisey River, fell to Cossack forces by the end of the 1500s. From there Cossacks pushed into central Siberia, lying between the Yenisey and Lena Rivers, at the beginning of the 1600s. By the 1640s, they had subdued most of the Tungu peoples who inhabited this territory. Beginning in the 1630s, adventurers and Cossacks moved into the eastern portion of Siberia, exploring northeastern lands and then about twenty years later reconnoitering the northern fringes of Mongolia and China. During the last half of the 1600s and the early 1700s, Cossacks attacked, plundered, and established themselves in the far eastern corner of Asia, setting up headquarters at Okhotsk on the Ulya River. The biggest disappointment in the eastern empire was the failure of Russian forces to take control of the Amur River basin to the southeast and along the northern border of China. With its temperate climate and fertile soil, the Amur basin offered the opportunity to develop an agricultural base for the eastern region of the empire. Russian empire building here though collided with the expansionist aims of the Chinese Qing emperor. Conflicts between the two produced the Treaty of Nerchinsk in 1689, which required Russia to abandon the Amur basin. Thus, by the early 1700s, Russian expansion had reached the Pacific, and three distinct regions comprised the empire in Asia: western, central, and eastern Siberia.

The central state in Moscow sought, like European empire builders in America, to remake Siberia into a commodity-producing region to serve Russian geopolitical ambitions in northern and eastern Europe. The first order of business for the Russian tsars was to mobilize local populations into a labor force to exploit the natural resources on behalf of the empire. In principle, this followed the tried and true practices of most empire builders in history, and it certainly corresponded to intentions of European colonizers in the western hemisphere. The unique aspect about the appropriation of labor and resources in Siberia was that colonization there did not have its roots in agricultural production as the American experience did. Rather, exploitation concentrated on the harvest of sable fur pelts. Russian colonizers did not hunt and trap sables themselves, but they demanded a quota of pelts from local populations in every region that came under their control. This system of tribute was known as *yasak* and it became an essential element of the early modern Russian empire from the Ural Mountains to the Pacific Ocean. According to the practice, Russian officials, or private brigands, held local leaders and their families hostage in return for an annual payment of pelts, the quota of which was determined by the number of native males at least fifteen years old. The administration of this tributary extraction in fur lasted until the early 1700s, when Peter I focused on mining metals for military purposes and when the sable population was almost completely depleted. The demand for tribute outlived the large-scale supply of fur, as tsars shifted to extorting monetary payments from Siberians.

The harvesting of fur as a commodity necessitated an organization similar in principle, at least, to the plantation complex in the Atlantic. Local peoples resisted Cossack incursions into their lands and the cruel *yasak* system. When Cossack forces established themselves in a given territory, the government authorized the construction of garrisons to maintain control over an area and to implement the tributary arrangements. In this respect, the policy of establishing military garrisons to control regions, combined with promoting peasant migration into them (as the Chinese did in Tibet and Turkestan) enabled Russia to colonize an extensive territory. Russian expansion into Siberia amounted to the conquest of one-sixth of the earth's surface area, making it the largest land empire in the world at the time.

Safavid Iran

Three Muslim regime states in the sprawling region from India to Hungary and from Egypt to Morocco contributed significantly to the interaction of peoples in western Asia, eastern Europe, northern Africa, the Mediterranean Sea, and the Indian Ocean. The Safavid Empire in Iran, the Mughal Empire in India, and the Ottoman Empire in Anatolia, all created large territorial empires and developed strong state systems that fostered trade, promoted the spread of the Islamic faith, and allowed for the diffusion of Asian culture into the wider world.

As we have seen in all early modern imperial regimes, state building was closely interwoven with empire in Iran. The Safavids, along with the Mughals in India, however, presented unique cases in that imperial conquests actually produced the need for a state. Conversely, the typical pattern – in Europe, China, Russia, and Ottoman domains – was for a comprehensive state or cluster of states to create an empire. Yet these two Muslim empires represent a reversal of the dominant trend.

Rising in the early 1500s, the Safavid dynasty took its identity and name from the Safaviyeh order, a mystical Muslim sect that traced its origins to sheik Safi al-Din, a fourteenth-century holy man from Ardabil in the region just southwest of the Caspian Sea. The Safaviyeh had designs on expansion as the rulers of a Mongol-Turkish dynasty in Iran began to go into decline in the late 1400s. An opportunistic fifteen-year old boy in the order, Ismail Safavi, rallied restive Turkic tribesmen in Azerbaijan, known as Qizilbash (redheads) for their distinctive red headgear, behind his messianic claims. Though they were Muslim, the Qizilbash held a number of heterodox beliefs, including reincarnation and ongoing divine revelation (after the death of Muhammad), that made them prone to fighting holy wars. Ismail appealed to their beliefs, claiming descent from Safi al-Din and even asserting his own divinity. Ismail urged the Qizilbash to take up religious revolution on his behalf.

In 1501, Ismail and his devoted following captured neighboring Tabriz, after which he proclaimed himself shah (emperor) in Iran. Subsequently, Ismail and the Turkic tribesmen went from one improbable victory to another from 1500 to 1502; they conquered Azerbaijan, Armenia, and Khorasan. Once in power, Ismail declared Shi'ite Islam as the religion of his empire in order to gain loyalty of Iranian elites, especially Shi'ite religious leaders (ulama). Ismail concocted a fictional genealogy that linked the Safavids to the family lineage of Muhammad. Shi'a Muslims were (and still are) a minority group within Islamdom, but maintain a majority in pockets of the middle east, including Iran and Iraq. Shi'ites recognize the family of the prophet Muhammad, through his cousin Ali, as the sole possessors of legitimate religious authority. Most Muslims identify with some branch of Sunni Islam, which holds that religious authority flows through broadly acclaimed leaders in the Islamic community who were not from the family of the Prophet.

Ismail and successive Safavid rulers expanded their rule across Iran, steadily curtailing the radical mysticism of the Qizilbash and promoting Shi'ism as a prevailing religious force. Until his death in 1524, Shah Ismail worked to consolidate his authority by crafting a state to govern his empire, though the most important steps in the centralization of authority followed later at the end of the sixteenth century. The ultimate result was a strong Iranian empire that lasted until 1722.

The political legitimacy of the regime relied heavily on the theocratic assertions of shahs for much of the Safavid period. They proclaimed that they ruled by God's favor, and some shahs, like Ismail, cloaked themselves in a divine status. In so doing, Safavid shahs combined ancient features of Persian kingship with long-held notions of Islamic authority to establish an unassailable theoretical basis for their rule. Since classical times, Persian rulers had declared their divinity, so the Safavids were appropriating a familiar political concept from the region. In addition, Ismail and the early Safavid emperors proclaimed that they were special representatives of the hidden Twelfth Imam. According to the prevalent version of Shi'ism in the area, twelve authoritative imams (religious leaders) had descended from Muhammad. The twelfth, Muhammad al-Mahdi, a ninth-century imam, never died, but was hidden by Allah; his triumphant unveiling would herald the end of time and the ultimate victory of Islam.

The rapid success of the Safavid dynasty and the exalted status of Shah Ismail encountered a major setback in 1514 with a momentous military defeat at the battle of Chaldiran. Turkish sultans had monitored the progress of the Qizilbash forces with alarm, since they represented a threat to the Ottomans, who held to mainstream Sunni Islam. Consequently, the Ottoman military mobilized to meet the Safavid threat on the plain of Chaldiran and dealt a crushing blow to the Qizilbash forces. Employing gunpowder weaponry, Ottoman musketeers positioned themselves behind wooden gun carriages and fired away at the charging Qizilbash cavalry. Shah Ismail had convinced the Qizilbash that his supernatural powers would protect his followers and lead them to victory. Thus, the mounted tribesmen, imbued with a holy warrior ethos, eschewed muskets and cannons and made one cavalry charge after another into the teeth of the Ottoman rifle corps. When Ismail and the Qizilbash eventually retreated, the Ottomans pursued them all the way to Tabriz with artillery fire. The old-fashioned warfare of the nomad and the mystical power of the shah succumbed to the real-world superiority of the Ottoman military.

The devastating loss at Chaldiran resulted in two critical changes in the Safavid realm. First, the stunning military reversal halted the westward expansion of the empire and temporarily marked the end of Safavid expansion outside Iran. Second, the failure at Chaldiran greatly undermined the Qizilbash's confidence in the spiritual powers of Ismail and subsequent shahs. The Safavid monarchy continued to embody the ideal of a sacred Shi'ite kingship, yet the special status of particular shahs became open to challenge. Relations between the

Turkish Qizilbash and Safavid shahs developed into the political tug of war between provincial aristocrats and centralizing rulers common throughout the early modern world.

The Safavids created an empire quickly, yet it took considerably longer to develop a state structure. In fact, the development of a stable government grew out of the particular needs in administering the empire. The most important architect of the Safavid state was Shah Abbas I (the Great, r. 1571–1629). One of his lasting achievements was to reduce the political influence and military presence of the Qizilbash. Before Abbas, these powerful warriors functioned as petty lords who collected taxes, enforced laws, and provided military support. Since their bases of power were local, the Qizilbash maintained a large degree of independence from the central government. Shah Abbas countered this provincialism by enacting a number of administrative and military reforms. On the administrative side, he divided the empire into royal provinces and appointed agents loyal to the government to collect taxes and carry out imperial edicts. A number of offices in the government whose responsibilities had been vague and whose jurisdiction had overlapped political and religious institutions became specified and bureaucratic. Under Shah Abbas, a sizable civil service emerged that carried out most governmental functions. The shah was able to hold the Qizilbash at bay and undermine their position through the creation of a standing professional army from enslaved Christians in Georgia, Armenia, and Circassia. Having eliminated the Qizilbash from military operations, the shah introduced gunpowder weaponry in the Safavid army.

Like most absolute monarchs, Shah Abbas ruled harshly and violently. Faced with Qizilbash insubordination and an unruly population, his armies spent much of their time engaged in military conflicts of one sort or another. Abbas put down rebellions mercilessly, and his troops massacred tens of thousands of Qizilbash. In 1590, he opened major offensives against the Uzbeks to the north and the Ottomans to the west; Safavid armies took Tabriz, Baghdad, Basra, and much of Iraq and the Persian Gulf. With the fervent support of the Shi'ite religious establishment, Abbas attempted to impose Shi'a orthodoxy across the empire, vigorously persecuting Sunnis and non-Muslims. By his death in 1629, the Safavid regime was a centralized state with an expansive empire that stretched from India through Iraq.

Despite the vigor of the Safavid empire in the early 1600s, one hundred years later it ceased to exist. Several factors account for the relatively rapid demise of the Iranian regime. Two powerful neighbors emerged, Russia under Peter I and Mughal India under Aurangezeb, who put constant pressure on the northern and eastern territories in Azerbaijan and Afghanistan. These external forces would have taxed a strong state, but after the 1660s Safavid rulers were weak and inattentive to governmental affairs. The consolidation of power that took place in the early seventeenth century allowed for a strong state under capable shahs, but proved calamitous under ineffective ones. In this power vacuum, conservative religious leaders (ulama) intervened more forcefully in political and social affairs. The ulama condemned technological and intellectual innovation and instigated bloody crackdowns on religious minorities, which destabilized the Safavid regime. In 1722, an Afghan army attacked the empire, besieged the capital of Isfahan, massacred thousands of Iranians, and forced the shah to capitulate. The Safavid empire had come to an end.

Mughal India

A second Muslim empire that appeared about the same time as the Safavid was the Mughal dynasty, which ruled over almost all of India, Pakistan, Bangladesh, and parts of Afghanistan. The area that came under Mughal control at its farthest boundaries in the early 1700s dwarfed the other two Muslim empires. Even though the culture and history of these empires differed markedly, many aspects of their rule and expansion share broad patterns. Paralleling Shah Ismail's speedy ascent in Iran, Zahiruddin Muhammad Babur, a strongman from a small territory in Afghanistan, succeeded after several tries in defeating a local Indian sultan in 1526 near Delhi and laying the basis for the Mughal Empire. The early Mughal elites were of Turkish and (after the 1550s) Persian stock and thus foreign to India. This victory provided the starting point for an Indo-Afghan empire, a multiethnic territory that necessitated the construction of a strong state. Thus, again an empire gave rise to a state.

Babur never really intended to establish a state centered in India. His primary interest was territorial control over Afghanistan and Uzbekistan from his original outpost in Kabul. Thus, unlike the religious motivations inherent in the origins of other empires, the Mughal dynasty owed its beginnings to the quite worldly minded quest of Babur to acquire an extensive central Asian empire in the tradition of his grandfather, the notorious Mongol-Turkish warrior Timurlane. Neither Babur nor his successors ever achieved the dream of central Asian glory, but they did succeed in establishing an expansive and prosperous empire that by 1700 comprised the entire south Asian subcontinent except for the most southern portion of the peninsula. Between 1526 and 1530, Babur's troops had taken control of the Punjab, Delhi, and large swaths of land in northeastern India (Bihar to Gwalior). From their capital in the city of Agra, successive Mughal emperors expanded beyond Babur's initial conquests. Most Mughal territorial gains came under the emperorships of Akbar the Great (1556–1605) and Aurangezeb (1659–1707). During Akbar's reign, the empire took in extensive portions of Pakistan and Afghanistan, as well as all of northern India as far east as Bengal. The last great imperial surge under Aurangezeb absorbed all of India except the very southern tip and extended Mughal influence north into Kashmir and the Himalayan Mountains.

Even though Mughal emperors adhered to Sunni Islam, they did not attempt to ground their political legitimacy primarily in a Muslim ideology until the reign of Aurangezeb. As promoters of Muslim piety, the Mughals expected – even demanded – obedience and loyalty from their Muslim subjects. Yet, Islam claimed only a small minority in India; most were Hindu. Thus, Mughal rulers identified themselves with, and rooted their claims to absolute rule in, their lineage from universal conquerors. Babur descended from both Chinggis Khan and Timurlane, a rather imperial pedigree if there ever was one. The cultural homeland for the Mughals lay in the central Asian steppe, and their political legacy resided in the Timurid-Mongol khans. Just as inner Asia drew Chinese emperors to the west and away from the sea, so also the northern territories of Uzbekistan and Afghanistan exerted a strong pull on Mughal emperors. As far as Mughal elites were concerned, their Timurid-Mongol identity represented the most important basis for imperial rule. Islam exercised a much greater force in the rule of Aurangezeb in the second half of the 1600s. He considered his domain a Muslim empire, and he sought to implement shari'a (Islamic law) in the territories under his jurisdiction.

Centralizing political authority did not become a high priority for the Mughal regime until the fifty-year reign of Akbar, which commenced in the mid-1500s. Widely regarded as the most capable Mughal ruler, Akbar instituted a highly centralized, bureaucratic state that was accountable solely to the emperor. He recruited imperial servants from a variety of ethnic backgrounds: Indians, Persians, Arabs, Uzbeks, Afghans, and others. Most officials were Sunni Muslims; however, Hindus and Shi'ites served as well. The criteria for service were merit-based qualities, such as performance of responsibilities and loyalty to the emperor. The Mughal state also rewarded capable civil servants and military officers generously, which fostered allegiance without coercion.

Civil officers, known as mansabdars, carried out a wide range of government functions. The Mughal bureaucracy administered most matters related to finance, revenue collection, military affairs, law enforcement, and patronage. Mansabdars had at their disposal a large retinue of clerks and assistants, making Mughal government quite comprehensive. This central administrative structure was replicated on the provincial level, though managed largely by nobles who received their posts and revenues, not from family dynasties, but through imperial patronage. The effectiveness of the Mughal state stemmed from the high quality of its officers. The creation of an effective, centralized state drove the expansion of the empire under Akbar and subsequent emperors, especially Aurangezeb in the early eighteenth century. John Richards, a leading historian of India, has observed that "the Mughal Empire was a war-state," meaning that the basic functions of the state, in the resources it extracted and allocated, were directed for the purpose of expansion and empire building.

Ruling as a religious minority proved to be one of the thorniest obstacles in the Mughal regime, particularly in the 1600s and 1700s. All of the emperors professed allegiance to Sunni Islam, though some less ardently and less militantly than others. Hindus comprised an overwhelming majority of Indians, though Shi'ites, Christians, Jews, Zoroastrians, Sikhs, and other sectarian groups lived within the empire. Until the death of Akbar, a significant degree of accommodation and coexistence characterized relations among various religious groups. Muslim Sufi mystics incorporated folk customs and Hindu devotions, just as gurus attempted to harmonize Hindu and Islamic practices. The height of this ecumenical trend occurred under Akbar who held to a mystical divine religion, who enjoyed theological debate, and who extended tolerance to all groups.

Conservative Muslim clerics found such accommodation to be blasphemous and complained bitterly about the moral pollution that came from tolerating infidels. After Akbar, conservative clerics gained more influence at court, and emperors adopted a much more orthodox Muslim stance. Consequently, Mughal society during the seventeenth and eighteenth centuries became re-Islamicized, as jurists applied shari'a law, emperors patronized clerics and theologians, and clerics pushed non-Muslims to convert. This trend intensified under Aurangezeb, who reissued the head tax (jizya) on all non-Muslims and pressured and actively persecuted Sikhs. The social division and cultural insularity created by the revival of a strident and uncompromising Islam contributed to the weakening of the empire in the early 1700s.

The Mughal empire, not unlike the Safavid, went into fast decline in the early eighteenth century and never recovered. Though the Mughal regime existed in name for another century and a half, effective government and expansion really ended in 1719 with the succession of Muhammad Shah (r. 1719–1748) as emperor. While a number of factors led to the deterioration of the empire, the fractious religious policy and the imperial overreach of Aurangezeb into southern India rank among the most important. The exclusion of non-Muslims from positions of influence drained away many talented military and civil officers from service. The policy also produced social discord, especially in newly conquered areas in south India such as the Deccan. In addition, from 1707 to 1720, the government was wracked with four major succession disputes among imperial candidates, leading to civil discord and war. Consequently, the centralized state system constructed at the end of the 1500s fell apart. Growing regionalism and fragmentation gave local powers the occasion to assert their independence and European imperial powers the opportunity to insert themselves more deeply into Indian society.

The Ottoman Empire

The Muslim empire that endured the longest and wielded the most wide-ranging influence in the early modern period had its origins in several Turkish tribes that settled on the eastern fringes of Byzantine territory in the late 1200s. Named for an early principal figure (Osman), the Ottomans were a Turkish people who came onto the world stage conquering areas in eastern Europe in the 1300s, overthrowing the Byzantine emperor in 1453, and expanding across north Africa, Arabia, Anatolia, Mesopotamia, and the Persian Gulf in the 1500s. Aggressive and ambitious, Ottomans struck fear in the hearts of chieftains, princes, kings, and emperors from Madrid to Moscow. One of the most enduring of all early modern empires, the Ottoman regime remained intact, albeit in a much diminished state, until 1923. Though Ottomans competed and warred with Christian kings in Europe and Shi'ite shahs in Iran, the empire created by Turkish sultans also produced merchants and missionaries, which fostered a rich economic and cultural exchange at a critical crossroads in Eurasia.

The early Ottoman advance into the Balkans and eastern Europe came about as a result of the swift Turkish cavalry brigades and the weakness of principalities in the region. The sultan Orhan took the city of Bursa in 1326 and from there moved into the Gallipoli peninsula in 1354, establishing a Turkish presence in Greece, Macedonia, and Serbia by the end of the 1300s. Terrified by the specter of Islam, European kings and Catholic authorities called for crusades and crafted alliances against the Ottomans. The real prize for Turkish sultans, however, was Constantinople, the capital of the Byzantine empire and the center of Orthodox Christianity. Despite the defensive efforts of European and Byzantine forces, Constantinople fell to Mehmed II (1444–1446, 1451–1481) on May 29, 1453. The conquest of Constantinople, afterwards renamed Istanbul, marked an extraordinary triumph for the Ottomans and a pivotal moment in western Asia and eastern Europe. From their new capital in Istanbul, Turkish sultans became a major power in the eastern Mediterranean and western Asia.

Sultans from the reign of Mehmed II throughout early modern Ottoman history presented themselves as the singular guardians of Islamic orthodoxy throughout the world. They assumed titles, such as "Warrior of the Faith" and "Defender of the Shari'a." These claims reminded Sunni Muslims of the glory days of universal unity in Islamdom under the Abbasid caliphs (750–1258). Within Islamic (and Christian) societies of the 1500s, powerful apocalyptic expectations reinforced the concept of the Ottoman sultan as a universal Muslim ruler to unite Christians and Jews to the true faith as the world came to an end. But Ottoman propagandists not only appropriated Islamic political theory, but they also cast the sultans as world conquerors in the tradition of Alexander the Great and Chinggis Khan. And, after the conquest of Constantinople, sultans even portrayed themselves as successors to the Byzantine emperors. Though the bases of political legitimacy came from several sources, the ideal of a universal Islamic empire ruled by a devout Muslim provided a fundamental rationale for Ottoman sovereignty.

Ottoman expansion relied heavily on effective military power and a strong state structure, enabling sultans to consolidate their authority over a range of different peoples and cultures. Ottoman elites, especially during the assaults on Christian principalities, attracted large numbers of warriors by appealing to the martial ethos of Turkish tribesmen and the Muslim concept of holy war. Thus, Ottoman fighters embraced the ideal of the holy warrior, or ghazi, of Islam. Though Ottoman conquerors did not, as a general rule, coerce non-Muslims into converting, the glory of battling for the faith against infidels supplied ample motivation for Turkish tribesmen who loved to fight.

In addition to a well-motivated military force, the Ottomans also utilized slaves, taken from Christian populations in the Balkans, known as Janissaries. The practice, referred to as the devshirme, imposed a levy of Christian children who were required to convert to Islam and enter the sultan's service. The Janissaries received a first-class education, learned to act as Turkish elites, and then served in the Ottoman army or civil administration. Those who served in the army did so in the infantry and cavalry corps, handling muskets, cannons, and the most current weapons. The Janissary and Turkish units together made up the most skilled fighting force in western Asia and eastern Europe.

The state structure that made such an effective military possible excelled in devising means for extracting revenue from the sultan's subjects and allocating it for imperial and royal needs. A chief administrator, called a vizier, oversaw the central administrative offices in Istanbul, while provincial governors regulated civil affairs in conquered areas outside the core region of Anatolia. Governors in the provinces came from two sources. One was the Turkish military personnel who resided on designated territories, known as timars, supported by local tax revenue in return for military and civil service to the central state. A second type of governor was the non-noble, salaried official who attained the office through royal appointment. In both cases, provincial governors managed the collection of taxes and enforced laws.

The actual application of the law to real-life circumstances fell to a variety of judges who ruled either from the shari'a or from a set of Turkish legal codes, referred to as kanuns. Islam shaped society and culture throughout Ottoman territories and the administration of the shari'a formed the most practical instrument for spreading and maintaining a Muslim identity. Steeped in Islamic law, Muslim judges (qadis) presided over courts throughout the empire. Sultans also issued laws and made decrees that became part of the kanuns, which supplemented the shari'a by filling in legal gaps on matters that the religious law did not specifically address.

Informal politics behind the scenes in the imperial household played a very influential part in the direction of the state and accorded women a critical place at court. Sultans had many wives and concubines, some of whom were slaves, secluded from society in a harem. Because sultans sired dozens of children, the anticipation of a sultan's death occasioned intense intrigues, as his sons competed for the throne or places of influence. Often upon the accession of a sultan, the new ruler would have his brothers and uncles murdered or blinded to eliminate threats to the throne. The women of the harem played a leading role in seeking to influence their husband to favor their own son and served as powerbrokers among their own sons. While women occupied a subordinate position in Ottoman society, wives and concubines at court wielded considerable influence.

Just as different factions struggled for power in other states around the world, Janissaries and timar holders sought to shape the character of the government. Janissaries served in important posts in the central government, managing the harem, accounting for revenue, and implementing royal policy. At odds with the centralizing tendencies of the sultan's government, nobles attempted to thwart the state-building efforts of the Janissaries. Decentralization enabled timars, who lived in the provinces, to operate more autonomously and to retain a greater share of tax revenue. As holy warriors, timar-holding ghazi aspired to campaign against Christian kingdoms in the west. By the reign of Suleyman I (known both as the Magnificent and the Lawgiver,

r. 1520–1566), the Janissaries in the military and the state gained the upper hand, ensuring the victory of strong central authority in the Ottoman Empire.

One of the most unique features about Ottoman society was the manner in which the Muslim government treated religious minorities, namely Christians, Jews, and other minority groups. For centuries Muslim governments had granted Jews and Christians a protected status whereby they received the privilege to worship in their tradition in return for paying a special tax, the jizya, and for agreeing to a host of sanctions that identified them as second-class citizens. The Ottoman government adopted this policy and allowed the dhimmis, as Christians and Jews were known, to organize themselves into semi-independent communities. In Anatolia and in Arab lands, many Christians and Jews converted to Islam, at least in part to avoid these financial and social burdens, yet in the Balkans, comprised overwhelmingly of Christians, few conversions took place. Forced conversions were uncommon and, while violence against Jews and Christians did occur, the normal state of affairs was a delicate coexistence between Muslims, Christians, and Jews. The accommodation of religious minorities in this manner was not quite religious toleration, at least as we understand it in the modern world. Few people in the early modern period conceived of an inherent right to the freedom of belief and expression. In the Ottoman Empire, concessions to dhimmis emerged as an effective means to manage religious difference in societies that were quite diverse culturally. Over the course of the early modern period, relations between these communities, known as millets, and Ottoman authorities became increasingly institutionalized. As a result, by 1700, millets largely governed themselves, though non-Muslims continued to exist in a subordinate social status.

The peak of the Ottoman Empire extended from the 1500s through the 1600s. After defeating Safavid forces at Chaldiran in 1514, Selim I (r. 1512–1520) swept into eastern Anatolia, Mesopotamia, and Egypt, along with Mecca and Medina in the Arabian peninsula. Ottomans and Safavids remained bitter rivals and fought intermittently during this period. Eventually, the Ottomans managed to absorb Iraq into their dominions. The present-day boundary between Iraq and Iran stems from the standoff between the two empires. Ottoman sultans also displayed a keen interest in developing a maritime empire to protect Mecca and Medina, Islam's holiest cities from Christian powers and to control trade in the eastern Mediterranean, the Red Sea, and the Persian Gulf. Selim I and Suleyman I effectively resisted Portuguese efforts to divert trade from the Persian Gulf and Mediterranean. Turkish commanders planted forts along the coasts of Arabia, Yemen, and east Africa, thwarting the Portuguese strategy of cutting off the Persian Gulf to trade.

In the west, the Ottomans competed with several European states and Russia for territory in eastern Europe, the Balkans, the Crimea, the Caucasus, and Ukraine. Suleyman rallied troops in eastern Europe pushing though Hungary in the 1520s and laying siege to Vienna in 1529. During the sixteenth and seventeenth centuries, the Ottomans struggled against the Hapsburgs who controlled large areas in central and eastern Europe through their ancestral homeland in Austria. Janissary and cavalry troops were never able to crack Austria, but they did pull Hungary, Moldavia, Transylvania, and Romania into the Ottoman dominions. By the second half of the 1500s, however, the Austrian Hapsburgs managed to check Ottoman expansion and regain control over Hungary and other eastern dominions at the end of the 1600s.

Ottoman conquests in north Africa – Egypt, Tunisia, and Algeria – stoked European fears that the sultans would turn the Mediterranean into a Muslim lake. The Hapsburgs once again opposed encroachment, this time into the Mediterranean, by challenging Turkish bases in north Africa and Turkish ships on the sea. Malta and Cyprus came within the orbit of Suleyman and Selim II by 1570, though the Hapsburgs scored a major naval victory at Lepanto a year later. By 1580, the Hapsburgs and Ottomans reached a stalemate so that the Ottomans held onto territory from Algeria to Egypt and Palestine (including Cyprus and Malta), but were not able to push farther.

In the 1700s, Ottoman expansion came to a standstill with several military reversals. The arrested empire building stemmed from imperial overreach and political fragmentation. The frontier areas of the Ottoman domain in the west – eastern Europe and the western Mediterranean – pushed up against the Russian and Hapsburg-Austrian empires, both of which were vigorous and acquisitive. To the east, the Safavid presence required extensive Ottoman resources to hold the borders. In the face of these external demands, and increasing pressure in the west, the central state gave way to provincial parties, such as nobles, local officials, and merchants, who longed for political and economic autonomy from an exploitive central government. A succession of incompetent sultans were unable to keep the central bureaucracy functioning so power devolved to the local level. Provincial authorities lacked the comprehensive resources to maintain a well-equipped and well-trained fighting force. Underpaid Janissaries abandoned their allegiance to sultan and state for wives, lands, and additional incomes. Finally, as the central authority waned, the ulama waged moral and religious campaigns that stifled innovation and intellectual advancement. Just as in the late Safavid and Mughal dynasties, cultural insularity in the Ottoman Empire denied political leaders tools that could have reversed the imperial slide. In the nineteenth century, stagnation gave way to contraction as the empire suffered losses to Russia and Austria and from local revolts. By that time, the once great Ottoman Empire of Suleyman the Magnificent had become known as the "sick man of Europe."

An Age of Empire Building in Asia

The early modern period was an age of remarkable empire building across Asia. As societies recovered from Mongols and Timurids, a slate of strong states appeared in China, Russia, India, Iran, and Anatolia. Dynasties crafted an array of creative ideologies, invoking the divine, a venerable lineage, or the practical need for stability to justify their rule. Across the political landscape, the elements of state building were noticeably similar: the subjugation of noble or provincial parties, creation of comprehensive bureaucracies, and construction of effective armies and navies. Empire building was a natural outgrowth of state formation, as powerful armies brought new peoples and lands under imperial control. The construction and maintenance of empire led to four critical processes of interaction – long-distance trade, migration, biological exchange, and spread of knowledge – that transformed world history.

Works Consulted

Babayan, Kathryn. "The Safavid Synthesis: From Qizilbash Islam to Imamite Shi'ism," *Iranian Studies* 27(1994), 135–161.

Brook, Timothy. *The Confusions of Pleasure: Commerce and Culture in Ming China*. Berkeley: University of California Press, 1998.

Brummett, Palmira. *Ottoman Seapower and Levantine Diplomacy in the Age of Discovery*. Albany: State University of New York Press, 1994.

Chaudhuri, K. N. *Trade and Civilization in the Indian Ocean: An Economic History from the Rise of Islam to 1750*. Cambridge: Cambridge University Press, 1985.

Dreyer, Edward L. *China and the Oceans in the Early Ming Dynasty, 1405–1433*. New York: Pearson Longman, 2007.

Dukes, Paul. *The Making of Russian Absolutism, 1613–1801*. New York: Longman, 1982.

Forsyth, James. *A History of the Peoples of Siberia: Russia's North Asian Colony, 1581–1990*. Cambridge: Cambridge University Press, 1994.

Hellie, Richard. "Migration in Early Modern Russia, 1480s–1780s," in David Eltis ed. *Coerced and Free Migration: Global Perspectives*. Stanford, Calif.: Stanford University Press, 2002, 292–323.

Hostetler, Laura. *Qing Colonial Enterprise: Ethnography and Cartography in Early Modern China*. Chicago: University of Chicago Press, 2001.

Inalcik, Halil. *The Ottoman Empire: The Classical Age 1300–1600*. New York: Praeger Publishers, 1973.

Lapidus, Ira M. *A History of Islamic Societies*, 2nd ed. Cambridge: Cambridge University Press, 2002.

Levathes, Louise. *When China Ruled the Seas: The Treasure Fleet of the Dragon Throne, 1405–1433*. New York: Oxford University Press. 1996.

Lieberman, Victor. "Transcending East-West Dichotomies: State and Culture Formation in Six Ostensibly Disparate Areas," in Victor Lieberman ed. *Beyond Binary Histories: Re-imagining Eurasia to c. 1830*. Ann Arbor: The University of Michigan Press, 1999, 19–102.

Madariaga, Isabel de. *Ivan the Terrible: First Tsar of Russia*. New Haven, Conn.: Yale University Press, 2005.

Menzies, Gavin. *1421: The Year China Discovered America*. London: Transworld Publishers, 2002.

Mungello, D. E. *The Great Encounter of China and the West, 1500–1800*. 2nd ed. Lanham, Md.: Rowman & Littlefield Publishers, 2005.

Perdue, Peter. *China Marches West: The Qing Conquest of Central Eurasia*. Cambridge, Mass.: Harvard University Press, 2005.

Pomeranz, Kenneth, and Topik, Steven. *The World That Trade Created: Society, Culture, and the World Economy, 1400 to the Present*. Armonk, N.Y.: M. E. Sharpe, 2006.

Richards, John F. *The Mughal Empire*. Cambridge: Cambridge University Press, 1995.

Roemer, H. R. "The Safavid Period," in Peter Jackson and Laurence Lockhart eds. *The Timurid and Safavid Periods*, vol. 6 *The Cambridge History of Iran*, 7 vols. Cambridge: Cambridge University Press, 1986, 203–456.

Savory, Roger M. *Studies on the History of Safawid Iran.* London: Variorum Imprints, 1987.

Seth, Michael J. *A Concise History of Korea: From the Neolithic Period through the Nineteenth Century.* Lanham, Md.: Rowman & Littlefield Publishers, 2006.

3

International Markets and Global Exchange Networks

The exchange of manufactured goods and cultivated foodstuffs has formed an integral part of human history in most every corner of the planet from the earliest days of our existence down to the present. Trading products has been such a profitable economic activity that countless merchants have been willing to travel long distances often on foot, astride a cranky animal, or inside a rickety sailing vessel to conduct business. Even in civilizations in the remote past – from 4,000 to 600 years ago – buyers and sellers trekked as far as from Mesopotamia (Iraq) to the Indus River Valley (Pakistan) in Asia, from southern Mexico to present day Vera Cruz in America, and from Mali to Morocco in Africa. As early as 2,000 to 3,000 years ago, long-distance traders moved along regularly traveled routes. The longest and the most renowned was the Silk Roads, a complex of routes that facilitated overland and maritime trade from the Mediterranean to the South China Sea. Despite all kinds of cataclysms, from falling empires in Persia, China, Guatemala, and Rome, to marauding Timurids in Asia, to ravaging plagues in Eurasia, merchant groups continued to ply their trade down to the early modern age of empire building.

Long distance commerce in this age of global engagement developed out of longstanding networks and all the financial mechanisms that made them work. Of all the commercial activity going on in various parts of the world, routes in Eurasia and Africa represented the strongest continuity with the international markets of the early modern period. Though age-old Afro-Eurasian circuits and mechanisms formed a vital element of continuity, the scale of exchange signified abrupt new changes in early modern trade. From the 1400s to the 1700s, large portions of sub-Saharan Africa, America, and Oceania became absorbed into commercial transactions that sent, among other things, American silver to Asia, American sugar to Europe, west African slaves to America, Siberian and Canadian furs to Europe and China, Indonesian and Indian spices to Europe, and European muskets to Africa and America. The potato migrated from Peru to Europe in the late 1500s, finding a welcome home in Ireland two hundred years later. Genuinely global economic networks emerged in this period.

Early modern international commerce differed fundamentally from modern configurations. Premodern commerce remained polycentric; that is, a plurality of overlapping but distinct economic spheres coexisted alongside one another. For example, fluctuations in sugar production in the Caribbean or tobacco yields along the Atlantic seaboard had little effect on consumption in southeast Asia. Likewise, the spice market in Asia bore little relation to commerce in the Atlantic. In modern times conversely, financial developments in one region reverberate throughout the world, such as the stock market crash in the 1930s and the financial meltdown in 2008. Early modern trade did not, therefore, constitute a comprehensive economic system.

The volume of long-distance trade, while significant in contemporary times, pales in comparison to international commerce in the modern era. The core European commercial states, England, the Netherlands, France, Spain, and Portugal, derived only about two percent of their Gross Domestic Product (or GDP, the sum of a country's economic production) from overseas trade. Yet, international trade as a portion of the GDP in these same countries in 2005 ranged from 28 percent (England and Spain) to 66 percent (the Netherlands). Nevertheless, the financial ramifications of early modern long-distance trade were far from insignificant, as a number of European states and merchant firms grew incredibly wealthy from commerce in the Atlantic.

Beyond pure economics, the most important features of international commerce were the large scale exchanges of material culture and the geopolitical implications of commerce. The trading structures that moved merchandise over long distances were closely interconnected with the expansion of empires that we examined in the previous two chapters. Consequently, international commerce was not simply the working of supply and demand in a free market. Rather, imperial regimes sought to influence the conditions of trade for their benefit, just as political powers had to accommodate and adapt to local circumstances. The global dissemination of material goods and the imperial dimensions of trade fostered broader awareness of foreign peoples and places, which contributed to greater cultural integration of world regions.

The Characteristics of Early Modern Trade

Long-distance economic exchange possessed a number of distinct characteristics that stemmed from the particular risks involved in trade and travel at the time. The challenges associated with breaking into markets sometimes far from home or wringing larger profits from those markets compelled individuals and organizations to blend traditional methods with new strategies. Mercantile associations were built on longstanding networks and time-honored mechanisms to manage the risks of intercontinental business operations.

Longstanding Networks

International commerce developed out of regional production and commercial operations around the world that had existed for centuries. The most intense commercial zone in the world – the one that tantalized mariners and merchants in Portugal – was along the coastline of the Indian Ocean basin. Ports along the coastlines of southern China, the Indonesian archipelago, India, the Persian Gulf, the Arabian peninsula, the Red Sea, and east Africa served as conduits, funneling products from the interior of these regions for collection and distribution to other lands. The most important ports of call across this vast maritime area included Macau, Guangzhou (Canton), and Quanzhou on China's southeast coast; Melaka on the southern tip of Malaya; Aceh on the northwestern edge of Sumatra; Surat, Bengal, Calicut, Goa, and Masulipatam along the Indian coastlines; Colombo on the island of Sri Lanka; Hormuz, an island itself just off the coast of Iran in the Persian Gulf; Aden on the tip of Yemen; and Mogadishu and Kilwa along east Africa. These port cities possessed a high degree of political and economic autonomy, thus bringing together buyers and sellers from all of these territories.

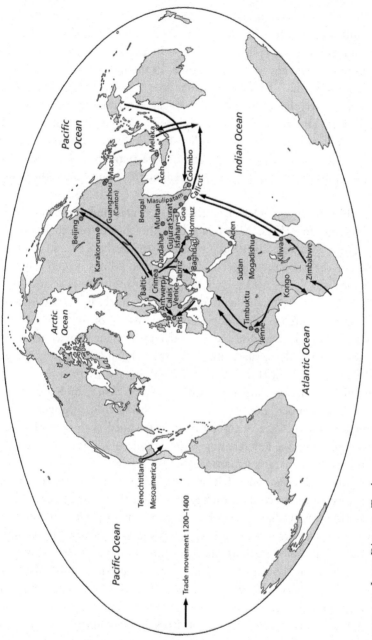

MAP 3.1. Long-Distance Trade, 1200–1400

The ebb and flow of exchange occurred along the annual rhythms of wind and weather in the Indian Ocean. In the spring and summer, monsoon winds pushed from southwest to northeast across the ocean into Asia's continental coastline. In the fall, the winds reversed themselves so that during the winter they gusted from northeast to southwest. Merchants timed their voyages according to the prevailing winds during the course of the yearly circuit. Persian, Indian, and Arab mariners utilized substantial wooden ships, known as dhows, some of which possessed a cargo capacity of more than four hundred tons. Chinese junks were even larger, with capacities of up to one thousand tons.

Within the Indian Ocean basin, many routes linked various cities and regions to others. Merchants brought cotton, indigo (used for dyes), and gold and silver bullion from areas in the Red and Arabian Seas via the western coast of India to the Malay archipelago in exchange for spices, silks, and porcelain from various islands and China. A second route from Gujarat in western India to the Swahili cities incorporated African goods into this whorl of material culture. The range of merchandise passing through the coasts was amazing: precious stones, dyes, rugs, silks from the Persian Gulf; cloth, indigo, and yarn from Bengal and Coromandel; cinnamon from Sri Lanka; rice, silks, and porcelain from China; slaves, ivory, and gold from Africa; and pepper, nutmeg, mace, and cloves from Indonesia. Just as remarkable was the variety of peoples engaged in these exchanges; most ports contained merchant groups of Gujaratis (Indian), Fujianese (Chinese), Persians, Armenians, Jews, and Arabs.

A part of the renowned Silk Roads, the overland routes of central Asia constituted a second distinct trading zone that complemented port trade along the Indian Ocean basin. Caravans of pack animals, usually camels or horses, transported merchandise typically consisting of lighter luxury items, such as silks, precious stones and metals, musks, dyes, woolen and cotton cloth, candles, and other small finished goods. One of the largest commercial streams of slaving in history was centered in the Crimean region on the Black Sea. Raiders captured Slavic peoples in the Ukraine, Poland, and Russia and sold them in Crimean cities to buyers from across Asia. In the 1400s, Ottomans and Tatars wrested this profitable enterprise from Italian merchants and continued it throughout the early modern period. The traffic in humans in the Crimea ensnared hundreds of thousands and became an important staple of the economy during the early modern period.

In central Asia, with the collapse of the Mongol Empire in the 1300s, trade became much more tenuous along the Silk Roads as warring Turkish nomadic tribes, unstable khanates, and opportunistic bandits threatened the security of travel. Nevertheless, the expansive territory made up of northern India, Pakistan, Iran, Iraq, Armenia, Afghanistan, and southern Russia still experienced vigorous commercial activity. Close family and personal connections between Indian, Armenian, and Persian merchant groups represented the driving forces of trade in this region. Merchant firms from these areas made contact with one another in a number of vital cities, such as Isfahan, Qandahar, Tabriz, Multan, and Baghdad. These cities had long histories as economic hubs along the Silk Roads, and they survived the tumult of the collapsing Mongol empires.

The conglomeration of states, territories, and cities in Europe from the Baltic to the Mediterranean Sea made up a third regional commercial zone. Two distinct circuits flowed into Europe, one from the Mediterranean in the south and the other from the Baltic Sea region into the northern regions. The southern flow, dominated by north Italian merchants in Venice, Genoa, Padua, and Florence, acquired Asian and African merchandise from their agents in Egypt, Constantinople, and various cities along the north African coast. Italian merchant houses, particularly Venetian ones, maintained a virtual monopoly on the Mediterranean mercantile economy, though merchants from southern France and Spain had managed to elbow their way into this trade. Italians brought the newly acquired Asian products, especially spices, but also silks and porcelain, and resold them at a cluster of fairs held in France in the county of Champagne, just northeast of Paris. Local people, elites, and their trade representatives purchased these items at the fairs for clients or for resale in urban areas across Europe.

The trade network predominating in northern Europe focused, unlike that in the southern circuit, on commodities: grain from the Baltic (Poland, Latvia, Lithuania) and wool from England. Since the middle ages, merchants from northern German cities formed a cooperative, known as the Hanseatic League, which dominated commerce in the northern seas, much like Venice did in the Mediterranean. Hanseatic merchants purchased wheat and other grains from areas in Poland, Latvia, and Lithuania and transported it in large carrying vessels to northern German cities. Individual merchant firms in each city then contracted to sell grain throughout Germany and the Low Countries, shipping the grain in barges along inland rivers. Separate from the Baltic grain trade, English merchants shipped wool to major cloth markets at Calais (France) and Antwerp (Low Countries).

Three principal circuits of trade, flowing through and outside Africa, comprised a fourth commercial zone. In the north, the trans-Saharan caravan traffic in gold and slaves to the coastal cities incorporated the Sudan (just south of the desert) into the Mediterranean networks. Arab Muslim merchants had discovered commercial opportunities in west African cities, where political elites had access to gold from the Senegal, Niger, and Gambia Rivers. As a result, a series of thriving merchant-based empires emerged in west Africa; at the beginning of the fifteenth century, the Songhay Empire controlled this territory and managed the trans-Saharan route.

On the southern end of the continent, a second intra-African commercial flow linked the Swahili cities of the east coast to a prosperous inland empire known as the Great Zimbabwe (in present-day Zimbabwe). In the early fifteenth century, the declining Great Zimbabwe gave way to the Mutapa Empire located in the same area. Local peoples mined gold from the rivers throughout the Zimbabwe Plateau and collected ivory, which they traded for cloth and beads in the coastal cities. Gold, ivory, and secondarily slaves, were the primary African staples in the vital trade with Gujarat in northwestern India. The Swahili-Gujarat connection brought African goods into the larger commercial network of the Indian Ocean, as African gold and ivory made their way as far east as China.

While the northern and southeastern routes connected lands in Africa to the larger Eurasian commercial world, a third transregional sector, situated in central sub-Sahara (present-day Kongo, Zaire, and Angola), was solely an internal exchange network. Because no written records existed before the arrival of Europeans, little is known about trade in this area. By the 1400s, the Kongo Kingdom dominated the region and exacted tribute in slaves, gold, and agricultural products from the scattered small villages.

Finally, the fifth major commercial zone lay in the Americas, situated in Central America and Mexico (also known as Mesoamerica).

South central Mexico, extending to the Yucatan peninsula, had been the site of a series of civilizations, beginning with the Olmec Empire, around 1400 B.C.E. The empires of this region fostered trade throughout a broad area, even as far north as what is today the southwestern United States. Precious stones, gold, cotton, tin, and birds (parrots and macaws) moved back and forth along several routes. On the eve of European contact, the Aztec Empire ruled over most of Mesoamerica from its capitol in Tenochtitlan. Emperors imposed tribute requirements among neighboring societies, requiring quotas in maize, textiles, jewelry, blankets, cacao, pottery, and human beings to be used in ritual sacrifices. The most significant commercial center lay just outside Tenochtitlan in the city of Tlatelolco that operated an extensive market, attracting merchants from across Mesoamerica. The lack of any indigenous pack animals, except for the llama, and the absence of a wheel meant that humans formed the primary source of portage in Mesoamerican trade.

Thus, long-distance trade was a widespread phenomenon before the advent of the early modern period. Not only did societies in almost every corner of the globe engage in trade across considerable distances, but commercial networks in Africa, Asia, and Europe also overlapped at key geographical points. The port city trade in the Indian Ocean, the overland routes in central Asia, the intra-European circuits, and the north African zone fed into one another at various points along the Mediterranean coast. The Swahili cities on the east African coast served as another point of transcontinental intersection as local merchants exchanged gold and ivory from the Zimbabwe plateau for cloth and spices from south and southeast Asia. By 1400, transcontinental trade had led to increasing integration of large portions of Africa, Asia, and Europe, an important precondition for the formation of a global commercial economy in the early modern period.

Organization of Trade

These networks offered merchants in the early modern period the possibility of great rewards, since products imported from far away were not readily available in the local economy. Yet this type of trade also posed daunting obstacles for those willing to conduct business over great expanses. Merchants who intended to profit from buying and selling in different lands not only had to contend with the issues faced by businesses in our world today, such as raising capital, identifying a market for certain products, and buying low and selling high, but they also had to deal with a range of issues more specific to circumstances in the premodern world.

Long-distance trade took a very long time – sometimes over a year – to complete a circuit and carried all sorts of dangers and uncertainties from sickness, banditry, malfeasance, warfare, shipwreck, spoilage, price fluctuation, and unstable political conditions. For seamen on transcontinental voyages, life onboard a vessel could be quite grim. Sanitation, hygiene, and diet were substandard for prolonged human duration, leading to wasting diseases and ailments, such as scurvy, rickets, and severe diarrhea, known as the "bloody flux." A deficiency of vitamin C, scurvy produced large discolored spots on the skin, led to the loss of teeth, and incapacitated victims with fatigue. As one can imagine, crews could easily become restive and even rebellious. To protect against mutiny, officers imposed a strict discipline, flogging seamen for indiscretions and hanging them for serious offenses.

In this precarious world of early modern trade, one basic type of risk was protection that necessitated a range of expenditures to safeguard all the activities associated with trading far from home. These costs involved such things as paying taxes or tribute to various officials to conduct business in or travel across their territories, hiring strongmen or soldiers for security during the voyages, and bribing (or paying extortion money) to whomever necessary to ensure a safe journey. Bandits on land and sea lurked on the periphery of every society around the globe, looking for opportunities to prey on unsuspecting travelers and traders. The pirate became a particular object of fascination for writers in the 1600s and 1700s looking for new exotic material to mesmerize audiences. Charles Johnson, an English writer in the early 1700s, for example, described Edward Teach, infamously known as Blackbeard, the scourge of the Carolina coast:

[His] Beard was black, which he suffered to grow to an extravagant Length; as to Breadth, it came up to his Eyes, he was accustomed to twist it with Ribbons, in small tails...and turn them about his Ears...and [he] struck a lighted match...on each side [of] his Face, his Eyes naturally looking Fierce and Wild, made him altogether such a Figure, that Imagination cannot form an Idea of a Fury, from Hell, to look more frightful.[1]

Underneath comic book characterizations such as Johnson's lay the awful reality of piracy and banditry for merchants and mariners. While pirates and bandits have always plied their trade, predation by gangs reached new heights in the early modern period. The growth resulted from the increase in long-distance travel and the inability of any state to control the high seas and highways effectively. Banditry became an acute problem in east and central Asia during the Ming period, and piracy posed tremendous dangers in the Caribbean, north African coast, western Indian Ocean around Madagascar, and the South China Sea. In a number of cases, women led pirate gangs. Jacquotte Delahaye led a gang of a hundred pirates that took a small Caribbean island from the Spanish in 1656 and died several years later in a shootout defending her "freebooter republic."

Beyond protection from bandits and pirates, another major expense that merchants faced was transportation costs. These represent the total outlay in transporting goods, currency, and human agents round trip. Protection and transportation costs rose proportionately with the hazards of a business journey forcing merchants either to raise prices for their products, to seek alternative trading locations, or to forego (or abort) a venture altogether. How did merchants manage these risks? And further, how did the management of risk influence early modern trade?

The workings of commerce required intensive partnering, for no single merchant could accomplish all the tasks, handle all the dangers, and raise all the capital necessary for such extensive undertakings. One well-established and forceful partnership throughout history was the alliance between the political state and the economic elite. The closest associations between state power and commercial enterprise developed in the European, Russian, and Ottoman Empires. According to mercantilist theory, the state should play a central role in directing foreign trade. Consequently, European governments either administered overseas commercial activity directly (Portugal, Spain, France) or closely supported the merchant companies it granted monopolies (England, the Netherlands). Likewise, Russian tsars and Ottoman sultans fused the expansion of trade with the interests of the state. The Safavid and Mughal dynasties took a middle position. Both regimes promoted trade. The Mughals granted tax privileges to European companies, while Safavid shahs uprooted Armenians just across the border from the Ottoman Empire and relocated their merchants to the newly constructed city of New Julfa so that they could trade with Russian, Dutch, Persian, and English merchants.

On the other end of the spectrum, imperial courts in China represented the most guarded stance toward commerce. Confucian mandarins regarded trade as an ever-present source of disorder that needed to be restricted and regulated. The government treated Chinese merchants who ventured into maritime Asia with contempt and refused to protect them when they encountered danger from other political powers. In most cases, however, imperial states played crucial roles in the growth of long-distance trade.

At the local operational level, the most elemental and enduring form of a mercantile partnership was the family. Family networks, originating in the immediate household and then, as opportunities expanded, extending out to cousins, uncles, aunts, and in-laws, provided stronger bonds of trust than relations with nonfamily members. Families could pool resources and keep profits within the domestic corporation. As operations grew and became more complex, family businesses took on additional partners and investors outside the bonds of kinship.

Most family merchant businesses in the early modern period remained small and local, though some became players in long-distance operations. In the early 1500s, the Stroganov family of Russia made a fortune by exporting salt from the lake Solvychegodsk in the extreme north. When Ivan IV began to open up Kazan in the Volga River basin in the 1550s, he granted Anika Stroganov large tracts of land in the region. The Stroganov family financed military operations and the construction of fortified settlements in eastern Siberia in return for a monopoly on most revenues. In the late 1500s and early 1600s, the Stroganovs became the richest family in Russia.

Throughout southeast Asia it was not uncommon for women to take the leading commercial role in a family, buying and selling in the markets in the port city trade. In Cambodia, Thailand, Sumatra, and Malaya, women played influential functions in family business operations. European merchants, almost all of whom were male, recognized and utilized the retail expertise of local women. They arranged temporary marriages whereby the merchant paid her a negotiated price to live with him as a partnered couple for a specific period. When he departed for Europe, often returning to his wife and family, the liaison came to an end, and she was free to find another short-term husband. Temporary wives proved extremely useful in helping European men develop familiarity with local markets.

Nonfamilial corporate organizations in this age of global networks borrowed heavily from long-established forms of partnership. Appearing in a variety of guises, merchant associations acted to bring together capital and labor as well as to reduce risk. One versatile form that prevailed throughout Eurasia was the *commenda*, which was common among Arabs in central Asia as early as the 600s and in north Italy in the 1200s. In a *commenda*, one partner supplied the bulk of the capital, while a second contributed most of the labor, making the voyage and carrying out all the assorted transactions. The more prosperous firms employed agents and sought to raise capital from a wide circle of investors. Displacing the traditional traveling merchant, salaried factors resided temporarily in the places where firms conducted a large share of business. Factors managed transactions, oversaw the organization's local affairs, and made periodic reports back home. For example, at the end of the 1400s, Mahmud Gâwân, an Iranian business owner and local ruler in southern India (Bahmani) dispatched factors annually to Bursa in Anatolia to sell Indian spices and textiles. Florentine factors in turn purchased these goods and imported them for resale in Europe. Many varieties of this basic organizational scheme existed across Asia, Europe, and north Africa. Islamic law sanctioned commercial partnerships, promoting the cooperative use of capital and a shared stake in profits and debts. In the Baltic, the Hanseatic League exemplified the strengths of collective resources in maritime trade.

The joint-stock companies chartered by the English and Dutch governments in the early 1600s (and later Swedish and Danish corporations) represent more abundantly capitalized and elaborately organized forms of these earlier partnerships. Traditionally, historians have hailed the overseas joint-stock companies as the first modern corporations. Given the previous forms of partnership, however, it is more appropriate to regard them as transitional organizations, bridging earlier collective efforts to later corporate structures.

English businessmen in London had formed collective merchant organizations in the 1500s, like the Company of Merchant Adventurers, as did Dutch commercial parties after the initial voyages into the Indian Ocean in the 1590s. From these associations emerged the English and Dutch East India companies in 1600 and 1602, respectively. These and later corporations differed from previous organizations in several respects. Joint-stock companies received a government monopoly for trade in a specific region. Later, trading corporations, such as the Virginia Company, South Sea Company, Dutch West India Company, and Levantine Company, were formed for exploration and settlement in America and Asia, obtaining exclusive rights to these territories. So governments allied themselves closely with these mercantile organizations. Second, a board of directors in the home country governed each company. Accountable to investors, directors maintained ultimate responsibility for the companies. In practical terms, they gave overseas administrators and officials a great deal of latitude in running regional operations. The directors raised capital by selling shares of company stock publicly to investors. Typically investors assumed all liabilities for losses and in return received a substantial percentage on any profits, as much as 100 percent on their investment in some cases. Directors answered to shareholders about the management and the profitability of the companies. Consequently, shareholder interest, or in other words profit, became the driving force behind the overseas trading organizations.

In addition to the institutions that facilitated long-distance trade, a wide array of financial technologies enabled merchants to obtain credit, transfer debts, and exchange funds. Commerce simply could not have developed without a means to transmit credit, payment, and debt, so these exchange mechanisms were critical to the growth of international markets. The origins of instruments, like the check, bill of exchange, and loans, arose long before the early modern period as common sense solutions to the risks caused by distance. Both the check and bills of exchange (promissory notes redeemable at remote sites) became widely utilized in Persia in the 1000s and 1100s, but were in use, along with rudimentary forms of the bank, in the central Asian zone centuries earlier.

Likewise, scholars have located extensive banking and accounting operations in Cairo dating from 1075. The Chinese first put paper money into circulation in the 1000s. Muslim merchants adopted technologies, such as bills of exchange, checks, double-entry bookkeeping (accounting system for recording debits and credits), and circulated them in the lands under their influence. As European traders, particularly Italians came into contact with Muslim merchants, Europeans discovered these financial instruments and utilized them in developing their own commercial enterprises. By the 1300s, these business practices were common in northern Italy.

Cities formed the spatial environment for exchange between foreign merchants and organizations in the early modern world. Situated strategically on overland or maritime commercial routes, cities and oases sometimes existed somewhat independently from central political control, as Gujarat and Calicut in India or Kilwa and Malindi in east Africa. Other municipalities, like Macau and Guangzhou in China or Aleppo and Baghdad in the Middle East, however, operated under closer government scrutiny. Regardless, cities provided a legal framework to resolve disputes and greatly diminished the threat of violence by private parties, which kept protection costs low. Falling within municipal jurisdiction, fairs, markets, and bazaars marked the designated spaces, carefully regulated by law and custom, for economic exchange. In the initial stages of development, towns held markets on specific days, then gradually over a long period of time, the periodic markets evolved into permanent ones.

Merchants from the region often traveled along a circuit of fairs, setting out their goods in the morning and then packing up for tomorrow's fair down the road. Booths, tables, vendors, moneychangers, local artisans and peasants, peddlers, animals, children, and all sorts of foreigners talking in many different tongues filled the smelly, smoky, and crowded markets. Cities within all the trading circuits of the early modern world, whether maritime or overland, were filled with these commercial spaces that connected local production of spices, metals, cotton, silk, and other goods to the wider world. Consequently, urban culture has, in most times, promoted a level of tolerance and cosmopolitanism to make buyers and sellers feel secure to transact business. Within the transregional commercial zones discussed previously, cities functioned as nodal points for exchange that connected local and regional producers to the wider world of international markets. As cities grew in Eurasia, along the coasts of Africa, and in America in the early modern period, their markets became even more firmly connected to a global flow of goods.

In most cases, merchants or agents did not work for businesses in the way we understand today. Individual merchants, agents, and investors often functioned as independent operators who partnered with different associates for specific operations. For example, a merchant in Gujarat might join with several associates, perhaps a brother and an uncle, to finance a trip to Kilwa (east Africa) to purchase gold. They might also seek additional investors and the assistance of local bankers from the Banyan Hindu caste. At the same time, our hypothetical Gujarati merchant probably was making plans to invest as a silent partner in a voyage to the Molucca Islands for cloves and nutmeg organized by a former associate in a previous operation. If he proved to be an enterprising merchant, he would engage in several other deals as well. The Florentine silk merchant, Gregorio Dati, for example, withdrew from a partnership with Buonacorso Berardi in 1395 and then eight months later formed an association with Michele di Ser Parente and Nardo di Lippo that they agreed would expire in 1403. Dati invested 1,000 florins in the business's total capital of 9,600 florins for an ownership stake of four and one-half shares out of twenty-four total shares. At the same time, Dati did business on his own and shipped cloth to his brother Simone di Stagio in Valencia (Spain) who sold Dati's merchandise on consignment. Merchants found abiding business partnerships, many times involving family members, yet commitments of this sort did not prevent them from acting as free agents to pursue other opportunities when they arose.

Trade Diasporas

Regardless of the specific institutional form of long-distance trade, doing business in a foreign land necessitated bridging the cultural divide with the host society. Throughout world history, cross-cultural trade was facilitated by settlements of foreign residents that resided in a particular district, city, or market. Referred to as trade diasporas by modern scholars, resident foreign communities acted as cultural mediators between merchant groups that came from their native lands and the host community. By learning the language and local customs, networking with suppliers and other alien merchants, and establishing a familiarity with political authorities, these agents cultivated good business relations and eased potential hostilities caused by suspicions toward foreigners. For example, Indian merchants planted themselves throughout commercial sites along caravan routes in central Asia in the 1600s, in Afghanistan, Iran, the Caucasus region, and Russia. Some 10,000 resided in the Safavid capital of Isfahan.

Two of the most extensive trade diasporas were Jewish and Armenian communities, serving as important cultural mediators in the early modern world. Fleeing violent conflict and taking advantage of commercial opportunities, both peoples migrated around the globe, turning up in such places as Bahia (Brazil), Boston, Kandahar (Afghanistan), Cairo, Istanbul, Aleppo (Syria), London, Astrakhan (Russia), and Macau. In the late 1400s, during the final campaigns to conquer the Islamic Moors in southern Spain, religious and political authorities took a dark view of Sephardic Jews (that is, Jews from Iberia) in their midst. Shortly after the last Moorish stronghold fell to Spanish forces in 1492, King Ferdinand and Queen Isabella, with the backing of church officials, declared that all Jews must convert to Christianity or leave. Over the course of the 1500s, Sephardic Jews immigrated into north Africa, Italy, the eastern Mediterranean, the Spanish and Portuguese empires, Amsterdam, and throughout Ottoman realms.

As a result of these circumstances, Sephardic Jews and New Christians (Jews who claimed to convert to Christianity) positioned themselves at key geographical points to take advantage of the growing global networks. In the Atlantic economy, New Christian communities became important agents in silver exports from Peru and Mexico and the sugar trade from Brazil in the 1500s, fostering exchanges between the colonies and European merchants. In 1644, there were 1,450 Sephardic Jews in Dutch-occupied regions of America. Sephardim and converted Jews also emerged in the major northern European commercial metropoles, becoming especially conspicuous in London, Amsterdam, and Hamburg. The Jewish populations peaked at 1,700 in London in 1740 and 4,500 in Amsterdam at the end of the seventeenth century. Likewise in the Mediterranean, New Christians formed a significant commercial presence along the Dalmatian coast, in Venice, Livorno, and Ancona. New Christians numbered well over 3,000 in Livorno.

Even though New Christians performed valuable commercial functions in the Atlantic economies, they were eventually forced to disband their communities and flee to safer environments. The Spanish and Portuguese inquisitions intensified their efforts against Judaizing backsliders in the American colonies in the first half of the seventeenth century. Colonial authorities in Spanish America prosecuted 188 cases and executed thirteen people for relapsing to Judaism between 1646 and 1649. The inquisition succeeded in driving out the remaining New Christians in Spanish America, and by 1654 the Portuguese had expelled all peoples of Jewish ancestry in Brazil. A number of these refugees settled in Caribbean islands not held by Spain, though in 1685 Louis XIV of France banished them from French colonies. For all intents and purposes, the most dynamic Jewish commercial networks had been driven from the New World by the end of the seventeenth century.

Outside of Amsterdam and London, Sephardic Jews found the most welcome refuge in Ottoman Muslim lands because of the relatively accommodating social policies toward religious minorities. Allowed to organize their own semiautonomous communities, Sephardic Jews were able to utilize their skills and extensive networks in the eastern Mediterranean and in Arab lands. They served as intermediaries between European Christian and Muslim merchants in the overland routes across western and central Asia and in the port cities of south Asia. Because of the nature of commerce, Sephardic Jews interacted closely with peoples in host societies, though in most cases they lived in distinct precincts, followed their own customs, and practiced their own religious observances.

The Armenian diaspora of the 1600s and 1700s paralleled in many respects the widespread Jewish migrations. Geographically, Armenia lay across some of the most profitable overland caravan routes between the Mediterranean and central Asia. Landlocked between the Black and Caspian Seas, Armenian merchants participated vigorously in the over land caravan trade that went north to Astrakhan on the Volga River, south into India and the Indian Ocean, west to the Mediterranean, and east to sites on the Silk Roads. Given their long commercial history, Armenian merchants had developed uncanny expertise in dealing with a wide range of people from various cultural backgrounds. Military conflict between the Ottomans and Safavids in the early 1600s led Shah Abbas I to resettle a large number of Armenians forcibly in a suburb of Isfahan. Named New Julfa, this settlement formed the basis of an extensive Armenian commercial matrix with the political support of the Safavid rulers. Unlike Sephardic Jewish communities, Christian Armenians enjoyed political patronage. In Iran, Shi'ite rulers gave them protection throughout the 1600s and, in most areas in Europe and Asia, Armenian merchants moved with relative ease in their host societies.

From New Julfa, and later Bandar Abbas in the Persian Gulf, Armenians established far-flung merchant communities throughout Europe and Asia, sending out tens of thousands to settle in commercial centers such as Amsterdam, London, Marseilles, Venice, Astrakhan, Gujarat, Aleppo, and Cairo, as well as many other places. In the seventeenth century, approximately 10,000 Armenians resided in Ottoman domains. Armenian fortunes turned sour in the early-1700s as Safavid shahs, influenced by conservative Muslim clerics, took a less favorable view toward these Christian subjects. As the Safavid dynasty deteriorated, Armenians scattered. Many fled into south Asia to connect with the British Indian trade. Armenians could also be found in almost any commercial venue in Eurasia, from Amsterdam to Melaka, brokering Persian silks, Indian spices and cloths, Russian furs, and European textiles. Throughout the early modern world, foreign agents in trade settlements greatly reduced protection costs and provided merchant firms information about conditions in lands where they conducted business.

The chief characteristics of long-distance trade resulted from the continuity with long-established networks and financial mechanisms that facilitated cross-cultural exchange. Merchants managed risk by allying with governments, forming partnerships, and relying on cultural networks in early modern trade. Despite continuity with the past, the expansive empires of the early modern period inaugurated a new stage of international commerce.

The Theatres of Long-Distance Trade

Out of the longstanding commercial circuits that crisscrossed regions of the world, the growth of trading networks in three theatres during the early modern period produced an integrated global economy. The expansion of commercial activity in the Indian Ocean basin and in the nexus of overland Eurasian routes, combined with the birth of international trade across the Atlantic, pulled regional economies into a global exchange network. The emergence of a worldwide economy in the 1500s and 1600s marked a clear departure from the transregional patterns of trade in previous periods. The scale of production grew substantially to meet consumer demand for foreign products. As the oceans became bridges rather than barriers to continents, hosts of peoples traveled to distant lands so that commerce became enmeshed in empire building, migration, biological exchange, and missionary endeavors. By the late 1700s, new technologies, from international banks, to joint-stock organizations, to artillery-laden warships, significantly altered the power relations of trade. As a result of these developments, economic supremacy began to shift from Asia to Europe by the end of the early modern period.

Maritime Trade in the Indian Ocean Basin

Trade along the ports in the Indian Ocean basin experienced a remarkable upsurge beginning around 1400, prompting historians to call this era in maritime southeast Asia, "the age of commerce." In China, the riches across the Indian Ocean stirred seafaring ambitions in the Yongle emperor who sponsored the grand expeditions of Zheng He in the early 1400s. The intense growth stemmed from rising demand for trade items, such as spices, ornamental wood, timber, cotton, textiles, grains, gold, and silver. As regions on the mainland recovered from the plagues of the 1300s, states expanded agricultural production, yielding prodigious population growth that started in the 1400s. The first Ming emperor came from peasant stock and thus realized the value of a productive and profitable peasantry. The agricultural policies that the Ming state instituted in the 1300s and early 1400s led to sizable surpluses in cereal commodities, which fostered population growth and provided valuable trade items to Indonesia and Malaya. China more than quarupled its population from 75 million in 1400 to 320 million in 1800, India's population hovered around 200 million in 1800, while the entire continent grew from 275 million in 1500 to 625 million in 1800, out of a total world population of 950 million people. Even with the Ming and Qing prohibitions and restrictions on trade after the mid-1400s, the expanding markets in east Asia proved a boon to mercantile activity throughout the Indian Ocean. Agricultural development in India also fostered population growth that facilitated and fueled commercial exchange. Intensive farming techniques created higher yields not only in food crops, but in commercial ones, such as indigo, cotton, sugarcane, and opium. By the 1500s, Indian producers were deeply enmeshed in trading

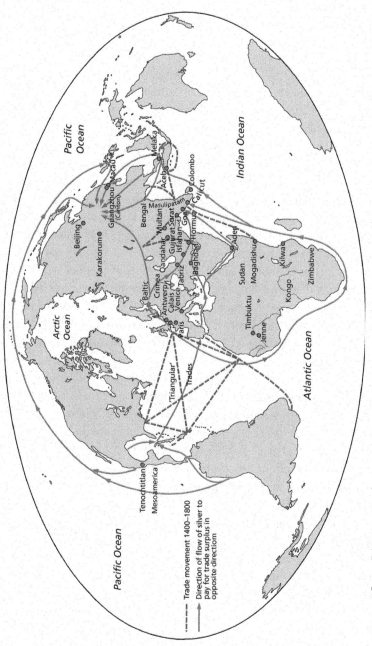

Pacific
Ocean

Indian Ocean

Melaka

Aceh

Colombo

Calicut

Macau
(Canton)

Guangzhou

Bengal

Masulipatam

Beijing

Multan

Surat

Aden

Karakorum

Qandahar

Gujarat

Goa

Hormuz

Mogadishu

Kilwa

Isfahan

Baghdad

Sudan

Kongo

Zimbabwe

Crimea

Tabriz

Arctic
Ocean

Baltic

Venice

Timbuktu

Antwerp

Calais

Jenne

Paris

'Triangular'

Trades

Atlantic Ocean

Tenochtitlan

Mesoamerica

Pacific Ocean

 Trade movement 1400–1800

Direction of flow of silver to
pay for trade surplus in
opposite direction

MAP 3.2. Long-Distance Trade, 1400–1800

87

connections in the Swahili cities in east Africa and the port cities of southeast Asia.

A secondary factor in rising commercial activity was the European appetite for Asian goods, especially spices from India and maritime southeast Asia. Spices occupied a central medicinal, culinary, and aesthetic place in European societies, especially among elites who could afford them. The old tale that Europeans craved spices to preserve meat and cover the taste of spoiled food is no more than a tale. Medical practitioners and folk healers employed spices, such as cloves, black pepper, and cinnamon, for a variety of ailments. The highly developed and flavorful culinary culture enjoyed by elites required sugar, black pepper, ginger, saffron, and other spices. In addition, households scented their dwellings with resins and incenses because people held a deep sensual appreciation for aromatic fragrances. By 1400, European societies had begun to regain stability from the devastation of plagues to such an extent that Italian and Portuguese mariners resumed the quest for an all-water route to gain access to Asian spices. Thus, agricultural development, population expansion, and acquisitive interest in key sectors of Eurasia quickened the tempo and elevated the level of trade in the Indian Ocean.

The major patterns of production, exchange, and consumption followed traditional routes until the Portuguese appeared in the Indian Ocean at the end of the 1400s. On the heels of Vasco da Gama's arrival in Calicut in 1498, the Portuguese entrance into the Indian Ocean commercial zone initially wreaked havoc on the balance and scale of trade for about fifty years. With the most heavily armed ships in the Indian Ocean, the Portuguese used force to control shipping, which greatly reduced the flow of traffic on the seas. At least until the 1530s, Portuguese commanders sank ships and plundered cargo at every opportunity, pursuing a strategy of choking off the flow of goods at critical locations. In 1510, Afonso de Albuquerque allied with local forces to conquer Goa, and then a year later his fleet of thirteen ships seized Melaka, a central entrepôt for spices; shortly thereafter Albuquerque oversaw construction of fortified factories. From these and other factories planted along the coastlines of the Indian Ocean, Portuguese officials wrung control of a significant chunk of the spice trade and diverted the normal flow of goods. During this period, Lisbon became the point of entry for spices into Europe from routes around the Cape of Good Hope rather than through the Mediterranean Sea to Italy.

Portuguese supremacy, however, was short-lived. Arab, Indian, Indonesian, and Chinese mariners found other routes and began to arm themselves for confrontation at sea. The Ottoman sultan's, Selim I (r. 1512–1520), conquest of Egypt, the western coast of Arabia in 1517, and the port city of Aden (in present-day Yemen) introduced a powerful new competitor in the Persian Gulf and Arabian Sea that checked Portuguese power in the region and thwarted Portugal's ability to divert trade. Venetian and Ottoman merchants revived the routes through the Red Sea and Persian Gulf, which endured as a major east-west thoroughfare through the 1500s. In the eastern sphere of the Indian Ocean, the sultan of Aceh (Sumatra) allied with the Ottomans in resisting the Portuguese and redirected local commercial traffic through the strait of Sunda, instead of the Portuguese-controlled strait of Melaka. In the face of such obstacles, Portuguese commanders and mercantile officers insinuated themselves more peacefully and collaboratively in the Asian maritime trade.

After the mid-1500s, the maritime Indian Ocean network settled into a rhythm of commercial prosperity that lasted for a century for regions in southeast Asia and throughout the early modern period for India, China, and Japan. The insatiable European demand for Asian goods sparked unprecedented levels of production for pepper, nutmeg, mace, cloves, cotton cloth, ivory, silks, and porcelain. Farmers across the Indonesian archipelago and Malaya expanded their cultivation of pepper so that production in these lands surpassed levels in southern India, which had previously ranked as the chief supplier.

In addition to the runaway European appetite for spices, the huge volume of silver, imported from Japan and America powered commercial growth. The rapidly expanding Chinese economy ran on silver currency, just as coined silver rupees circulated widely in India; thus, demand certainly kept pace with supply. Newly tapped Japanese mines supplied merchants who transported excessively large amounts to maritime ports for purchase largely by Chinese firms. After 1600, Japanese traders sailed into maritime Asia in ships displaying red seals to demonstrate that they had gained the government's permission; the red seal ships remained active in the Asian seas until the 1630s, when the shogun, Tokugawa Iemitsu (r. 1623–1651), adopted a severe isolationist policy, prohibiting the Japanese from foreign trading. American silver, extracted from the rich mine at Potosi in present-day Bolivia and other sites, entered the Indian Ocean initially via the Portuguese and then the Spanish who colonized the Philippines beginning in 1565. An annual shipment, known as the Manila galleon, sailed the length of the Pacific Ocean from Mexico to Manila, carrying silver from the New World to the Old. Most European shipments, however, traveled along the maritime routes around the Cape of Good Hope or through the eastern Mediterranean into the Red Sea and Persian Gulf. Indian and Chinese merchants in markets such as Manila, Melaka, and Macau contracted for enormous amounts of American silver. At the end of the 1500s, Portuguese and Spanish ships were carrying more than seventy tons of silver per year into Asia, only to be exceeded by the Japanese.

In the mid-1600s, the trading networks in the Indian Ocean experienced some significant changes that produced a sharp downturn of commerce in southeast Asia. A number of factors conspired to retard commercial growth throughout many parts of the world in the 1600s. There is evidence that climate change in the form of a general cooling of world temperatures played some role in economic retraction. In Europe, a century-long trend of colder and wetter weather, known as the "little ice age," reduced crop yields, causing malnutrition and lower population levels. In many parts of Asia, anecdotal evidence suggests that cooler temperatures created dryer than normal conditions that plagued crop production. Widespread droughts were recorded in China, India, Vietnam, and Thailand in the early 1600s, while crop failures gripped Java, Makassar, Melaka, and other areas of maritime Asia.

Climate change in the 1600s coincided with a number of economic problems and political crises. The large influx of silver from America and Japan decreased considerably. In Spanish America, the deep veins of American mines began to yield considerably less silver in the 1630s. At roughly the same time, the Tokugawa shogun Iemitsu decreed that, upon pain of death, no Japanese merchant could travel outside the country and no foreigner could enter for any reason. In 1638, he did grant the Dutch minimal commercial contact from Deshima, an island constructed in Nagasaki Bay. Dutch middlemen took over the silver trade between China and Japan that had previously taken place in Indonesian and Malayan ports, though at sharply reduced levels. In addition to the silver crunch, China underwent an acute political crisis in the 1630s and 1640s, resulting in the fall of the Ming and rise of the Qing dynasty. China did recover in the second half of the century to become a major world power in the Qing era; civil war embroiled the Middle Kingdom in the mid-1600s.

Despite the relevance of all these factors, the most immediate and direct event in the economic reversal of maritime Asia was the arrival of the Dutch in Indonesia. The VOC used unremitting force to oust their Portuguese rivals and intimidate local rulers for the purpose of controlling spice production. Historians regard the Dutch practice as a strategic one to reduce protection costs. Rather than outsourcing protection through bribes, equal partnerships, and the like, the VOC "internalized" protection costs by using military force to achieve company aims.

Though the VOC established a number of factories across maritime Asia from India to Japan, it was their presence in Indonesia and Malaya that enabled them to put a stranglehold on the spice trade. While a great variety of trade goods changed hands in this commercial zone, spices held the key to trade in the region because they attracted so many merchants with so many different goods. The VOC set up its Asian headquarters in Jakarta, renamed Batavia by the Dutch, on the island of Java in 1619 and planted strategic outposts along the Moluccas in Ternate in 1607 and Amboina in 1623. Jan Pieterszoon Coen (1587–1629), an unyielding governor of the VOC, realized that if the company could control spices at the point of production, then it could monopolize the trade. This strategy was possible because nutmeg, mace, and cloves grew within a very circumscribed geographical range. Nutmeg and mace were native to the Banda Islands, while cloves came from the Moluccas; both island groups were located in the eastern Indonesian archipelago. Banda, for example, grew 95 percent of the world's nutmeg supply. Consequently, Dutch forces, joined by Japanese mercenaries, invaded the Banda Islands in 1621, massacred almost all the natives, and subsequently imported African slaves to cultivate nutmeg and mace. At other locations, VOC forces eliminated rivals, ousting the Portuguese from Melaka in 1641 and subduing

Makassar (in Sulawesi) in 1669. In islands that the Dutch did not actually conquer, VOC governors attempted to coerce local sultans into agreements that gave exclusive rights to the company.

By the mid-1600s, then, the VOC monopolized the spice trade from its central outposts in Indonesia, due to its ability to deploy military power in the region. The company did not have nearly as much success with pepper, which was cultivated more widely across maritime Asia and southern India.

Because of its commercial leverage and military ruthlessness, the VOC became the major carrier in the north-south network from the mainland to the southeastern islands. In so doing, the company managed to overcome a basic obstacle for European merchants in Asian markets. Europeans had complained since the 1400s that their trade products attracted little interest among Asian buyers, forcing Europeans to purchase Asian goods with silver, which inflated costs. The Dutch broke through this dead end by becoming the chief carrier in what Europeans called the "inter-Asian trade," that is the port city trade encompassing Indonesia, China, India, and Japan. The VOC became the most important link that connected ports in these regions, trading for local products – spices, silks, cotton, silver – in the various Asian ports. Circumventing the need for silver, the VOC enjoyed enormous success as the most profitable trade organization in the world, selling spices in Europe for three times the purchase price in Asia.

What was profitable for the VOC, however, was disastrous for commerce among Asians. The general commercial decline of southeast Asia and overproduction of spices eventually took its toll even on the company, as profits grew thinner and expenses thicker in the 1700s. Because of the VOC's financial woes, the government of the Netherlands abandoned the trading company approach in the 1800s and made Indonesia a colony known as the Dutch East Indies.

Other regions connected to the Indian Ocean commercial zone resisted European incursions more successfully and thus adapted more constructively to a western presence. After the Qing dynasty brought stability to Chinese society, the Shunzhi emperor (r. 1644–1661) infused new vigor into anticommercial policies. In 1656, Shunzhi prohibited Chinese maritime trade, forbidding "even a plank from drifting into the sea." In the 1660s, the Kangxi emperor (r. 1661–1722) went further by forcing the population in the southern coastal regions to move inward, away from foreign pirates and traders. Despite these measures, thousands of Chinese merchants left the Middle Kingdom for port cities in southeast Asia where they formed sizable communities that partnered with the Dutch in Indonesia and the Spanish in the Philippines. Allied with European agents, Chinese merchants in maritime Asia continued to conduct business with their countrymen along the southern coastlines. The Qing state softened its stance against foreign commerce in the 1680s, allowing for limited and heavily regulated trade with European merchants at specific port cities.

The presence of European trading companies in India, for the most part, actually proved beneficial to regional economies until the demise of the Mughal state in the mid-1700s. English, Dutch, French, Danish, and Swedish companies constructed factories along the Indian coastline in the 1600s and 1700s with the approval of local rulers and Mughal emperors. Acquiring cotton, spices, and indigo for export to Europe, the trading companies stimulated regional production in Surat, Coromandel, and Bengal. The cotton cloth industry in particular benefited since it employed a range of workers, including peasants, spinners, weavers, and merchants. European companies also pumped large quantities of American and Japanese silver into the Indian economy, which contributed to the financial well-being of the Mughal regime. The emperors themselves, however, took little notice of commercial affairs with Europeans on the coast.

By the end of the early modern period, the intensified commercial activity in the Indian Ocean basin produced significant disparities. The broad regional prosperity that had reigned from 1400 to the mid-1600s contracted in the face of climatic changes, economic challenges, and Dutch military aggression. Japan turned inward, China remained guarded, southeast Asia collapsed, while India and their European trading partners prospered. Even in India, however, the decline of the Mughal Empire in the mid-1700s set in motion a process of growing English colonization.

Overland Eurasian Networks

The conglomeration of overland Eurasian commercial networks that stretched across the continent mirrored the same general patterns as the maritime sector in the early modern period. Traditional historical interpretations have cast overland trade Asia as a declining, passive phenomenon in the early modern period, outpaced by the high-powered maritime networks. Historians since the early 1990s, however, have shown that trade in many regions complemented the maritime networks and prospered into the mid-1700s. The general worldwide economic contraction of the 1600s (discussed previously) hurt some areas in central Asia, yet most regions were able to adapt effectively to changing circumstances.

The key factors that played a part in the development of commerce throughout Eurasia centered around the formation of empires friendly to trade. As the three large Muslim empires (Ottoman, Savafid, and Mughal) imposed a more stringent sense of order over central and western Asia, Russia was also taking control over the Volga River basin from the Tatar khans. Consequently, in the 1500s the traffic in trade items picked up considerably and remained strong in many areas to the mid-1700s. The deterioration of the Muslim states, combined with expanding European power, brought about a decline in exchange and opened the way for direct western influence in many parts of Asia.

Traveling by camel, horse, sled, or riverboat, merchants had made their way throughout the world's largest continent for many centuries. By the 1500s, a number or north-south and east-west routes connected even the most remote reaches of Asia. Roadbeds and river ways extended from Moscow to the port city of Astrakhan on the northern Caspian Sea and southward from there to Tabriz and Isfahan in Iran. From urban centers in Iran, several western arteries ran across Mesopotamia (Iraq), Syria, and Anatolia to the eastern Mediterranean and Black Sea. The Tigris and Euphrates Rivers emptied into the Persian Gulf and thus provided access to the Indian Ocean. The cities of Baghdad, Aleppo, Alexandria, Smyrna, Bursa, and Istanbul stood out as major commercial sites along the eastern thoroughfare from Iran to the Mediterranean. The most significant eastern highways from Iran either headed into Uzbekistan and eastern Turkestan (Turan) along the northern Silk Roads into Tibet, Mongolia, and China or into Afghanistan and a more southerly bearing into northern India.

Three developments in the 1500s allowed for the expansion of trade in the Asian overland networks. First, after the Ottoman, Safavid, and Mughal Empires consolidated their authority, the regimes promoted trade along the traditional caravan routes. Since its inception, Islam had always fostered a robust commercial ethos. Muhammad and his first wife Khadijah were successful merchants, and shari'a law laid down a long list of stipulations to ensure fair and honest trade. So it was natural that empires claiming to uphold Islam endeavored to expand commercial opportunities. The extraordinarily immense territorial expanse of these empires ensured a broad commercial zone in western and central Asia. One way the Muslim states advanced mercantile interests was by reducing banditry. To be sure, merchants traveling in Asia frequently had to pay protection money to local strongmen and opportunistic nomads. Nevertheless, all of these regimes acted consistently to make travel more secure, thereby stimulating trade. From time to time, emperors pushed infrastructure initiatives, like building bridges and repairing roads. Shah Abbas sponsored sweeping reconstruction of Iran's transportation system in the late 1500s.

Second, the early imperial push of Ivan IV into Kazan in the mid-1500s opened up the Volga River basin, permitting more sustained commercial contact between Russia and central Asia. The city of Astrakhan, lying at the mouth of the Volga River and the Caspian Sea, became an important point of exchange between Russian, Indian, Armenian, Persian, and Tatar merchants. The subjugation of this region also made possible the conquest of Siberia, which yielded the furs that found such enthusiastic markets in China, central Asia, and Europe.

Third, new maritime connections between Europe and Russia signified another portentous development for central Asian trade. In 1553, Richard Chancellor discovered a route around Scandinavia, docked at the Russian port of Archangel (Archangelsk), and then journeyed over six hundred miles to the court of Ivan IV who received him warmly. Chancellor's voyage initiated new commercial linkages between Europe, Russia, and Asia, which trading companies, such as the (English) Muscovy Company, soon exploited.

Owing to these developments, commerce across Asia's overland networks brought a diverse array of people to buy and sell goods from around the world. The volume of trade is hard to gauge because of scarce financial records; nevertheless, it is clear that thousands of merchants, organized generally into trading diasporas, journeyed across the chief routes of Eurasia and took up residence, for varying lengths of time, in the urban commercial centers. Merchants from Uzbekistan, Afghanistan, Turan, and Transoxiana fanned out into India and Iran.

Large numbers of Indian firms, both Hindu and Muslim, organized themselves in Turan, Afghanistan, Iran, the Caucasus, and Russia. Indian communities in Moscow, St. Petersburg, and Astrakhan connected the northern and southern borders of Asia, bringing cotton textiles, spices, indigo, and slaves to Russia for furs, woolen cloths, and salt.

Europeans also infiltrated overland networks through trade with Russia in northern ports, active engagement in Ottoman emporia, and direct participation in Safavid commercial traffic. Hoping to find a northern route to China, Chancellor and his crew opened the door not only to English trade in Russian markets but also to Dutch and Scottish firms. Dutch ships began to show up in the White Sea in the 1560s, and in 1584 Ivan IV ordered the construction of a port at Archangel to accommodate trade with western European companies. The English Muscovy Company swapped textiles for furs, hides, and Persian silks, whereas the Dutch could offer silver, which was vital to the Russian economy. Better financed than the English, Dutch merchants maintained the strongest position in the Russian trade, sending more than two hundred ships per year in the 1630s. In 1703, Peter I established St. Petersburg at the preferred port for western trade, leading to the decline of Archangel.

In spite of the growing prevalence of the Cape routes around Africa, the markets in the Levant (eastern Mediterranean) continued to draw considerable European attention. The city-state of Venice had monopolized commerce in the region since the 1100s, but the rise of the Ottomans in the 1300s and 1400s challenged this supremacy. Venetians, Genoese, and their Christian allies fought a series of wars with the Turks in the 1400s and 1500s for control over the sea routes and for the defense of their faith. These military engagements did not stop Italian and French merchants from venturing into the lands of the infidel to pursue profit. Indeed by the early 1500s, Venetian and Ottoman firms fully realized that they both stood more to lose from the Portuguese Cape route than from their own conflicts.

The Levantine trade network that connected Venice to the Ottoman Empire more broadly linked Europe, north Africa, and Asia via the routes that flowed through Egypt to the Red Sea and through Mesopotamia to the Persian Gulf. These routes revived, after taking an initial hit from the Portuguese entreé into the Indian Ocean, and prospered into the 1700s. Dutch, English, and French Levantine companies joined Venetian and Genoese firms in the eastern Mediterranean in the 1500s and 1600s, receiving special trade privileges, known as capitulations, from Ottoman sultans. In cities such as Istanbul, Izmir, Aleppo, and Baghdad, mercantile exchanges between these companies and Arab and Turkish agents were brokered by Greek, Armenian, and Jewish middlemen. The English East India Company obtained permission in 1616 to plant factories in Iran, and seven years later company forces helped Shah Abbas oust the Portuguese from Hormuz. Dutch and French East India Companies soon followed. Corsairs (pirates) along the north African coast formed the most menacing hazard to trade, preying on any ship vulnerable to attack. Nevertheless, goods from all over the world passed through the Levantine routes, the most important of which included Siberian furs, Persian silks, American silver and sugar, Asian spices, Chinese porcelain, central Asian horses, eastern European and African slaves, English textiles, and Indian cloths. Thus, growing economic integration between Africa, Asia, and Europe figured as a remarkable feature of the overland routes for most of the early modern period.

Several critical geopolitical and economic developments that produced a number of realignments in the overland Eurasian networks occurred in the 1700s. The Muslim empires entered a period of steep decline or, in the case of Safavid Iran, disintegrated altogether. As a result, European companies that had pushed into these lands acquired more control over routes and regulated trade to their advantage. With the rapid decline of the Safavid state in the early eighteenth century, Dutch, French, and especially the English, gained a mastery over trade. Since these companies no longer needed cultural mediators, Armenian merchants in New Julfa lost their western allies at a time when shahs were taking a harsher stance against them. Most Armenians dispersed across Asia and Europe. In the Ottoman Empire, commercial traffic continued to move steadily, but English, Dutch, and French companies supplanted Turkish and Arab firms, which enabled them to import manufactured items (textiles, glass, clocks) and export raw materials (iron, wood, lead, grain). The fragmentation of the Mughal Empire allowed English factories in southern India to expand their influence over local economies and dictate the terms of exchange. In northern India, where Europeans had not established a foothold, Indian merchants continued to export cotton cloth and other items into central Asia for horses.

Whereas the decline of Muslim states allowed networks to slip increasingly into western European hands in western and south Asia, the expansion of Russia and China brought central Asian systems under the sway of these two empires. At the direction of Peter I, Russian merchants, with Cossack backing, adopted a more assertive strategy in central Asia. The Russian tsar wanted to dominate commerce between Iran, India, Afghanistan, and Uzbekistan. To that end, Russians constructed fortified trading outposts in the region around Orenburg between the Caspian and Arial Seas on the Ural River in the early 1700s. The project enticed trade with Uzbek, Afghan, and Indian merchants and placed Russia in a powerful position in central Asia. Taking place at the same time, the Chinese conquest of Tibet, Turkestan, and Mongolia incorporated much of central Asia's production into the centralized economic structure of the Qing dynasty.

Thus, the overland Asian routes, connecting east Asia to the Mediterranean, endured, prospering in some areas and declining in others, throughout the major geopolitical realignments of the early modern period. As western European, Russian, and Chinese powers intervened more directly, the overland networks became more fully integrated in the global economy.

The Early Modern Atlantic Economy

It was in the quest to find more efficient routes to India and China that mariners, in the pay of Spanish and Portuguese monarchs, inadvertently stumbled upon the American continent. The unintended consequence of voyaging to Asia resulted in one of the most important episodes in world history, crucial to the development of globalization in modern times. In the early modern period, an extensive international nexus of trade emerged in the Atlantic out of European conquests in the Americas and partnerships in west Africa.

Unlike the continuities between longstanding routes in Eurasia and early modern networks, the rise of a transnational commercial structure in the Atlantic was a new and revolutionary event. Bridging Africa, America, and Europe, the emergence of the transatlantic economy marked the formation of genuinely global commercial networks. The patterns of economic exchange in the Atlantic contrast sharply with those in the Indian Ocean in several respects. First, European countries and firms did not begin to gain economic and political leverage in Asian maritime or overland trade until the later 1600s and 1700s; they played a central role in the Atlantic economy much more quickly. Second, the overriding European approach to Asian networks focused on controlling trade, while in the Atlantic Europeans attempted to organize resources and people. As a result, a much greater level of coercion accompanied European ambitions in America. One similarity between the Asian and Atlantic economies was that European mercantile enterprises became chief agents for distributing goods worldwide.

Over the course of the 1500s and 1600s, commercial traffic linking economies in western Africa, the Atlantic coast of America, and western Europe developed into a general pattern often referred to as the "Triangular Trade" or the "Atlantic Trade." Traveling between three continents, ships sailed in segmented relays that formed a single international circuit. In general, items manufactured in Europe, such as textiles, guns, and rum, were exchanged in Africa primarily for slaves. Slave ships then crossed the Atlantic in the infamous middle passage to American ports at which point the slaves who survived the ordeal were sold for cash, sugar, molasses, and other American products, depending on the location. Circuits also sailed from the Atlantic seaboard to the Caribbean to Europe and from New England to Africa to the Caribbean.

Despite the efforts of European governments and merchant firms to control commerce, it was far beyond their capacity in the early modern period to police trading and shipping on the distant seaways and ports. The mercantilist theories subscribed to by government officials enjoined naval forces to regulate trade within their colonial regimes, yet also too encroach on commerce with other colonies. Governments issued laws prohibiting their colonies from trading with individuals or merchants from other European countries. At times, however, governments were willing to overlook, even condone, violations of monopolies. In the 1700s, English shippers regularly violated the slave trading monopolies (the *asiento*) granted by the Spanish crown for its colonies in the Caribbean. The English government even declared war on Spain in 1739 in response to the legal Spanish boarding of an English vessel in search of contraband. The English captain, Robert Jenkins, created a stir, claiming atrocities against his crew and alleging that the Spaniards had cut off one of his ears. Before the House of Commons, Captain Jenkins produced in a dramatic fashion a jar containing his severed ear as proof of Spanish cruelty.

Despite governmental attempts at regulation, commercial parties traded directly with one another all across the Atlantic. Many merchants, shippers, and planters acted primarily in their own private interests for their own profits. For example, a Dutch shipper, skimming profits from the Dutch West India Company, might also contract with a French planter to smuggle slaves from an African trader who had signed a contract with the Spanish government to supply slaves only to Cuban plantations. Throughout the 1500s, British activity in the Americas centered around preying on Spanish and French ships and cutting in on the slave trade to the Caribbean. Francis Drake, John Hawkins, Martin Frobisher, and other British privateers enjoyed great celebrity for their naval exploits, real and exaggerated, against Spanish galleons and colonies. One of the most recounted stories was Drake's raid of a gold and silver convoy in the Spanish port of Nombre de Dios in 1573, which fabulously enriched the commander and his crew. Thus, distinctions between legal trade and contraband, company policy and private trade, naval vessels and pirates, were quite murky in the early modern period.

Underneath the transcontinental exchanges in the Atlantic world, the dynamics surrounding trade in each region differed considerably. The growing integration of Africa into global networks brought about major changes across the continent. The growth of maritime commerce in the Atlantic Ocean created prosperity in cities and states along the western coast and in central interior regions. Increased trade, however, escalated conflicts even in areas that prospered as states, cities, and tribes vied for control over commercial rights and trade routes. Portuguese, then Spanish, Dutch, English, French, Swedish, and Danish merchants and military personnel plied the islands and coasts on the western side of the continent, setting up fortifications at numerous locations. These included Elmina (Ghana), Arguin (Mauritania), Cape Verde Islands, Loango (Kongo), Senegal, and the area along the Guinea Coast.

Throughout the early modern period, Europeans traded from the coast, seeking slaves, gold, copper, ivory, and cloth. In exchange, Africans traded for guns, textiles, iron, liquor, and cowry shells, which many societies utilized as currency. Muskets gave some states a military advantage over territorial rivals, though firearms had limited impact in Africa before 1800. Coastal commerce proved extremely lucrative for merchants and rulers who could negotiate effectively with Europeans and could control access to commodities in the interior.

The prodigious increase in the trafficking of slaves greatly affected all coastal areas in the sub-Sahara and even penetrated central territories in the seventeenth and eighteenth centuries. The slave trade enriched some states, such as Oyo, Asante, and Dahomey on the west coast, but it did so at the expense of heightened violence and warfare needed to capture and enslave people from other regions. The number of Africans enslaved for American plantations reached between 10 million and 12 million, in addition to 1.7 million others ensnared in the trans-Saharan and Indian Ocean trade (see also Chapter 4). The hardest hit areas demographically stretched along the western coast from Angola to the Guinea Coast, a district that supplied 85 percent of all slaves destined for America. At its peak in the eighteenth century, slave trafficking spread into the eastern Kongo and Lunda. Slave extraction drove the prosperity and expansion of the Lunda kingdom, in the interior of the continent.

Growing out of traditional indigenous slaveholding practices, the pernicious trade always remained under the control of African societies and not of European powers, which were largely confined to the coasts. The profits from enslavement bred violence, since states, rulers, and privateers regularly conducted raids, attacks, wars, and kidnapping ventures to supply the demand for labor. Many societies also suffered internally from a breakdown in law and order due to a rise in banditry associated with kidnapping. Areas in the Kongo, Angola, and along the Gold Coast were virtually swept clean of civilian males between the ages of fourteen and thirty-five. Two-thirds of all enslaved Africans were male, which skewed gender relations considerably in affected regions. Women took on increased roles in agricultural and industrial production, and the low density of males added incentive to polygamous marital arrangements.

The importation of foreign goods – cassava, maize, tobacco, and peanuts from America, cowry shells and spices from Asia, and guns, iron, and textiles from Europe – affected domestic patterns of production and consumption. Peanuts first appeared in the Kongo in the sixteenth century via the Portuguese and disseminated throughout west, central, and southern regions. Africans referred to the peanut as nguba, which over time, as it rumbled through discourse between African and European creoles in America, became pronounced as goober, a term still prevalent in the southern United States. Maize and cassava also spread in various western, southern, and eastern regions of Africa because of their adaptability in a range of climates, elevations, and soil types. The Portuguese also introduced Asian strains of rice and sugarcane, which developed into significant crops in the Kongo River basin and along western coastlines. American and Asian crops supplemented African diets, contributing to population growth on the continent in the early modern period despite the loss of millions to the slave trade.

European manufactured items, such as iron and cloth, found markets in societies connected to the Atlantic trade. Yet, Africans also produced various types of iron, steel, and cloth that they sold for export to Europeans, so commerce in manufactured wares occurred as a two-dimensional exchange. It is often assumed that European production overmatched African industry and thus brought about a rapid decline in indigenous industry. This view does not hold for most of the early modern period, as African production levels met local demand. By the end of the 1700s, the decline of productivity as a result of the slave trade and the increasing accessibility of European items did begin to damage African industrial production seriously.

Spanish empire building in Central and South America in the 1500s had two important ramifications for long-distance trade: the large-scale circulation of gold and silver bullion and the extensive production of agricultural commodities. Conquistadors discovered and expropriated enormous deposits of silver and gold. Historians have documented that from 1493 to 1800 American mines produced 2,490 metric tons of gold, accounting for 71 percent of the world's total and a whopping 102,000 metric tons of silver, 85 percent of the world's total. Some historians claim that these sums represent only half of American bullion mined. The silver mine in Potosi and others in southern Mexico possessed the richest veins, though the precious metals were found throughout Central and South America.

The production of gold and silver, mined by coerced natives or enslaved Africans, greased the wheels of a burgeoning international economy. The worldwide movement of bullion flowed from American mines to Asian destinations, especially China and India, though the metals moved along two different directions. The transpacific Mexico to Manila route formed the first direct commercial link between Asia and America. The bulk of American metals, however, traveled to Asia via Europe. Offloaded in Cadiz and Seville, the bullion was minted and then shipped to European financial centers, such as Genoa, Padua, Antwerp, Amsterdam, or London. Dutch, English, and Italian merchants then purchased gold and silver through banking connections and transported them to India and China to pay for Asian spices, cloths, silks, and assorted luxury items. The Dutch also utilized bullion for its lucrative Baltic Sea trade with Polish and Russian merchants. In return for silver and gold, the Dutch acquired commodities, including wheat, rye, timber, leather, and furs, for resale in northern and central Europe.

Even though Brazil could not offer Portuguese explorers enormous reserves of gold and silver, it did possess a lucrative resource vulnerable to exploitation, fertile land. In the 1530s, Portuguese settlers began to establish plantations in Brazil. Arising in the middle ages, plantations were large agricultural estates that could encompass hundreds of acres and were devoted to the production of a single crop, cultivated by either low-wage, coerced, or enslaved laborers. Arabs had operated sugar plantations in the Levant, where Europeans, including the Portuguese, came into contact with this system of production. In the earliest days of Portuguese exploration in the Atlantic, entrepreneurs sought to implement this large-scale agricultural organization to the Madeira, Canary, and Cape Verde Islands. By the mid-1400s, sugar plantations appeared in the Madeiras, and by 1500, planters were importing enslaved Africans to toil in the plantations on the island of São Tomé. Thus, the Portuguese transplanted the plantation system, ideal for the production of sugar, from the Mediterranean to several Atlantic islands to Brazil by the early sixteenth century.

Portuguese settlers combined all the fundamental elements of the plantation structure in Brazil and made it a staple of the Atlantic economy in the early modern period. Extremely strong European demand made sugar highly profitable and suitable for high-volume production. Brazil possessed the ideal climate, boasted some of the world's most fertile farmland, and contained a flat topography near the coastlines.

Through their connections in west Africa, the Portuguese also had access to an abundant supply of slave labor. This became crucial by the 1530s, as falling native populations at the hands of European diseases created a critical labor shortage. Dominating the slave trade in the sixteenth century, Portuguese merchants poured thousands of Africans into the cruel cane fields of Brazil. Soon sugar emerged as the prime Brazilian cash crop. By the late sixteenth century, Brazilian sugar mills were turning out 130 tons of sugar per year, as plantations had become highly capitalistic organizations.

Introduced by the Portuguese in Brazil, the plantation system became the model for commodity agricultural production throughout the Americas. In the 1600s, as Dutch, English, and French entrepreneurs and merchant organizations planted colonies in the Caribbean and on the Atlantic seaboard, they set up plantations for the production of sugar, cotton, tobacco, and indigo. The wide dissemination of this agricultural organization produced a regional economy known to historians as a "plantation complex." Accompanied by rapid and almost complete native depopulation, a relatively small number of European settlers took control over lands and repopulated them with millions of enslaved Africans to produce agricultural commodities for export to international markets. Stretching largely across the tropical climatic zone, this plantation complex lay at the center of an Atlantic economy linked to global trade networks.

Outside of the plantation economy in North America, native tribes traded animal furs and skins to a robust European market in return for firearms, wampum beads, alcohol, knives, axes, and other manufactured goods. This lively commerce had an important impact on the economic and political development in the eastern half of North America in the early modern period. The size and political organization of the North American peoples, especially in relation to the much smaller population of European settlers, enabled them to engage Europeans on much more equal terms for a much longer period than the native peoples of South America. Once the Aztec and Inca Empires succumbed to the Spanish, the relatively smaller indigenous societies of Central and South America became subject to extensive colonization in the 1500s and 1600s. Thus, commercial exchange in these regions was rather meager.

In North America, the hides from deer, moose, foxes, raccoons, and squirrels, but most especially beavers, were immensely popular among

European elites, prompting traders to make contact and negotiate with native tribes for pelts from these animals. Profitable for all parties, the trade in furs fed a ravenous European demand that by the early 1700s had outpaced supply in North America. Native tribes highly valued this trade, placing great store in wampum beads, used for symbolic and artistic purposes, and in firearms for efficiency in hunting and in military affairs. Liquor, namely whiskey, rum, and brandy, found an enthusiastic market as well, though its overconsumption produced high rates of alcoholism that sapped the vitality of many indigenous societies.

The mutual profit in these commercial exchanges produced rivalry and conflict as European and American groups competed with one another for access to these goods. Dutch, English, French, and Spanish traders fought with one another to gain access to Iroquois, Huron, and Algonquin merchants, as well as to traders from smaller tribes along the Atlantic coast. Likewise, American nations waged wars with each other to manipulate trade and to control hunting lands. One of the fiercest and most widespread conflagrations was the so-called Beaver Wars, which took place in the mid-1600s. In this conflict, the Iroquois responded to the depletion of beaver populations in their lands by seeking to take over trade conducted between the Huron and the French in the western Great Lakes. The Iroquois managed to dominate the region until the end of the seventeenth century when isolation and factionalism among the nations left them vulnerable to French and native forces. The beaver population experienced such intense overhunting that it went into decline at this time. Nevertheless, European traders continued to trade with Algonquin-speaking peoples in the northeast, Cherokee and Creek tribes in the southeast, and other indigenous societies for pelts and slaves.

The Portuguese endeavor to reach Asia and the Spanish discovery of America set in motion processes that led to the formation of an Atlantic economy. For global markets, this sector produced precious metals, timber, and agricultural commodities, including sugar, cotton, tobacco, and indigo. The various regions that comprised this commercial zone fared very differently. International trade and colonization generated enormous capital for European countries and merchant organizations. The Atlantic made Europe wealthy, providing the necessary capital for investment in industrialization. Many African cities, such as Asante and Dahomey, profited greatly from transcontinental commerce, but at the expense of a pernicious slave trade that destroyed many societies in Benin, Guinea, Angola, and other areas. Decimated by disease and colonization, most American peoples lost control of land and became dependents in trade relations with Europeans.

The Rise of Global Trading Networks

New patterns and structures in long-distance trade led to commercial networks that came to span the world in the early modern period. These international markets did not constitute a global system like that which makes up modern commerce, but rather they developed into porous sectors of exchange through vast geographical spaces. Changing hands many times, goods like silver, spices, cotton, and sugar traveled across continents to meet specific regional demands. Early modern commercial economies grew out of long-established ways of doing business, from the ancient Afro-Eurasian routes, to age-old trading diasporas, to customary financial instruments. Out of these older forms emerged joint-stock companies, merchant empires, banks, and newly discovered lands. The overall result was greatly elevated volumes of trade that endured, despite fluctuations and regional deviations, throughout the period. The merging and overlapping of commercial networks was not a peaceful affair that benefited everyone. Wars, exponentially higher levels of enslavement and coercion, piracy at sea, and other forms of violence accompanied the increased levels of long-distance trade. And there were clear winners and losers in the world economy. By the end of the period, European countries and companies had gained at the expense of Africa, America, and southeast Asia; China and Russia profited at the expense of central Asia and Siberia. The blending of continuity with innovation, the rise of one region beside the fall of another, and the coexistence of violence with prosperity symbolize the paradoxes in the integration of global networks in the early modern age.

Works Consulted

Abu-Lughod, Janet L. *Before European Hegemony: The World System* A.D. *1250–1350*. New York: Oxford University Press, 1989.
Armstrong, Terence. *Russian Settlements in the North*. Cambridge: Cambridge University Press, 1965.

Barrett, Ward. "World Bullion Flows, 1450–1800," in James D. Tracy ed. *The Rise of Merchant Empires: Long-Distance Trade in the Early Modern World, 1350–1750.* Cambridge: Cambridge University Press, 1990, 224–254.

Bentley, Jerry H., and Ziegler, Herbert F. *Traditions and Encounters: A Global Perspective on the Past,* vol. 2 *From 1500 to the Present.* 2nd ed. New York: McGraw Hill, 2003.

Braudel, Fernand. *Civilization and Capitalism 15th–18th Century,* vol. 2 *The Wheels of Commerce,* trans. Siân Reynolds. New York: Harper & Row Publishers, 1982.

Broeze, Frank ed. *Brides of the Sea: Port Cities of Asia from the 16th–20th Centuries.* Honolulu: University of Hawaii Press, 1989.

Brook, Timothy. *The Confusions of Pleasure: Commerce and Culture in Ming China.* Berkeley: University of California Press, 1998.

Brucker, Gene ed. *Two Diaries of Renaissance Florence: The Diaries of Buonaccorso Pitti and Gregario Dati.* Julia Martines trans. New York: Harper and Row Publishers, 1967.

Charlton, Thomas H. "The Aztecs and their Contemporaries: The Central and Eastern Mexican Highlands," in Richard E. W. Adams and Murdo J. MacLeod eds. *The Cambridge History of the Native Peoples of the Americas,* vol. 2, pt. 1 *Mesoamerica.* Cambridge: Cambridge University Press, 1996, 500–558.

Chaudhuri, K. N. *Trade and Civilisation in the Indian Ocean: An Economic History from the Rise of Islam to 1750.* Cambridge: Cambridge University Press, 1985.

Cipolla, Carlo M. *Before the Industrial Revolution: European Society and Economy 1000–1700,* 3rd ed. New York: W. W. Norton & Company, 1993.

Curtin, Philip D. *Cross-Cultural Trade in World History.* Cambridge: Cambridge University Press, 1984.

————. *The Rise and Fall of the Plantation Complex: Essays in Atlantic History.* Cambridge: Cambridge University Press, 1998.

Dale, Stephen Frederic. *Indian Merchants and Eurasian Trade, 1600–1750.* Cambridge: Cambridge University Press, 1994.

Ehret, Christopher. *The Civilizations of Africa: A History to 1800.* Charlottesville: University of Virginia Press, 2002.

Fisher, Alan. *The Crimean Tatars.* Stanford, Calif.: Hoover Institution Press, 1978.

Foltz, Richard C. *Mughal India and Central Asia.* New York: Oxford, 1998.

Freedman, Paul. *Out of the East: Spices and the Medieval Imagination.* New Haven, Conn.: Yale University Press, 2008.

Goffman, Daniel. *The Ottoman Empire and Early Modern Europe.* Cambridge: Cambridge University Press, 2002.

Gorenstein, Shirley S. "Western and Northwestern Mexico," in Richard E. W. Adams and Murdo J. MacLeod eds. *The Cambridge History of the Native*

Peoples of the Americas, vol. 2, pt. 1 *Mesoamerica*. Cambridge: Cambridge University Press, 1996, 318–357.

Heath, Byron. *Discovering the Great South Land*. Dural, New South Wales: Rosenberg Publishing, 2005.

Inalcik, Halil. *The Ottoman Empire: The Classical Age 1300–1600*, Norman Itzkowitz and Colin Ember trans. New York: Praeger Publishers, 1973.

Israel, Jonathan. *European Jewry in the Age of Mercantilism, 1550–1750*. Portland, Ore.: Littman Library of Jewish Civilization, 1998.

Klausmann, Ulrike, Meinzerin, Marion, and Kuhn, Gaberiel eds. *Women Pirates and the Politics of the Jolly Roger*. Tyler Austin and Nicholas Levis trans. Montreal: Black Rose Books, 1997.

Levi, Scott C. ed. *India and Central Asia: Commerce and Culture, 1500–1800*. Oxford: Oxford University Press, 2007.

_____. *The Indian Diaspora in Central Asia and its Trade, 1550–1900*. Leiden: Brill, 2002.

Lincoln, W. Bruce. *The Conquest of a Continent: Siberia and the Russians*. New York: Random House, 1994.

Mintz, Sidney. *Sweetness and Power: The Place of Sugar in Modern History*. New York: Viking, 1985.

Nash, Gary B. *Red, White, and Black: The Peoples of Early North America*. 3rd ed. Englewood Cliffs, N.J.: Prentice Hall, 1992.

Pearson, M. N. *The New Cambridge History of India*, vol. 1 *The Portuguese in India*. Cambridge: Cambridge University Press, 1987.

_____. *Port Cities and Intruders: The Swahili Coast, India, and Portugal in the Early Modern Era*. Baltimore: Johns Hopkins Press, 1998.

Pomeranz, Kenneth, and Topik, Steven. *The World That Trade Created: Society, Culture, and the World Economy, 1400–The Present*. New York: M. E. Sharpe, 1999.

Reid, Anthony. *Southeast Asia in the Age of Commerce 1450–1680*, vol. 2 *Expansion and Crisis*. New Haven, Conn.: Yale University Press, 1988.

Richards, John F. *The New Cambridge History of India: The Mughal Empire*. Cambridge: Cambridge University Press, 1995.

Salisbury, Neal. "Native People and European Settlers in Eastern North America, 1600–1783," in Bruce G. Trigger and Wilcomb E. Washburn eds. *The Cambridge History of the Native Peoples of the Americas*, vol. 1, pt. 2 *North America*. Cambridge: Cambridge University Press, 1996, 399–426.

Sharer, Robert J. "The Maya Highlands and the Adjacent Pacific Coast," in Richard E. W. Adams and Murdo J. MacLeod eds. *The Cambridge History of the Native Peoples of the Americas*, vol. 2, pt. 1 *Mesoamerica*. Cambridge: Cambridge University Press, 1996, 449–499.

Steensgaard, Niels. *Carracks, Caravans, and Companies: The Structural Crisis in the European-Asian Trade in the Early Seventeenth Century*. Lund: Studentlitteratur, 1973.

Thornton, John. *Africa and Africans in the Making of the Atlantic World, 1400–1800.* 2nd ed. Cambridge: Cambridge University Press, 1998.

Turley, Hans. *Rum, Sodomy, and the Lash: Piracy, Sexuality, and Masculine Identity.* New York: New York University Press, 1999.

Vries, Jan de, and Woude, Ad van der. *The First Modern Economy: Success, Failure, and Perseverance of the Dutch Economy, 1500–1815.* Cambridge: Cambridge University Press, 1997.

4

The Movement of Peoples and Diffusion of Cultures

Today, one of the most striking consequences of globalization is the wide-reaching movement of peoples and their cultures around the planet. A person can virtually encounter the world – see distinctive attire, smell exotic cuisine, and hear all sorts of mysterious verbal cadences – on a stroll through almost any big city. In terms of language, a survey conducted in the United Kingdom in 2005 found that at least 104 languages were spoken among school-aged children in Scotland, 98 languages in Wales, and 300 in England. In London alone, one can hear 196 different spoken languages.[1] No doubt, studies of New York, Paris, Buenos Aires, Tokyo, Jakarta, and a host of other cities would yield comparable statistics. At no other time in history have so many different people resettled in so many different lands.

The roots of modern migration patterns, and ultimately cultural diffusion in the twenty-first century, extend back to the substantial movements of peoples in the early modern age. Empire building in America, Siberia, and central Asia spawned large-scale migration movements that repopulated these world regions. Africans and Europeans mixed with native Americans in the western hemisphere, Russians and Siberian peoples remade northern Asia, and Chinese emigrants reshaped large areas of central and southeast Asia. As different ethnic communities established new homes in new places, various peoples interacted with one another on an extensive scale for the first time and thereby created new societies.

These massive migration streams also paved the way for the movement of people in modern times. The reason nineteenth-century European migrants poured into temperate zones around the world is because their ancestors had carved out territorial empires in North America, South Africa, Australia, New Zealand, and Argentina in the 1500s and 1600s. As a result, Irish, Italian, German, and Scandinavian peoples could envisage overseas destinations that contained communities with familiar customs, patronage networks, and often family connections. Similarly, the Russian migration into Siberia and Chinese diaspora into other parts of Asia followed on the heels of early modern movements. Migration between 1400 and 1800 laid the basis for new ethnic and cultural identities in the world we inhabit.

The primary dispersions of people occurred across two hemispheres, a transatlantic and a trans-Eurasian zone. In the transatlantic, enslaved Africans and Europeans crossed over the ocean to exploit the resources of America. Across Eurasia, two separate migration patterns emerged: a Russian movement eastward across the Ural Mountains into Siberia and an extensive Chinese resettlement in both southeast and central Asia. Many smaller-scale migrations occurred throughout this period, such as religious refugees resettling in various parts of Reformation Europe, native American societies relocating in the face of European incursions, and Bugis from Sulawesi dispersing en mass into Sumatra and Malaya. Although regional movements such as these are certainly worthy of study, this chapter focuses on the migration streams that had global implications in the transatlantic and trans-Eurasian passages.

Land and Labor in the Atlantic World

The expansion of European empires into America formed the initial catalyst and the ongoing force behind early modern transatlantic migrations. Acquiring land for agricultural cultivation provided a compelling motivation for European overseas ventures and America afforded them the most opportune circumstances to put these ambitions into place. After realizing that Columbus had not landed off the coast of China, the Spanish started appropriating land for mining and farming operations in the early 1500s in Central and South America. Over the course of the 1500s and 1600s, other European powers followed suit.

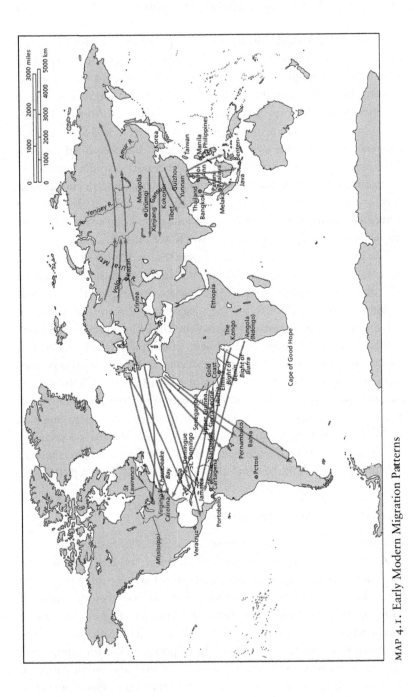

MAP 4.1. Early Modern Migration Patterns

Land drew Europeans across the Atlantic, but the organization of cultivated terrain required intense labor to extract wealth from the earth. The earliest land tenure arrangements after the Spanish arrival in the Caribbean, Mexico, and Peru stipulated that indigenous peoples perform labor services for Spanish landlords. Forced labor initially took the form of a repartimento arrangement whereby a certain segment of an indigenous population had to work in mines or in agricultural settlements. The Spanish crown attempted to eliminate abuses in the repartimento system by introducing the encomienda, which represented the transplanting of old feudal traditions about land organization to Spanish America. Under the encomienda structure, the monarchy endowed the labor and income of native inhabitants residing on a parcel of land to a Spanish colonist. In return for "protecting" local tribes and teaching them the Christian faith, the landlord received income that the land produced and the labor required to make it productive. In practice, Spanish repartimentos and encomiendas amounted to little more than slavery. The lack of any effective legal restraint on Spanish colonists and the resistance of American peoples led to their virtual enslavement for agricultural and mining labor. The coercion of labor at the outset, therefore, went hand in hand with the control over land in America, a tradition with a very long history in European societies.

In North America, conflicts over land between European colonists, especially English settlers, and American tribes poisoned relations throughout the 1600s and 1700s. Dutch and French colonies remained relatively small, and migrants contented themselves with trade to American tribes. Because of heavy demographic settlement, English colonists came into bitter disputes with American nations. Proponents of colonization, realizing that American tribes possessed basic rights to the land, developed theories to rationalize the appropriation of landed resources. As the Reverend Robert Gray mused in 1609, "By what right or warrant can we enter in the land of these Savages, take away their rightful inheritance, and plant ourselves in their places?"[2]

Colonialists approached the dilemma differently. Some, such as the Quakers (known as Friends) in Pennsylvania, purchased land, others simply occupied it on the grounds that no one was developing, that is farming, it. But native societies utilized land area for hunting, which often precluded settled agriculture in sizable spaces. Though tribes and colonies frequently negotiated treaties, migrants regularly ignored boundaries and settled into native lands, provoking bloody reprisals. Incidents like this led to fierce wars, such as the Pequot War in 1637 and King Philip's War in 1675–1676. Bitter disputes over land shaped English and native American relations throughout this period and beyond.

In the sixteenth and seventeenth centuries, two major developments intensified the demand for agricultural and mining labor in the Atlantic world. First, the catastrophic collapse of native populations from exposure to Eurasian disease strains brought on a labor crisis for European empire builders. The lack of American immunity to Old World pathogens led to devastating outbreaks of smallpox, measles, and other infectious diseases that annihilated populations. The impact on labor, especially since farming and mining were work-intensive occupations, proved profound; Spanish and Portuguese colonists began to rely completely on slave labor, almost completely from Africa, by the second half of the 1500s.

A second critical factor that exacerbated labor demands occurred as the French, English, Dutch, Swedes, and Danes settled into the Caribbean islands in the mid-1600s. The French colonized Martinique and Guadeloupe, the Dutch moved into St. Maarten and Aruba, and the English came into possession of the Bahamas and Barbados. The sole purpose for the colonization of the islands in the Caribbean revolved around sugar production, which had found a ravenous market in Europe. Planters established vast capitalist undertakings in their Caribbean holdings, employing the plantation model of agricultural production that Portuguese colonists were perfecting in Brazil. The development of an extensive plantation complex in Brazil, the Caribbean, many places across Central and South America, and on the Atlantic seaboard in the English colonies of Virginia, the Carolinas, and Georgia, created enormous labor requirements. As they developed into mature form, plantations contained anywhere from fifty to hundreds of laborers at one time. And because of unhealthy conditions and the exhaustive work, most laborers, at least initially, did not survive for more than several years. Consequently, the demand for agricultural labor remained intense for commodity production in the Atlantic throughout the early modern period.

European colonialists found in Africa a seemingly unending source for the rigorous labor demands of American agriculture and mining. Africa had long functioned as a reservoir for slave labor in other parts of the world. As early as the eighth century, Muslim Arab merchants sought slaves from the east coast of Africa. Swahili merchants in what is today Kenya and Tanzania sold captured peoples as slaves to Arab middlemen who resold them to markets in the Mediterranean, Arabia, India, southeast Asia, and China. Long before the demographic collapse of native American peoples, Portuguese explorers had taken slaves as they probed Africa's western coastline in the fifteenth century. The first known instance occurred in 1441, when Antam Goncalves led a party that captured ten to twelve men and brought them back to Portugal. The Portuguese began scrambling right away to acquire as many slaves as possible for service in Portugal, and elsewhere in Europe, as well as for agricultural labor in the Atlantic islands they were colonizing. Rather than raiding for slaves, Portuguese commanders established regular trade relations with African merchants who trafficked in human cargo. By 1456, trading surpassed raiding as the means to obtain slaves. Soon thereafter, Portuguese traders were transporting five hundred African slaves per year into Europe and the Atlantic islands.

The pace of the slave trade picked up considerably after Portuguese and Spanish colonialists began to come to grips with the richness of the natural resources in America. Although some disagreement exists about the volume of the trade, the most widely regarded estimates have calculated that approximately two thousand slaves per year were shipped to America in the 1500s. This number jumped considerably to twenty thousand per year in the 1600s, as sugar plantations in Brazil and the Caribbean gained momentum. The 1700s proved to be the high-water mark for slaving, as figures rose to fifty-five thousand early in the century and even to eighty-eight thousand at century's end. By the end of the Atlantic slave trade in the nineteenth century, between ten million and twelve million Africans had been enslaved for American plantations and mines. Perhaps as many as ten million fell victim to the Islamic slave trade in north and east Africa, which continued, albeit illegally, into the twentieth century.

Though Africa yielded millions to servitude on American plantations, raiding and seizing indigenous peoples for enslavement also formed a significant enterprise in the southern English colonies in North America. Native societies in America customarily enslaved enemies captured in war and sometimes even went on the warpath to acquire slaves. Upon the arrival of the Portuguese and Spanish, native Americans experienced labor coercion at the hands of conquistadors and colonialists in Central and South America. English slave traders operating in the southeastern regions of North America, but concentrated in South Carolina, greatly expanded the scale of buying and selling indigenous peoples. The historian Allan Gallay has calculated that English traders purchased between 24,000 and 51,000 native Americans between 1650 and 1715. Traders shipped most of the enslaved natives to plantations on Caribbean islands colonized by the English, including Barbados, Jamaica, and Bermuda.

Just as in Africa, the traffic in American slaves developed out of longstanding practices that expanded from European demand for agricultural labor. Native tribes participated fully in the trade, as Chickasaw, Savannah, Creek, and other groups joined with English forces or embarked on predatory sweeps on their own. The extensive scope of slave raiding in this period fostered an increasingly violent environment in the geopolitics across the southeastern region. Native tribes sought to take advantage of English demand by partnering with colonial forces, manipulating Europeans into attacking their enemies, and enriching themselves in the trade. Conversely, some tribes such as the Apalachee and Choctaw incurred heavy losses from war and slave raiders. A series of intense military conflicts between the Carolina colony, the Yamasee, Creeks, and Cherokee from 1715 to 1717 sent the slave trade into a steep decline. Lack of trust in English traders and officials, as well as a war weariness, convinced native tribal leaders to discontinue their slave raiding alliances with colonial forces. Since the Carolina slave traders depended heavily on native assistance, the American slave trade dwindled to a trickle, as the traffic in Africans grew to extraordinary proportions in the eighteenth century.

Eighty-five percent of the Africans destined for America came from coastal regions that stretched from the Guinea Coast to Angola. Areas that yielded an especially high volume included Upper Guinea, the Gold Coast, the Bight of Benin, the Bight of Biafra, the Kongo, and Angola. As the demand for slaves increased beyond the human supply of the coastal regions in the 1600s and 1700s, slavers pushed farther inland to find adequate human pools. Due to the type of labor needed in America, two out of every three African slaves were male, and most slaves were between the ages of 14 and 35 at the time of capture.

Enslavement derived from European labor demands, but the entire process on the continent from capture to disembarkation remained largely under the control of Africans. Made possible by the prevailing views of wealth in Africa, slave holding on the continent had a very long history. Societies in the sub-Sahara conceived of land as common property, so no one could make an absolute claim of ownership over a parcel of ground. Any person could cultivate a plot of land, provided no one else was using it. The means by which one obtained wealth was through control over labor, as the human capital that produced prosperity from the earth. Thus, buying and selling slaves formed an integral part of African society long before the Portuguese arrived. Before the Atlantic trade, enslaved people were usually either victims of warfare, judicial punishment, or indebtedness. The circumstances of enslavement in Africa contrasted sharply with the brutal conditions of chattel slavery in the Atlantic trade. Slaves in Africa performed a wide variety of tasks from grueling agricultural labor, to domestic work, to cattle ranching, to high-level administration. Consequently, in general the lot of an enslaved person in Africa differed substantially from those in America whose primary purpose was to toil on a plantation or in a mine.

On the violent journey from Africa to America, the initial step involved either abduction of some sort or a transaction by which a prisoner, criminal, or debtor was sold to slave merchants. Some communities also paid regular human tribute to powerful neighboring tribes to preempt raiding. Upon taking possession of enslaved men and women, traders transported their human property to market locations on the coast by chaining the prisoners together and marching them. Upon arrival, the slaves were placed in holding cells, called barracoons, until purchased by European slave traders. As part of the negotiations over price and quality, prospective buyers inspected the human merchandise carefully, probing orifices in the search for physical defects. Once sold, the ship's crew prepared the slaves for departure by stripping, shaving, and branding them. As the Africans boarded, the crew divided them according to gender and chained them either in the cargo hold or on the deck. The ship then embarked on the middle passage to America.

The voyage lasted, depending on the weather, from four weeks to two months. Conditions on board varied from one ship to the next, though they were dreadful at best. Generally conditions improved over the course of the early modern period, since ship owners came to realize that greater profits – and the slave trade above all was an economic enterprise – required enough food, water, exercise, and medical attention to deliver their merchandise alive. Weather permitting, the crew brought the captive peoples on deck for periods during the day, feeding them a mixture of rice, beans, yam, and palm oil in the mornings and late afternoons and forcing them to exercise by jumping and dancing. The Africans usually remained chained in groups to make resistance or flight more difficult. After a late afternoon meal, the crew repacked the men in the cargo hold below the deck for the night. In most cases, women and children remained on deck unless the weather made it necessary for them to be placed in the hold. The spatial constraints in the hold relative to the size of the cargo led to cramped quarters, stifling heat, and unsanitary conditions. Slaves were packed with an eye for efficiency of space and allotted about twenty inches between them and given only enough room to sit up. Space allotments fluctuated significantly between "tight packed" and "loose packed" slaving ships. Some ships contained a few portholes on the sides and grates covering the hold, but these provided little ventilation in the tropical climate. Suffocation and debilitating seasickness were not uncommon.

These conditions proved ideal for the spread of disease, and most ships in the early trade sustained heavy loss of life among both the captives and the crew. By the late seventeenth and early eighteenth centuries, most slave ships employed medical personnel to reduce losses. Those who died were tossed overboard, and in many instances the crew pitched sick slaves over to stall the spread of disease. Insurance companies provided compensation only for dead slaves who were thrown over, requiring profit-minded captains to decide whether to keep the sick onboard or to pitch them and misrepresent their status.

Nevertheless, mortality on ships preoccupied both contemporary slave merchants trying to protect profits and subsequent historians attempting to reconstruct African slaving. The topics of death rates and patterns over the early modern period have provoked strong debate among scholars. The broad consensus today is that onboard death rates were very high at the outset of the trade, figures that could reach as high as 50 percent. Yet as slavers ordered larger ships, equipped the ships with better provisions and minimal medical treatment, and refrained from packing ships as tightly as possible, the mortality rate receded considerably over time. In the 1790s, for example, the average onboard death rate from five hundred ships (whose records have survived) fell under 7 percent. In general, it is estimated that 25 percent of all Africans making the middle passage died during the voyage.

Those who did survive the transatlantic crossing entered a new world of bondage labor upon reaching their American destinations. African slavery extended to every land colonized by European settlers in America. Merchant companies, like the Dutch West India Company and the British South Sea Company, or private traders licensed by a European government, delivered slaves to specific markets in the Caribbean and along the extensive coastline from Brazil to Maryland. The Spanish crown issued highly coveted and expensive licenses (the *asiento*) to merchants to deliver slaves within Spanish-held areas. Some of the most active slave ports in America included Barbados, Jamaica, Cuba, and Santo Domingo in the Caribbean; Veracruz, Portobello, Cartagena, Pernambuco, and Bahia in Central and South America; and Virginia and the Chesapeake Bay in North America. By granting or selling monopolies, each country attempted to control the importation of slaves into its own colonies, which led to bitter colonial conflicts and even wars in the 1700s. After arriving in port, enslaved people were inspected and delivered to owners who either had contracted for them earlier or bought them at a public auction. Across the early modern period, approximately 40 percent of enslaved Africans were transported to Brazil, 40 percent to the Caribbean, 15 percent to Spanish America, and 5 percent to British North America.

The mortality rate for imported slaves was high, especially in the sugar-producing regions of Brazil and the Caribbean. The work regime on any plantation imposed intense physical demands on laborers that, combined with inadequate food and medical attention, led to early death. Yet sugar plantations produced the highest mortality rates of enslaved Africans throughout America, necessitating a steady stream of imported labor to meet the losses. Not only was the labor on sugar plantations especially debilitating, but the tropical regions where they were located confronted Africans (and Europeans) with new disease environments. Africans had to endure a period of "seasoning" in which their immune systems had to adapt to new world pathogens or die of disease. It is estimated that 7 percent of Africans in Cuba and 10 percent in the British West Indies succumbed to disease during the seasoning period.

The conditions that led to high mortality also ensured that fertility rates of African women in America remained low. The grueling conditions of bondage were hardly conducive to a successful pregnancy and childbirth. Furthermore, slavers imported far fewer women than men, especially in the Caribbean, as well as in Central and South America. Enslaved populations in the British North American colonies (later the southern United States) were better able to sustain themselves demographically than those to the south. The disease environments proved far less ravenous, and plantation owners in the 1700s began to import a larger number of females to encourage reproduction to counter the rising prices of slaves. For example, 350,000 slaves were imported into North America between 1700 and 1770, and the slave population grew from 22,000 to 434,000 during this period. But in the Caribbean, almost a million Africans arrived during the same period, but the slave population only grew from 115,000 to 315,000. It took three slaves to increase the slave population by one person in the Caribbean. In Virginia, slaves were able to maintain themselves demographically in the later 1700s.

Captive Africans responded to their bondage in a variety of ways; many resisted their captors by committing suicide, fleeing servitude, carrying out acts of sabotage, or by staging revolts. Studies of slave mutinies in the 1700s have indicated that revolts onboard were common. Resistance to slavery also took place as a regular matter of course on plantations, as many Africans damaged equipment and worked halfheartedly, while a much smaller number tried to escape. Many of those who were successful in fleeing their masters established communities of runaway slaves, known as Maroons, in frontier regions. Often these communities harassed slave establishments and encouraged others to join them. Since the number of black slaves outnumbered whites, slave masters possessed a healthy fear of revolt and made bloody examples of those who fomented insurrection. As revolts became more common in the 1700s, owners expended significant resources on armed patrols to keep revolts in check, which cut into the profits derived from the use of slavery.

The most dramatic slave revolt occurred in St. Domingue in 1791, when slaves joined with free blacks and mulattos ("gens du coleur") under the leadership of Toussaint L'Ouverture to wage a revolution against the French colonial government. After thirteen years of intermittent fighting between local forces and French troops, the victorious black general Jean-Jacques Dessalines declared the independence of the island nation in January 1804. In naming their new country, the revolutionaries adopted the local native appellation, Haiti. A result of the most successful slave revolt in history, Haiti became the second republic formed in America, after the United States.

Why did coerced labor, primarily from enslaved Africans, emerge as the most viable form of human production in the economy? Control over land in America promised enormous wealth for European colonizers willing to shoulder the financial risks. Given all of the economic factors, coerced labor (slavery and indentured servitude) on plantations and in mining operations represented the most cost-effective means to produce profits from the land. For us today, these economic calculations gloss over the moral outrage of slavery. This moral problem, however, is one that only emerged in the 1700s when a principled opposition to slavery emerged, three hundred years after it had gotten underway in the Atlantic. For at least five thousand years, since the formation of the first civilizations, most societies throughout the world have practiced slavery; some, like ancient Greece, Rome, and the Aztec Empire, quite extensively. One of the longest and most active slave regimes appeared in Crimea on the Black Sea, as Italians, then Tatars, and then Ottomans after them sold Slavs into bondage for Asia and Europe. African societies had also engaged vigorously in buying and selling slaves for many centuries.

Most people recognized that bondage was an unfortunate circumstance for the bound, and some moralists advocated humane treatment for slaves; nevertheless, almost everyone accepted enslavement as a legitimate social condition. Europeans employed forms of bondage on other Europeans and coerced them into transatlantic migration, but not as chattel slaves. From 1607 to the Revolution, more than half of the English migrants that came to America did so as indentured servants. To pay for the Atlantic crossing or to repay debts at home, men and women contracted with employers to work for a specified period, normally from four to seven years. After this period of servitude, indentured servants were freed from their obligations and could pursue their livelihood in their transplanted homes. The employer guaranteed servants shelter, food, and clothing, but nothing more in return for their physical labor. Though hardship, and occasionally abuse, filled the lot of indentured servants, their treatment does not compare to African slaves who had little hope of freedom. Europeans also shipped around 50,000 convicts to North America, primarily Georgia, and approximately 160,000 to Australia from 1788 to 1868. The forced exile of criminals and the practice of indentured servitude mark the limits that Europeans placed on claiming possession of other Europeans.

Thus, as the Atlantic slave trade commenced, there were no major debates about the morality of enslavement. In fact, Bartolomé de las Casas, a Catholic priest and one of the most ardent critics of Spanish brutality toward native American peoples, at one point called for the enslaving of Africans as a means of alleviating the suffering of Americans. He wrote in his autobiography:

There were even some...who promised the cleric Bartolomé de las Casas that if he brought, or gained permission to bring, a dozen Negroes to this island, they would give up their Indians so these Indians could be set free. When the said cleric understood this...he secured this [permission] from the King: that in order to free the Indians the Spaniards of these islands would be allowed to take some Negro slaves.[3]

After witnessing the treatment of African slaves, however, de las Casas strongly regretted his proposal.

Many Europeans, Africans, and Americans benefited from the trade. For European merchants and plantation owners in America, Africa offered the most cost-efficient source for slave labor. The middle passage formed the shortest distance between supply and demand for low-cost labor, after the demise of native American populations. European slavers, for the most part, did not have to expend the effort to collect, transport, and process slaves within the African mainland, so merchants enjoyed an economy of effort in procuring labor. Thus, the geographic twist of fate that made the African western coast accessible to European ships, along with the presence of native elites skilled at the supply end, made the trade profitable for European merchants and plantation owners. At the same time, labor needs in America also represented a tremendous boon to African traders along the coast. Slave traders demanded specific goods and set prices at levels in accordance with their own expectations for profit. In cases of power disparities, indigenous traders enjoyed the upper hand, so Europeans could not dominate the market for slaves but had to negotiate at rates heavily influenced by local conditions. The presence of so many competing European powers – Portuguese, English, Dutch, French, and to a lesser extent Danes and Swedes – enabled Biafrans, Senegalese, Beninese, and others to tilt the balance of trade in their favor.

Falling transportation costs in the Atlantic greatly contributed to Africa's long life as the chief source of agricultural and mining labor in America. During the second half of the 1400s, the Portuguese led the way in building better ships, exploring the African coast, and developing expertise with wind patterns and ocean currents in the Atlantic. Technological know-how enabled Europeans to plant themselves on the African coastline and carve out empires in America. As Portuguese and Spanish merchants, then later Dutch, English, and French, developed the Triangular Trade, they remained highly sensitive to profit margins, which shaped their decisions on the particular goods they extracted, traded, and shipped. Since shipping merchandise across the Atlantic formed the greatest expense, merchants calculated quite carefully the cost-yield ratio for transporting goods. In the slave trade, shipping accounted for three-fourths of the selling price for an enslaved African in America. The concern with reducing transportation costs forced mercantile enterprises to invest in improved ship design on an ongoing basis. As a result, transportation costs fell over time, and European maritime shipping became the most cost-efficient form of intercontinental transportation until the Industrial Revolution of the nineteenth century. In sum, the absence of moral scruple about enslavement; the financial rewards of slaving to merchants in Europe, Africa, and America; and maritime technology created and maintained the Atlantic plantation complex.

The Atlantic slave trade had a long life; it endured for around 350 years, roughly from 1450 to 1831, when Brazil finally joined the ranks of all other American and European nations in abolishing the traffic. Denmark outlawed the trade in 1803, Britain in 1807, the United States in 1808, the Netherlands in 1814, France in 1815, and Spain in 1820. Slavery itself, however, did not come to an end in the western hemisphere until 1888, when Brazil, again the most reluctant signatory, adopted abolition, and even then not without great bloodshed. Britain abolished slavery in 1833, France in 1848, and the United States in 1865. The Islamic slave trade persisted well into the 1900s.

Two factors figured into the demise of enslavement in the Atlantic world. In the 1700s, criticism of slavery grew with the Enlightenment, which stressed innate human dignity and equality under the law. In addition, a number of Christian denominations, especially Quakers, called for the extermination of slavery on moral and religious grounds. Freed and escaped former slaves, most famously Olaudah Equiano, lent their voices, publicizing the inhumane treatment of the victims, and decrying the inherent immorality of the institution. Fueling an abolitionist movement, critics and activists placed slaveholders on the intellectual defensive and assisted slaves in the southern United States in fleeing their bondage. Alongside the rising moral critique, the economic vitality of slaving also began to wane in the early 1800s. Slave revolts and fear of new uprisings raised the cost of maintaining control on plantations, while overexpansion in the sugar industry led to declining profits. Historians have engaged in a running debate over the relative weight of moral objections or economic considerations in bringing an end to slaving. No clear consensus has emerged, but the persistence of the debate suggests that both factors played important roles in the breakup of the Atlantic slavery regime.

New Societies in the Atlantic World

The involuntary migration of perhaps as many as 12 million Africans into America marked the most extensive long-distance movement of peoples in the early modern period. The rate of African immigration dwarfed that of the European exodus, as approximately 1.4 million migrants from Europe, including indentured servants, crossed the Atlantic before 1800. European populations did grow prodigiously across America, however, due to natural increases through reproduction. Even though enslaved peoples suffered much higher rates of mortality and much lower rates of fertility than other immigrants, Africans still greatly outnumbered peoples of European descent in Brazil and in most of the Caribbean. And, throughout all settled American lands, Africans and their descendants formed a conspicuous demographic presence. The magnitude of the diaspora guaranteed that these enslaved peoples would exert substantial influence on the development of American culture.

Enslaved Africans and their descendants retained deeply ingrained cultural traits from their homelands, especially in religious practices, musical expressions, and culinary traditions. Yet because of the circumstances of migration, it became necessary to accommodate these customs to very different physical environments and social organizations. In crossing the Atlantic, Africans underwent a cultural transformation that compelled them to adapt, and thus alter, traditional forms to new surroundings. Europeans who made their way across the Atlantic experienced a similar cross-cultural process, as they implanted themselves across the American landscape. A number of Americanized Africans who obtained their freedom actually returned to their ancestral homeland and played an important role in spreading Christianity. This reverse migration accelerated at the end of the 1700s and through the 1800s, when Sierra Leone and Liberia were founded in west Africa for former slaves. As a result, Europeans with a host of distinct national identities, Africans from a wide variety of tribal backgrounds, and native peoples interacted in various American settings, producing multicultural societies. In terms of economy, society and culture, the Atlantic migrations indeed created a new world.

During the 1500s, Spain led the way in European migration, but in the 1700s England caught up and surpassed all other countries. By the time that northern European colonization was just getting underway in 1600, 125,000 Spaniards were living in Central and South America, primarily in urban centers like Mexico City, Potosi, and Cartagena. Brazil contained around 25,000 Portuguese. An important shift took place in the 1600s, when northern Europe began to cultivate colonies in North America and plantations in the Caribbean. The first permanent English colony in Jamestown put down roots in 1607 and by 1670, some 100,000 migrants populated settlements along the east coast. Dutch and French migrations lagged considerably at 10,000 each at the end of the 1600s. Northern Europeans poured into North America in the 1700s; by 1780, 722,000 immigrants from the British Isles had made their way to the English colonies. By 1700, Spanish immigration reached 500,000 and Portuguese around 100,000. Migration from other European countries picked up steam too, as the French added 50,000 between 1700 and 1750 and the German 111,000.

On the other side of the Atlantic, the Cape of Good Hope on the tip of South Africa developed into a small Dutch settler colony over the course of the 1600s and 1700s. From its inception in 1652 to its capitulation to the English in 1806, the Cape colony drew approximately 15,000 Dutch people looking for farmland, as well as a number of German, Scandinavian, and French migrants. The Dutch settlers, later known as Afrikaners, pushed aside the Khoikhoi and Xhosa peoples and set up farms and ranches.

Women played important functions in the formation of settlements in new environments. All colonizing powers realized the importance of women in establishing a permanent demographic presence in America, Africa, and Asia. The initial strategy involved recruiting women to migrate overseas, though few women displayed much interest in traveling so far from home in such precarious circumstances. Women comprised less than 20 percent of the Spanish and the Portuguese immigrants for the entire period, though the English achieved much higher rates of female migration in North America. Very few Dutch women moved into overseas colonies. Consequently, Dutch, Spanish, and Portuguese authorities decided to send girls (as well as boys) from orphanages to find their fortune overseas, though these schemes also came to naught for various reasons. Eventually, colonial authorities concluded that native women needed to assume the primary role as wives to repopulate colonial societies, and as concubines or prostitutes to satisfy male sexual needs.

As men and women from three continents converged in America, a primary characteristic underlying all societies that developed across the continents was a social hierarchy based on ethnic gradations. The percentage of males outnumbered females in both European and African migration streams, and gender disparity was much more pronounced among Spanish and Portuguese settlers in Central and South America. The disproportionate number of Spanish and Portuguese men bred a broad pattern of miscegenation and intermarriage among men with connections to Iberia and American and African-American women. The children of European unions in America were known as creoles, those of European-American unions were known as mestizos (females as mestizas), European-African unions as mulattos (mulattas), and

African-American unions as zambos (zambas). In the English stream that dominated migration to North America, a much larger percentage of women crossed the Atlantic, in some cases almost as much as 50 percent, as in the Carolinas in the 1700s. As a result, sexual engagements between Europeans and Americans or Africans were less common than in Central and South America.

As peoples from different ethnic backgrounds intermarried, or had informal sexual relations, ethnicities merged, blending European, American, and African peoples. The Protestant religious teachings of the English and Dutch colonists placed higher demands on indigenous people for converting to Christianity than the Catholic traditions of the Spanish, Portuguese, and French. English and Dutch Protestant missionaries, unlike their Catholic counterparts, resisted baptizing Americans and Africans as infants in most circumstances, contributing to a much lower rate of conversion to Christianity. Since no Christian denomination condoned intermarriage with non-Christians, far fewer marriages between English and Dutch men and native women took place than in the Iberian empires. This does not mean, however, that colonial men did not have informal relations – sometimes forced – with nonwhite women. In the British colonies, white colonists generally did not acknowledge these liaisons or their offspring. Contact between native American or African-American men and European women in these colonies was regarded as a heinous sexual taboo and surely led to severe punishment, if not death, for the males.

Within the multiethnic societies of South and Central America, a hierarchy emerged that privileged connections to European ancestry. The uppermost elites were settlers who could trace their birth back to Spain or Portugal, known as peninsulares, followed by creoles and then by mestizos. In the initial waves of Spanish migration in the early 1500s, conquistadors and other elites actually sought wives from the Mexican and Peruvian nobility. Following a traditional European practice, they did this to cement political alliances with indigenous elites. For local families, marriage to a European afforded the opportunity to retain or to advance their social status so they also found such marriages to their advantage. Over time, as mestizo populations grew significantly, they became important economic producers, yet chafed under the rule of peninsulares or creoles. Mixed-race zambos and mulattos filled a similar function in Brazilian society. Likewise, in Africa a growing racial complexity marked the Senegambia region controlled by the French – Gorée, Rufisque, and Saint Louis – as European males intermarried with indigenous women. Swahili and Arab intermarriages in the eastern coastal cities of Africa functioned in a comparable manner. In all territories ruled by European colonists, however, native peoples and enslaved peoples languished at the bottom of society.

Within the social hierarchies that emerged, societies throughout this new world reflected the intermingling of African, American, and European cultures. Since peoples of European descent dominated political, social, and economic life, the features they contributed became institutionalized in all American lands. The impact of European culture manifested itself primarily in the areas of government and law, religion, and language. First, European structures of government and law, from monarchical models to aristocratic and more representative systems, found their way across the Atlantic. The vast territories in the Spanish Empire adopted a monarchical model for governance, with viceroys ruling from Mexico and Peru, along with a committee of ministers, the Council of the Indies. Likewise, the king of Portugal sent a royal governor to rule over Brazil, which had already been divided into territories under the control of Portuguese nobles. To the north, French territories in the Mississippi and St. Lawrence River valleys came under the control of a royal governor. Since monarchs governed Spain, Portugal, and France, it made sense to them to plant royal structures in their colonial territories. English colonies operated somewhat differently, but also reflected the political structure back home. Though subject to a monarch, they contained representative institutions that gave nonnoble, political elites a large voice in community affairs. These assemblies functioned similar to the House of Commons, a chamber in Parliament. Thus, colonizing elites adapted European styles of governance into American contexts.

Europeans also introduced Christianity to America, especially among indigenous peoples in Central and South America and among enslaved Americans. By virtue of the missionary efforts of Catholic Jesuits, Franciscans, and Dominicans, Central and South America became heavily Catholic. French Jesuits and Recollects (an Augustinian religious order) also made significant inroads with native tribes in North America. Protestant denominations prevailed in the English colonies and New Netherlands, not surprising since England and the Netherlands had adopted Protestant creeds during the Reformation. Protestant missionaries, however, failed to attract large numbers of converts among native Americans because the ministers insisted prospective converts had to become "civilized," that is adopt a European lifestyle before baptism. Protestants did, however, devote much more effort and attained greater success at converting slaves.

Finally, European dominance in America led to the establishment of European languages as the primary linguistic forms of discourse in the various territories. Though the spread of Spanish, Portuguese, English, and French spread haltingly and blended with American and African tongues, European languages were the linguistic expressions of the powerful. As a result, it behooved native and African-American peoples to acquire some facility in them in order to have any hope of dialoguing with those in power. As these languages extended their reach, they facilitated the spread of European ideas and customs.

Even with the widespread influence of European institutions in America, cultural expressions from native American and African societies played an important role in the development of popular culture. Peoples from very different ethnic backgrounds lived in close proximity to one another and even married one another in the Iberian empires, leading to an extensive cross-fertilization of cultures. Religious beliefs and practices were particular cultural expressions in which a blending of different traditions was most apparent. As native Americans adopted Christianity, they did so from their own conceptual framework, and so they continued to cling to the supernatural power of their own rites, which were alien to Europeans. Sometimes taking a relativistic approach to indigenous cultures, Catholic missionaries often overlooked pagan traditions for attaining immediate material needs, such as rituals to provide an abundant harvest. Especially in the early missionary forays, religious orders found that accommodating Christian practices to native religious customs served as an effective strategy for converting American peoples.

The most prominent example of this blending was the cult of Our Lady of Guadalupe, based on the legend involving a peasant's visions of the Virgin Mary near Mexico City in 1531. Church authorities constructed and promoted a shrine commemorating the apparitions of the Virgin located on the site of a popular pre-Columbian lunar and corn goddess, Tontantzin. Visual depictions of the Virgin incorporated similar features as the native goddess and, by the mid-1600s, she enjoyed immense popularity in Mexico for the miracles people claimed she performed. Baptizing local religious traditions played no small role in aiding the spread of Catholicism and, in so doing, added indigenous American elements into Catholic Christianity.

A similar syncretism occurred in African practices and European Christianity in the 1700s. Blacks in America who converted to Christianity embraced African saints, such as St. Elesbaan and St. Iphigenia, both from Ethiopia. It was not coincidental that St. Elesbaan won notoriety as an avenging warrior, while St. Iphigenia gained fame as a stalwart virgin, symbols of resistance for enslaved men and women. African-Americans introduced novel forms of worship in all Christian denominations, by including lively music, dancing, and theatrical elements that recalled African spirits and deities. African belief in the omnipresence of spirits in the natural world infused Protestant churches with a more sharpened sense of the supernatural in everyday life. Many of the hymns in Protestant churches originated as "Negro spirituals" sung as declarations of perseverance and hope amidst the oppression of bondage. Further, African views of death, afterlife, and time informed cultural attitudes in the southern United States in the 1700s and 1800s.

Another notable area marked by African-American influence was the evolution of languages in America. Enslaved peoples came from a very diverse array of linguistic backgrounds in Africa and found it necessary to develop means to communicate with each other, as well as with slave masters. Gradually the interaction among peoples from various parts of Africa and among colonial populations fostered a number of creole languages used by blacks, which bled into the different European vernacular dialects. Slaves in Suriname, for example, formed a language known as Sranan, a hybrid of Dutch, English, and African expressions. The best documented examples in North America were the Gullah and Geechee linguistic systems that emerged in Georgia and South Carolina. Below is a passage from the New Testament in Gullah compared to an English translation.

Now Jedus been bon een Betlem town, een Judea, jurin de same time wen Herod been king. Atta Jedus been bon, some wise man dem dat study bout de staa dem come ta Jerusalem fom weh dey been een de east. And dey aks say, "Weh de chile da, wa bon fa be de Jew people king? We beena see de staa wa tell bout um een de east, an we come fa woshup um op.

Now Jesus was born in Bethlehem town, in Judea, during the same time when Herod was king. After Jesus was born, some wise men that studied about the stars came to Jerusalem from where they were in the east. And they asked, "Where is the child, who was born to be the Jewish king? We saw the star which told about him in the east, and we came to worship him.[4]

These creole languages had a strong influence on linguistic usage in the southern United States, and Gullah is still spoken today in parts of Georgia and South Carolina.

The transatlantic diasporas of African and European peoples produced new societies in America, which one historian, Mechal Sobel, has appropriately described as "the world they made together." The colonial demand for labor in the early sixteenth century brought together Africans, Americans, and Europeans who formed multiethnic societies in the early modern world.

Resettlement Across Asia

At the same time that new societies were taking shape in America, halfway around the world Russians and Chinese were embarking on empire-building campaigns that reshaped northern and central Asia. Russian migration across Siberia, stretching from the Ural Mountains to the Pacific Ocean, constituted the second largest resettlement of populations in the early modern period and established the basis for massive eastward migration in the modern era. In fact, trans-Siberian migration in the 1800s and 1900s ranks as the third largest movement of peoples in all of world history, behind European and African migrations to America. The Russian population of Siberia grew from 300,000 in 1710 to 2.7 million by 1850 and to 5 million by 1900. The immigration rate across the Ural Mountains was not nearly as prolific in the early modern period: from 1550 to 1710, the Russian populace in northern Asia grew to 300,000, and all but 66,000 lived in western Siberia, between the Urals and the Yenisey River.

The significance of European Russian settlement into northern Asia in the early modern period, then, lies not only in the raw numbers of migrants. Rather, the importance of early modern migration was that it sufficiently Russianized Siberia to make it an outlet for the mass resettlement in the 1800s and 1900s. In terms of early modern global interactions, Russian eastward expansion exhibited a number of striking parallels with the transatlantic migrations. These similarities include the ruthless colonization of a vast territorial expanse, inhabited largely by seminomadic peoples, the decimation of aboriginal populations due to disease, the exploitation of land and coercion of labor that fueled the rise of a colonizing power to world prominence, and the transformation of indigenous cultures into new multiethnic societies.

The diffusion of Russians throughout Siberia was closely intertwined with empire building from the 1500s through the 1700s. Strategic geopolitical concerns prompted Ivan IV to expand into the Kazan region, yet the value of lands that lay to the east piqued the interest of subsequent tsars and pulled thousands of adventurers, military men, missionaries, brigands, administrators, and peasants into this immense landscape. Just as the desire for land drove western Europeans across the Atlantic, the riches derived from native habitats spurred the ambitions of the imperial state and Russian peoples. Large-scale mercantile operations, such as the one operated by the Stroganov family, unearthed large veins of valuable resources, like salt, gold, and copper. The most prized commodity from Siberia, however, neither grew in the soil nor resided within the earth's crust, but rather lived in the coniferous forests and open plains: fur-bearing animals.

The fur pelts of squirrels, rabbits, foxes, martens, and most especially sables found an unquenchable market in Europe, China, and the Middle East. North America offered beavers, minks, and other animals whose hides formed a lively source of trade to Europe. Siberia, however, emerged as the most fertile source of furs, particularly the highly sought-after sable, native to northern Asia and Scandinavia. From the end of the 1500s to the close of the 1600s, hunters pulled tens of thousands of sables out of Siberia every year, peaking at 100,000 at century's end. No other region in the world could compete with Siberian fur production until the 1700s, by which time the sable and other animals had been driven almost to the point of extinction. Revenue from the Siberian fur trade made up 10 percent of the annual imperial treasury. As sugar was to the Caribbean and South America and tobacco and cotton to North America, furs were to Siberia.

As Russians chased the sable across northern Asia, pushing ever farther east as they depleted one region after another, land provided a source of income for a second wave of immigrants in the 1600s and 1700s, peasants. As Cossacks in the pay of emperors besieged and conquered lands in western Siberia, a substantial stream of peasants followed. Serfdom endured in Russia until 1861, which placed onerous burdens on peasants. Many came to see Siberia as an opportunity to flee a life of subjugation. Much to the chagrin of Russian landlords, the state actually encouraged peasant migration into western Siberia and sought to control it. The Russian government did prohibit migrants from going beyond the reach of garrisons it had established in order to protect peasants from slave raids. By 1670, 34,000 peasants lived in the western regions of Siberia, turning the forests and plains into agricultural settlements.

If the pursuit of worldly fortune inspired most Russians to head into Siberia, the Russian Orthodox Church threw its wholehearted religious support into the colonization effort as well. Like the Roman Catholic Church and various Protestant denominations in the western hemisphere, the Russian Church attempted to live up to the Christian mandate to "go into all the world" to preach the gospel and make converts. Missionaries posted themselves in colonial settlements and used them as a base to repudiate the shamanistic religious practices of Siberian peoples and to confront Islam along the northern corridor of the central Eurasian steppes. Peter I pursued a rigorous program of Christianizing lands under Russian control, outlawing all non-Christian practices. Political officers and missionaries persecuted local religious men and destroyed local religious artifacts, though they proved unable to stifle shamanism completely. Later Catherine II relaxed these strictures, and indigenous religious cultures melded into the Orthodox faith in Siberia.

Eastward migration into Siberia conformed to the specific character of Russian empire building. The presence of military and administrative personnel, missionaries, and hunters in the fortified settlements called for the migration of all sorts of artisans to provide goods for the community. Since local peoples did not farm on any substantial level, the colonial population required a much larger migration of peasants to provide an agricultural infrastructure to support the settlements. Almost all of the peasants, which made up the bulk of the migration streams in the early modern period, settled in the western zone of Siberia. The forbidding climate in the central and eastern regions, except for the verdant Amur River basin (on the northeastern Pacific Ocean), made crop agriculture impossible. Consequently, before the migratory onslaught in the 1800s, over 75 percent of Russian settlers made their homestead west of the Yenisey River.

Russian migration generated far-reaching interactions with indigenous populations and native ecosystems that fundamentally altered the peoples and places of Siberia. It is a common misperception, promoted by colonizing interests, that Siberia, like North America, was an empty landscape ripe for Europeans to turn it into a productive environment. The Khantys, Mansis, Selkop, and Ket societies occupied the west, Tungus and Yakuts lived in central Siberia, and Eskimos, Chukchis, and Yugakirs lived in the far northeast. Just as hundreds of thousands of natives inhabited North America, so also did tens of thousands of aboriginals populate Siberia. These distinct peoples had organized their societies according to oral, informal, and tribal customs that emphasized mutual responsibility. Elders ruled in conjunction with a tribal leader or chief.

The introduction of the *yasak* system produced profound social changes that eroded the fluid social relations between members and brought about a more western and hierarchical organizational structure. Tribal leaders took on the attributes of a hereditary aristocracy, prevalent in Europe, and ordinary people found themselves under greater economic demands. Over time, as Russian peasants settled in western Siberia, they experienced the same type of restrictions and financial exactions that they had attempted to flee in Muscovy. Thus, colonizers reproduced Russia's hierarchical and coercive social organization – replete with nobles, serfs, and surplus extraction – in the nomadic frontier of Siberia.

While western societal structures displaced many Siberian forms, sexual interaction between Russians and aboriginals produced mixed-race peoples that blended ethnicities imperceptibly over time. A much greater ratio of males migrated than females, creating a strong demand for women on the frontier. To satisfy this need, Russian males intermarried and entered into extramarital sexual relations with native women. Often, the means of sexual partnering was extremely violent: Cossacks raided settlements, seizing wives and daughters, taking them as their own or selling them to third parties. Many Siberian women were sold into slavery. Nevertheless, in most areas a rather high degree of miscegenation occurred so that distinctions between Siberian and Russian ethnicities became hardly discernable over time.

Though much less known to history students than the Atlantic migrations, the eastward flow of Russians into Siberia nevertheless formed one of the most extensive transcontinental interactions in the early modern period. Just as the European and African diasporas reshaped America, Russian immigration carried dramatic implications for northern Asia. Perhaps the most significant changes were the conversion of the landscape in western Siberia into a more densely populated agricultural region, the institutionalization of exploitive social and economic hierarchies among tribal peoples, and the encasement of Siberian ethnic identities into a Russian Slavic cultural matrix. Many processes that shaped trans-Siberian migration bore basic similarities to European migration to America: the quest for economic opportunity afforded by land, the appropriation of non-European labor for commodity production, the displacement of indigenous peoples in service of colonial interests, and the blending of diverse cultural values in the emergent societies. The most obvious difference between the two was the triangular dynamic in America, as colonized Europeans, enslaved Africans, and indigenous peoples came together to form a new world. In the long term, both the transatlantic and trans-Siberian migrations established the bases for the massive transoceanic flow of peoples in modern times.

A third major migratory movement of the early modern period was the dispersion of Chinese peoples into the maritime territories of the Indian Ocean and across the grassy steppes of central Asia. Unlike the previous two migration streams, the Chinese outflows moved in two different general directions for two different reasons from the 1500s to the 1800s. Reaching its zenith in the mid-1600s, migration into southeast Asia grew out of a long-established pattern of Chinese merchant activity, which endured despite restrictions and even prohibitions from the Ming and Qing dynasties. The push across central Asia happened primarily in the 1700s, when Qing emperors sought to colonize Mongolia, Turkestan, Tibet, and other regions of central Asia. They undertook this colonial enterprise to protect China from powerful nomadic confederations and to assert the empire more firmly into geopolitics of central Asia.

The Chinese diaspora into southeast Asia was born out of the opportunities for trade in the commercial expansion of the Indian Ocean from the early 1400s to mid-1600s. As the Ming dynasty concentrated its attention on the northern and western plains in the early 1400s, it banned all foreign trade, except for tribute missions to the imperial court, and prohibited emigration. These missions, in which foreign ambassadors brought local exotic goods in return for Chinese gifts, constituted the only legal avenue of international exchange. Over the course of the 1400s, Ming emperors lost interest in the tribute system and the exchanges dwindled to nothing. Despite the imperial prohibitions, the demand for Chinese goods remained high, so merchants from the southern regions sought to capitalize on this trade by migrating to the vital port cities in southeast Asia, such as Melaka, Bangkok, Manila, and Jakarta. Chinese involvement in maritime commerce grew, as a new emperor relaxed the prohibitions on foreign trade in 1567. Consequently, Chinese outward migration grew significantly during the late sixteenth and seventeenth centuries. During this time, Chinese numbered in the thousands in the ports of Hoi Ann (Vietnam), Patani (Thailand), and Java (Indonesia) and reached as high as 20,000 in the Philippines in 1603.

Chinese migration into southeast Asia entered a new phase in the mid-1600s, when northern Manchu forces overthrew the Ming regime in 1644. The supporters of the old dynasty fled to southern China, Taiwan, Korea, Thailand, Malaya, and islands in the southeast. Initially, this Manchu (Qing) dynasty was hostile to trade and cracked down on the trading ports that had grown up in the Fujian regions on the south China coast under the Mings. Large numbers of people who made their livelihoods from commerce also poured out into regions already well populated by Chinese. The rise of the Qing dynasty, then, boosted emigration as its political enemies and economic refugees fled into areas throughout southeast Asia. The Qing dynasty softened the enforcement of its anticommercial edicts at the end of the 1600s, allowing foreign trade to recommence at a level that the imperial court could regulate closely. Because of the pulsating flow of migrants at various junctures from the sixteenth through the eighteenth centuries, the Chinese presence in southeast Asia was substantial. By 1810, people of Chinese descent reached almost 100,000 in Java, around 120,000 in the Philippines, over 230,000 in Thailand, and perhaps as many as one million were scattered across southeast Asia.

Chinese migration across this diverse region led to varied patterns of interaction with indigenous populations. In many circumstances, Chinese immigrants became absorbed into the host society and surrendered much of their native identity, especially when assimilation offered the potential of upward mobility. Spanish colonial authorities ruling over the Philippines pressured Chinese immigrants, as well as native Filipinos, to convert to Roman Catholicism. Colonial law stipulated that when Chinese men married Filipina women, the latter were to remain Catholic and their children reared in that faith. On the other hand, many Chinese throughout Indonesia, which was largely Muslim, willingly converted to Islam and blended into local society. Wherever it took place, the process of assimilation usually involved male immigrants marrying indigenous women and then later their mestizo children likewise would wed native spouses whose offspring would again marry locally. Chinese ethnicity in these situations eroded over the course of several generations, just as Sinitic cultural identity gave way to native religious practices and local customs.

The Chinese diaspora also produced distinct mestizo societies informed by both Chinese and local traditions. Almost no women migrated until the nineteenth century, a basic demographic reality that gave rise to mixed ethnic communities. Men sought wives or concubines among the local peoples, producing a very large mestizo population. In situations where neither political pressure nor economic advantage compelled assimilation, Chinese immigrants formed their own independent communities and retained their distinct identity. These communities were able to maintain a strong sense of "Chineseness" because of the regular immigration of males, who were looking for wives among mestiza daughters, as well as among indigenous women. Rather than repeatedly marrying mestizo offspring to native spouses, families in these hybrid ethnic societies matched their children with other mestizos or with recent immigrants from China.

Analyzing the aspirations and expectations of Chinese immigrants, who found themselves wedged between their native and the indigenous culture, scholars have identified them as sojourners. That is, male migrants in creole or mestizo communities rarely stopped considering themselves as Chinese who would return one day to their homeland after making their fortunes abroad. The irresistible draw of the Middle Kingdom pulled at emigrants instinctively so that they regarded their migration as a temporary stay, or sojourn. In fact, the Chinese term for these emigrants, *huaqiao*, translates as "Chinese human bridge," suggesting that the overseas journey was temporary. The sojourners of the Chinese diaspora developed their communities in phases over time. In the first phase, males that migrated into a particular territory, such as Java, bound themselves together into a self-supporting community. In the second phase, they either returned home or married local women, merging their families into a semiautonomous society. Finally, the last phase occurred as new male immigrants matriculated into the community, married, and reinfused the mestizo society with Chinese values. Some males did return to China after marrying either to resettle or to visit; when doing so, they left their indigenous wives and mestiza daughters, but took their sons with them. Across southeast Asia, Chinese mestizo communities created their own social institutions, religious organizations, and regulatory agencies to solidify communal feeling and to police their own affairs under the watchful eye of local or colonial authorities.

The Chinese found homes, whether temporary or permanent, throughout southeast Asia because host societies regarded them as useful for their own purposes. This outlook was especially true in areas controlled by European powers in the east, namely in Melaka, held by the Portuguese and the Dutch; in the Philippines, conquered by the Spanish; and in Batavia, taken by the Dutch. European merchants from these colonial outposts were quite eager to profit from the China trade, yet they encountered numerous cultural, economic, and political obstacles. These barriers became much more problematic under the growing restrictions of the Mings and the outright prohibitions of the Qings. Chinese mestizo merchants served as critical mediators for European mercantile enterprises in China and across the ports of southeast Asia. With their extensive contacts, mestizo merchants brokered trades and navigated through the loopholes and lapses in the official Chinese bans.

Even though they proved to be valuable assets to the Europeans, Chinese diaspora communities existed in insecure, often vulnerable environments. While the Chinese government gave tacit recognition to the economic necessities driving some emigrants, most came under suspicion as criminals, political dissidents, and rootless vagrants. In general, the imperial court and Confucian elites remained baffled that Chinese people left the Middle Kingdom for lands inhabited by inferior and barbarous peoples. Consequently, the Chinese state during the early modern period offered no support or protection to the diaspora communities in southeast Asia. The absence of state support to sojourners and settlers left them at the mercy of colonial authorities.

Even though the Portuguese, Spanish, and Dutch valued the economic utility of Chinese and mestizo merchants, the colonial regimes also harbored a great deal of concern about losing control over their colonial enterprise. Ever mindful of political insurrection, colonial authorities placed many controls and restrictions over Chinese and mestizo communities. The Dutch isolated the Chinese, mestizos, and other Asian immigrants, from the Javanese, while the Spanish segregated the Chinese from mestizos and Filipinos. Both colonial regimes upheld distinct laws and customs for each group and prohibited them from buying land. Although European authorities allowed the communities to govern themselves, they did so only under the jurisdiction of colonial governors who deputized a mestizo to maintain order and obedience. Fearing conspiracies and uprisings, Spanish and Dutch at times harassed, expelled, cracked down on, and even massacred those of Chinese descent. The Dutch annihilated 10,000 Chinese and mestizos in 1740, and the Spanish carried out severe pograms in 1603 and 1764. Throughout this period, the imperial government in Beijing offered no response to these atrocities and other crackdowns on the Chinese diaspora communities.

Chinese emperors during the Qing dynasty did, however, wholeheartedly promote a systematic program of large-scale migration, a movement west into the immense open spaces in central Asia. Rather than expanding into the maritime regions of the southeast, the Qing dynasty embarked on a massive colonial enterprise across central Asia in the 1600s and 1700s, which paralleled the Russian conquest of Siberia. Qing landward expansion marked a momentous turning point in world history, as China doubled its size and became a dominant power in central Asia.

The overriding geopolitical concern of the Qing dynasty in the 1600s and 1700s was to provide security along the western frontier against restive Mongol khanates and to counter the Russian push into northern Mongolia and the Amur River basin. Qing emperors embraced a bold offensive strategy to subdue Mongol and Russian threats. From 1683 to 1760, a succession of Qing emperors waged an unyielding, though intermittent, campaign that ultimately brought Tibet, Gansu, Kokonor (Qinghai), Mongolia, and Xinjiang into its colonial empire. In addition, the dynasty also annexed Yunnan and Guizhou in the southwest and Taiwan, the center of Ming resistance under the Koxinga emperor.

In much the same way that Russia imposed its authority over Siberia, the Qing state used mass migration as a tool in its empire-building program in central Asia. The first step, as the Chinese gained control over a territory, necessitated the construction of garrisons to maintain Qing rule and to outfit military colonies to strike deeper into unconquered regions. After pacifying a territory, the military colonies became the site for extensive civilian migration, made up mostly by Chinese peasants who came to clear lands and create an agricultural basis for more densely populated provinces out of the sparsely inhabited, semi-nomadic regions. The central government offered incentives to stimulate migration, such as four acres of land, tools, seeds, a horse, and financial assistance. The incentive program worked extremely well, for by the early nineteenth century, 155,000 Chinese peasants had settled in northern Xinjiang, comprising a significant portion of the local population.

The Chinese also sent criminals and political dissidents into exile in settlements across central Asia. Though the figures for Chinese migration into these conquered territories remain vague, the movement of peoples was quite extensive. Between 1758 and 1911, the government exiled 160,000 people to Xinjiang, and by the early nineteenth century, 100,000 civilians lived in Ili in the western region of the province, and 155,000 in the nearby cities of Berköl and Ürümqi.

Thus, like the Russian imperial project in Siberia and the European enterprises in America, the Chinese expansion across central Asia launched multiethnic settler societies under Qing imperial control. In modern times, the Chinese government has officially recognized fifty-six ethnic groups living within its borders. In the early modern period, these included a diverse array of Turkic peoples, such as the Uighur and Kazakh, as well as Kirghiz, Mongol, Uzbek, Zunghar, and Tatar groups. In the southwest provinces, Chinese migrants encountered Tai,

Mon-Khmer, and Tibeto-Burma peoples. In this pluralistic empire, the government promoted a traditional universalism, supported by Confucianism, which emphasized the comprehensive reach of the emperor over all peoples in the Middle Kingdom, regardless of their ethnic background. Fearing that cultural intermixing could lead to rebellion, Qing officials worked to manage ethnic pluralism by establishing policies to keep peoples separate. In settlements in Xinjiang, peoples were segregated from one another, in some cases by walls. Laws mandated that Manchu and Chinese immigrants had to continue to wear their hairstyle in the traditional Manchu queue, shaved from the forehead to above the temple with the remaining uncut hair pulled into a long, tight braid. Local men were not permitted to wear the queue unless given special permission as an honor. Provincial governments throughout the empire used local leaders of ethnic groups to implement laws dictated by central authorities. Manchu officials also sought to advance the use of Mandarin Chinese in these territories as a means to solidify a broad sense of community among the distinct peoples of the empire.

Attempting to foster a universal spirit obedient to the emperor, the Qing state strongly opposed intermarriage across ethnic boundaries. From the Qing point of view, sexual relations across ethnic lines violated the fundamental necessity of cultural order and political submission to the emperor. James Millward, a historian of China, has aptly observed, "cross-cultural drift was considered sedition." Enforcement, however, was another story. The effort at which the Qing pursued marital prescriptions suggests that intermarriage did take place, though probably at fairly low levels in the western provinces. Yet studies of the southwest provinces in Yunnan and Guizhou show that Han males married Tai females in significant numbers, just as the religious practices, languages, and social customs of these groups coexisted and blended together in these regions.

The Chinese diaspora, then, moved in two different directions in the early modern period. Migration into the maritime regions of southeast Asia was rooted in the pursuit of economic opportunity born from the vigorous commercial networks in the Indian Ocean. Despite restrictions and prohibitions by Ming and Qing authorities, hundreds of thousands of migrants from the Fujian districts on the southern Chinese coast poured into Thailand, Melaka, Java, the Philippines, and other territories. There they intermarried, assimilated, or established distinct mestizo communities, but nevertheless interacted closely with indigenous peoples. Vulnerable to exploitation from local regimes and scorned by their own government, migrants, whether returning, sojourning, or settling, retained close ties to their homeland. The westward migration of the eighteenth century, by contrast, was a central element of Qing imperial expansion across central Asia. Soldiers, merchants, administrators, and peasants provided the military, political, and economic infrastructure that brought China fully into the interior corridor of Asia. In Xinjiang, and other western lands, Chinese peoples held onto their ethnic and cultural heritage. In areas where enforcement of ethnic distinctions was lax, such as in Yunnan and Guizhou, however, Chinese migrants proved just as willing to encounter indigenous cultures as their compatriots who were settling into southeast Asia.

Migrants Interconnect World Regions

These extensive currents of migration call attention to the profound global interconnections that developed in the early modern period. The ambitions that pulled world regions closer from 1400 to 1800 came not only from kings and merchants, for ordinary men and women – millions of them – resettled in new lands and created new societies. Many people migrated for many different reasons and under disparate circumstances, but trading opportunities and agricultural expansion formed two general inducements. Perhaps a million people from the southern coastal regions of China poured into maritime southeast Asia to partner with European and indigenous commercial enterprises.

The demand for land and agricultural labor generated massive migration streams across the Atlantic and Eurasia, as Chinese, European, and Russian empires facilitated the rise of large-scale agriculture. Africans and Europeans in the transatlantic migrations created a complex of plantations, haciendas, and family estates that produced sugar, cotton, tobacco, and indigo for international markets. Russian tsars and Chinese emperors launched major resettlement projects from the late 1500s through the 1700s. Peasants from Russia settled across Siberia, while Chinese farmers moved into Tibet, Turkestan, Mongolia, Guizhou, and Yunnan.

The coming together of so many people created new societies across America and Asia. Yet the patterns of cultural interaction varied appreciably across world regions. Americans, Europeans, and Africans produced multiethnic societies characterized by social hierarchies that were reflected in pigmentation. Peoples of European descent thoroughly dominated all American societies, though African and indigenous motifs infused cultural forms. In southeast Asia, Chinese immigrants both assimilated in some regions (Indonesia) and retained distinctive mestizo communities in others, such as the Philippines. Fearing the collusion against political authority, the Qing state attempted to keep ethnic Han segregated from central Asian peoples with varying degrees of success. Repeated miscegenation and ongoing migration led to the near total absorption of western Siberian peoples within Slavic Russian culture and ethnicity. In so many ways, the currents of migration interwove the destinies of people around the world in the early modern period.

Works Consulted

Bentley, Jerry H., and Ziegler, Herbert F. *Traditions and Encounters: A Global Perspective on the Past*, vol. 2 *From 1500 to the Present*. 2nd ed. New York: McGraw Hill, 2003.

Brook, Timothy. *The Confusions of Pleasure: Commerce and Culture in Ming China*. Berkeley: University of California Press, 1998.

Curtin, Philip D. *Cross-Cultural Trade in World History*. Cambridge: Cambridge University Press, 1984.

———. "The Epidemiology of Migration," in David Eltis ed. *Coerced and Free Migration: Global Perspectives*. Stanford, Calif.: Stanford University Press, 2002, 94–116.

De Nyew Testament: The New Testament in Gullah Sea Island Creole with Marginal Text of the King James Version. New York: American Bible Society, 2005.

Eltis, David. "Coerced and Free Migrations from the Old World to the New," in David Eltis ed. *Coerced and Free Migration: Global Perspectives*. Stanford, Calif.: Stanford University Press, 2002, 33–74.

———. "Introduction: Migration and Agency in Global History," in David Eltis ed. *Coerced and Free Migration: Global Perspectives*. Stanford, Calif.: Stanford University Press, 2002, 1–32.

Forsyth, James. *A History of the Peoples of Siberia: Russia's North Asian Colony, 1581–1990*. Cambridge: Cambridge University Press, 1992.

French, Katherine L., and Poska, Allyson M. *Women and Gender in the Western Past*, vol. 2 *Since 1500*. Boston: Houghton Mifflin, 2007.

Gallay, Allan. *The Indian Slave Trade: The Rise of the English Empire in the American South, 1670–1717*. New Haven, Conn.: Yale University Press, 2002.

Games, Alison. "Migrations and Frontiers," in Toyin Falola and Kevin D. Roberts eds. *The Atlantic World, 1450–2000*. Bloomington: Indiana University Press, 2008, 48–66.

Giersch, C. Pat. "A Motley Throng: Social Change on Southwest China's Early Modern Frontier, 1700–1880," *The Journal of Asian Studies* 60 (2001), 67–94.

Harris, Joseph E. "The Transatlantic Slave Trade and the Making of the Modern World," in Sheila S. Walker ed. *African Roots/American Cultures: Africa in the Creation of the Americas*. Lanham, Md.: Rowman & Littlefield Publishers, 2001, 104–117.

Hellie, Richard. "Migration in Early Modern Russia, 1480s–1780s," in David Eltis ed. *Coerced and Free Migration: Global Perspectives*. Stanford, Calif.: Stanford University Press, 2002, 292–323.

Hostetler, Laura. *Qing Colonial Enterprise: Ethnography and Cartography in Early Modern China*. Chicago: University of Chicago Press, 2001.

Israel, Jonathan. *European Jewry in the Age of Mercantilism, 1550–1750*. Portland, Ore.: Littman Library of Jewish Civilization, 1998.

Levathes, Louise. *When China Ruled the Seas: The Treasure Fleet of the Dragon Throne 1405–1433*. New York: Simon and Schuster, 1994.

Mackie, J. A. C. "Introduction," in Anthony Reid with Kristine Alilunas Rodgers eds. *Sojourners and Settlers: Histories of Southeast Asia and the Chinese: In Honour of Jennifer Cushman*. St. Leonards, New South Wales: Allen & Unwin, 1996, i–xxi.

Millward, James A. *Beyond the Pass: Economy, Ethnicity, and Empire in Qing Central Asia, 1759–1864*. Stanford, Calif.: Stanford University Press, 1998.

Nash, Gary B. *Red, White, and Black: The Peoples of Early North America*. 3rd ed. New York: Prentice-Hall, 1992.

Palmer, Colin. "Afro-Mexican Culture and Consciousness during the Sixteenth and Seventeenth Centuries," in Joseph E. Harris ed. *Global Dimensions of the African Diaspora*. 2nd ed. Washington, D.C.: Howard University Press, 1993, 125–137.

Pan, Lynn. *Sons of the Yellow Emperor: A History of the Chinese Diaspora*. Boston: Little, Brown, 1990.

Perdue, Peter C. *China Marches West: The Qing Conquest of Central Eurasia*. Cambridge, Mass.: Belknap Press of Harvard University, 2005.

Pomeranz, Kenneth. *The Great Divergence: China, Europe, and the Making of the Modern World Economy*. Princeton, N.J.: Princeton University Press, 2000.

Reid, Anthony. "Flows and Seepages in the Long-Term Chinese Interaction with Southeast Asia," in Anthony Reid with Kristine Alilunas Rodgers eds. *Sojourners and Settlers: Histories of Southeast Asia and the Chinese: In Honour of Jennifer Cushman*. St. Leonards, New South Wales: Allen & Unwin, 1996, 15–49.

Reynolds, Edward. *Stand the Storm: A History of the Atlantic Slave Trade*. New York: Allison & Busby, 1985.

Sanderlin, George, ed. and trans. *Bartolomé de las Casas: A Selection of His Writings*. New York: Alfred A. Knopf, 1971.

Skinner, G. William. "Creolized Chinese Societies in Southeast Asia," in Anthony Reid with Kristine Alilunas Rodgers ed. *Sojourners and Settlers: Histories of Southeast Asia and the Chinese: In Honour of Jennifer Cushman*. St. Leonards, New South Wales: Allen & Unwin, 1996, 51–93.

Sobel, Mechal. *The World They Made Together: Black and White Values in Eighteenth-Century Virginia*. Princeton, N.J.: Princeton University Press, 1987.

Thomas, Benjamin. *The Atlantic World: Europeans, Africans, Indians, and their Shared History, 1400–1900*. Cambridge: Cambridge University Press, 2009.

Thornton, John. *Africa and Africans in the Making of the Atlantic World, 1400–1800*. 2nd ed. Cambridge: Cambridge University Press, 1998.

Walsh, Lorena S. "The Differential Cultural Impact of Free and Coerced Migration to Colonial America," in David Eltis ed. *Coerced and Free Migration: Global Perspectives*. Stanford, Calif.: Stanford University Press, 2002, 117–151.

Wang, Gungwu. *China and the Chinese Overseas*. Singapore: Times Academic Press, 1992.

———. "Sojourning: The Chinese Experience in Southeast Asia," in Anthony Reid with Kristine Alilunas Rodgers ed. *Sojourners and Settlers: Histories of Southeast Asia and the Chinese: In Honour of Jennifer Cushman*. St. Leonards, New South Wales: Allen & Unwin, 1996, 1–14.

5

The Formation of New Demographic
and Ecological Structures

The ways in which human societies have provided for themselves, whether it was the hunting and gathering strategies of native tribes in North America or the extensive cereal agriculture of peasants in China or the seasonal whaling expeditions of coastal communities in Siberia, have exacted a toll on their physical landscapes. Settled agriculture, the caloric basis of all civilizations around the world, makes exacting demands on natural ecosystems and imposes drastic changes on virgin terrains. Despite the destructive environmental effects that sometimes accompanied large-scale crop cultivation, agriculture has without a doubt enabled human societies to grow at a prodigious rate, allowing for much more concentrated population densities than were otherwise possible.

The practice of extensive agriculture throughout history, however, has not freed human populations from their fragile relationship with natural habitats. At the end of the eighteenth century, Thomas Malthus, an English clergyman and economist, identified clearly the limits of agriculture in his influential treatise, "An Essay on the Principle of Population." Malthus argued that societies based on agriculture will always tend to outgrow their food supply. According to the Malthusian calculus, "population[s], when unchecked, increased in a geometrical ratio, and subsistence for man in an arithmetical ratio."[1] That is, humans reproduce at a much greater rate than their capacity to produce food and thus at regular intervals stand at the brink of their own destruction. Though many economists and historians dispute the

146

applicability of Malthus's theory, all accept the premise that human societies dependent upon agriculture put significant pressure on the natural resources that sustain them, which in turn can jeopardize the welfare of those societies.

Writing at the end of the early modern period, Malthus derived his theory in part from his observations on the rapidly expanding world population brought on initially by transatlantic migration to America. He wrote, "it has been universally remarked that all new colonies settled in healthy countries, where there was plenty of room and food, have constantly increased with astonishing rapidity in their population."[2] Historians who study population movements have confirmed Malthus's observations. The intensified land use in expanded frontier settlements produced foodstuffs that enabled the world population to double from 400 million to 500 million in 1500 to 950 million in 1800. In China during this period, the population rose from 100 million to 320 million, in Europe from 80 million to 180 million, and in Africa, despite losses of in the tens of millions to slave traders, the population also rose from 34 million to 60 million.

What Malthus failed to appreciate was that the extensive movement of peoples and goods in the early modern period opened a new chapter in the interaction between human societies and natural ecosystems in world history. The effects of these interactions carried far-reaching ramifications for environments, plants, animals, and peoples. Much more substantial populations required bringing more soil under the plow, cutting more forests, draining more swamps, domesticating more livestock, hunting more animals, and hauling in more fish. As adventurers, merchants, and settlers moved into frontier regions, they exploited, what must have seemed like at the time, limitless resources, including timber, precious metals, prized stones, furs, hides, whales, and fish. Further, these migrants killed many large land mammals, for protection and sport, some almost to the point of extinction. Global expansion had significant environmental consequences.

Migrants not only acted as agents of change but also functioned as carriers of biological systems. Historians have shown that, as people moved into new lands, they purposely brought familiar animals, such as pigs, horses, and cattle. Yet they also inadvertently ferried rats, all sorts of bugs, weeds, parasites, and disease pathogens, which made their homes in completely new environments. These organisms interacted in a variety of ways in their host communities. The most dramatic was the catastrophic smallpox, measles, and influenza pandemics in the Americas, which killed perhaps as many as 100 million native peoples. Other effects of early modern biological exchange were not nearly as spectacular, but they were still profound, in that they contributed to the remaking of ecosystems in world societies.

Global Dissemination of Disease

In 1518, just over twenty-five years after Christopher Columbus first set foot on Hispaniola, Spanish colonists noticed that the indigenous Arawak (Taino) population began dying at dramatic rates from a disease well-known in Europe. The disfiguring boils that covered the bodies of infected Arawaks left no doubt that smallpox had, after two decades, found its way to the Caribbean. Two years later, as Spanish forces under Hernán Cortés were penetrating the heart of the Aztec Empire in Tenochtitlan, smallpox struck the natives with devastating results. As a result of these outbreaks, the Arawak peoples came to the brink of extinction from a population level in 1492 of 500,000, and the Mexicans sustained losses of over 50 percent by the early 1600s. Wherever Europeans ventured in the Americas, indigenous peoples underwent similar degrees of devastation at the hands of Old World diseases. Thus, one prevailing trend in early modern biological exchange was the destruction of indigenous peoples, who had been cut off from Afro-Eurasia, through contact with transoceanic settlers. This outcome not only played itself out across America but also characterized encounters in South Africa, Siberia, and Oceania.

The most extensive demographic repercussions from the spread of disease-bearing bacteria and viruses occurred in America. Two factors account for native peoples' vulnerability to European diseases: biological assimilation throughout Afro-Eurasia and the geographical isolation of America. Since the end of the last glacial period (ice age) about ten thousand years ago, large-scale migrations across Eurasia had occurred with some regularity. Between 3,000 and 1,500 B.C.E., different strains of Indo-European peoples migrated from southern Russia across Europe and central Asia into Spain, Greece, Mesopotamia, Iran, and India. They established new societies and civilizations throughout these regions. In the classical and postclassical periods (500 B.C.E. to

1000 C.E.), large groups of Huns, Germans, Arabs, Magyars, Norse, and Turks moved across Asia, Europe, and northern Africa, imposing themselves on local peoples. Later in the 1200s and 1300s, Mongols, Timurids, and Ottomans conquered large swaths of territory across Eurasia. During this period, merchants, missionaries, and diplomats traveled from Europe to destinations in Asia, seeking profits, alliances, and souls. Thus, Europeans had exposed themselves to a host of disease environments either directly through migration or indirectly through contacts with Asiatic societies.

As a result, contagious diseases formed a regular feature of life for Europeans. The most widespread and devastating pandemic was the fourteenth-century plague that swept across Eurasia from the 1320s to the 1360s. Known by Europeans as the Black Death, the plague was probably a combination of diseases associated with the bubonic plague. Infected fleas formed a primary vector of the disease, which lived on rats and traveled with them across the Silk Roads that linked east Asia to western Europe. Fleas inevitably passed from rodents to humans, transmitting the plague bacillus by biting their hosts. The bacillus also spread through the exhaled breath of infected persons to new victims. Traveling across east and central Asia, the plague struck trading ports in the Black Sea in the 1340s, and made its way into southern Europe in 1347. Estimates of the death toll in Europe range from 20 million or 40 million, and they reached 75 million for all of Eurasia. The plague returned to afflict Europe periodically until the 1700s.

While devastation on this scale was unique, Europeans routinely experienced a range of lethal or debilitating diseases, including smallpox, measles, influenza, mumps, and dysentery. Since these pathogens were prevalent, most people encountered them as a child, and the diseases thinned out population densities. In some parts of Europe, 10 to 15 percent of children died from smallpox. Yet those who survived acquired an immunity from the pathogen for life. The inspiration to create vaccines from weak viruses grew out of the realization that exposure and survival resulted in immunity. Consequently, most adult Europeans by the early modern period had acquired physiological protection for some very contagious and lethal diseases.

By contrast, native American peoples and aborigines in Siberia and Oceania were cut off from Eurasian pathogens and did not have the opportunity to develop any biological resistance to these diseases. It is not yet clear why the pathogens that emerged and evolved in Afro-Eurasia did not germinate in America, Siberia, and Oceania. Asians did migrate across land and ice bridges from Siberia to Alaska during the last glacial age. Perhaps low population densities in these regions for thousands of years sufficiently isolated viral strands so that they ultimately died out before the establishment of complex societies in the Mississippi River valley, Mesoamerica, and the Andes Mountains. Unfortunately, we know far too little about pre-Columbian peoples to answer the question. For now, it remains a mystery. What is quite clear is that by the 1500s indigenous peoples in America, Siberia, and Oceania lacked immunity to Old World pathogens.

The results for native American peoples were catastrophic, leading to severe decline and subjugation of indigenous societies almost every-where. After the onset of smallpox in Hispaniola, it quickly spread across the Caribbean islands, carried along by human vectors. As the Spanish began to import slaves to replenish the local labor supply, Africans introduced malaria and yellow fever, which infected both Spanish and Arawak alike. The 1520–1521 smallpox epidemic in Tenochtitlan laid waste to perhaps as many as half the population, which numbered between 250,000 and 400,000. Over the course of the 1500s, other severe outbreaks of smallpox, measles, typhus, and mumps battered the peoples of Mesoamerica; several even proved more lethal than the 1520–1521 pandemic. A sudden occurrence of typhus in 1576 left two million people dead by 1580. In all, the native population of Mesoamerica plunged from 14 million before 1519 to just less than 3 million in the 1620s.

As the Spanish expanded out from their bases in the Caribbean and central Mexico, pathogens, especially the smallpox virus, became a constant and lethal companion. Smallpox was contracted in two ways. One was through physical contact with the scabs or pustules that covered the skin of a smallpox victim; the other was by inhaling a victim's exhaled air. After contact, symptoms began to appear in eight to twelve days, including headache, nausea, skin boils, followed by massive internal bleeding that usually led to death. The disease wreaked havoc on the extensive Inca Empire. Claiming the lives of several Inca chieftains, the disease reached Peru even before Francisco Pizarro and his men launched their conquest in the 1530s. Over the course of several years, 60 to 90 percent of the native population within the Inca Empire had succumbed to the disease.

During the 1500s, a number of Spanish explorers pushed north into northern Mexico and into what today is the southeastern and southwestern United States, from Florida to California. The same pattern prevailed in these parts. In the region stretching from southern Arizona and New Mexico to northwest Mexico, pandemics of measles, typhus, and dysentery struck time and again, killing off 900,000 out of one million inhabitants by century's end. In the early phase of the Portuguese settlement of Brazil in the mid-1500s, diseases ravaged the populous Tupi tribes that had managed to resist Portuguese encroachments. The usual culprits, smallpox, measles, dysentery, along with the plague, laid local peoples low. Diseases, in conjunction with Portuguese military assaults, reduced the Tupi population to 800,000 by the 1570s, a fraction of the 2.4 million the Iberians originally encountered in 1500. Colonized by Spain and Portugal, Central and South America's most densely populated regions fell victim to a variety of European diseases and underwent a rapid decline in the 1500s, from approximately fifty million in 1492 to around five million to six million in the early 1600s.

The native tribes of North America practiced less-extensive forms of agriculture than the peoples to the south, utilizing foraging and crop farming as means to supplement the protein mainstays of their diet, wild game and fish. Their slighter population levels corresponded to their smaller agricultural scale: the population for all of native North America lay somewhere in the neighborhood of 3.8 million in 1492. Population densities in the north were far lower than South America, since tribes inhabited more space per capita and they periodically moved about in search of game. These conditions meant that the total loss of life due to European diseases was far less spectacular than the levels at which Mexicans or Peruvians died. Nevertheless, the patterns of infection and rates among native peoples in North America paralleled those in southern lands colonized by the Iberian powers. The first smallpox epidemic occurred in North America in 1616 along the Atlantic coast, and in the ensuing decades virtually no native American society went unscathed. For example, the Hurons inhabiting the St. Lawrence River valley engaged in regular commerce with French fur traders. Through this contact, the Hurons acquired influenza pathogens between 1634 and 1637, and a devastating outbreak of smallpox followed in 1639. Roughly half of the 18,000 Hurons died in this five-year period. In New England, smallpox spread out along the Connecticut River valley in 1633 and 1634, killing perhaps three-quarters of the 12,000 natives. Throughout the 1600s and 1700s, the English, French, and, for a brief time, the Dutch expanded settlements along the Atlantic seaboard, the Great Lakes, and Mississippi River. In the process, Old World pathogens touched every native American society, in most cases with debilitating results that facilitated European conquest over land and resources.

The only possible disease that America bequeathed to Europe was syphilis, though the evidence is far from conclusive and historians disagree on its origins. Nonvenereal strains of syphilis existed both in the Mediterranean and America before 1500, and a limited quantity of skeletal evidence suggests that the venereal form was present in pre-Colombian America. One theory posits that the disease mutated into a sexually transmitted strain before the Spanish arrival and entered Europe from a returning ship. Due to the sexual nature of its transmission, syphilis made a dramatic psychological impact in Europe in the 1500s and 1600s, though its demographic effects were slight. Even if venereal syphilis did originate in America, the disease exchange between the two continents remained extraordinarily imbalanced.

For Europeans at the time, these massive mortality rates only confirmed their own confidence in divine favor for their conquests. A Frenchman in Natchez, Mississippi, wrote in the first half of the sixteenth century that "touching these savages, there is a thing that I cannot omit to remark to you, it is that God wishes that they yield their place to new peoples." John Winthrop, governor of the Plymouth Bay colony, came to the same conclusion a century later, "for the natives, they are neere all dead of small Poxe, so as the Lord hathe cleared our title to what we possess." In contrast, Europeans withstood these diseases, indicating that God was punishing the heathen tribes and bestowing their land on good Christians. William Bradford commented from Plymouth in 1634, "those Indeans that lived aboute their trading house there fell sick of the small poxe, and dyed most miserably...not one of the English was so much as sicke, or in the least measure tainted with this disease."[3]

Africans also functioned as key vectors of diseases, first introducing yellow fever and malaria to the Caribbean in the early 1500s. As the slave trade picked up momentum, slave ships became highly effective incubators of contagious diseases, spreading among the human cargo and crew on the middle passage and importing strains of pathogens from Africa to America. Malnourished and dehydrated slaves packed into cargo holds became ready targets for infection from their fellow passengers, particularly from exposure to intestinal pathogens carried through body fluids. Conditions in the hold produced seasickness, fear, and all sorts of ailments that caused frequent vomiting and defecating, which on some ships did not get cleaned up during the passage. The stench from slave ships was legendary; inhabitants from coastal areas could tell from the odor if a slaver was approaching port. Typhoid fever, measles, smallpox, malaria, and dysentery posed constant threats that could wipe out an entire cargo. The death rate on slave ships during the course of the trade averaged around 25 percent.

Exposed to such lethal diseases on board, many Africans brought pathogens ashore and infected local communities. Portuguese colonists, for example, reported that African slaves had started epidemics in Brazil in 1616 and 1617. Over the course of the seventeenth century, Africans instigated a number of very serious outbreaks in Brazil, the Caribbean, Colombia, Venezuela, and Virginia. In order to avoid direct contact with diseases from Africa, English plantation owners in North America frequently purchased African slaves from Barbados, where they had undergone a period of "seasoning" that acclimated them to New World pathogens and acculturated them to the gruesome life of labor servitude. The disease networks that emerged from the transatlantic migrations directly contributed to European colonization of American lands and enslavement of African labor, which gave birth to new societies in the New World.

Though the scope of the disease encounter in the Americas was beyond compare in world history, the global interactions of the early modern period did produce other cases of widespread devastation of indigenous peoples at the hands of European pathogens. Disease accompanied Russians in their quest for furs and for land across Siberia in the 1600s. The indigenes of Siberia, not unlike American societies, had virtually no contact with outside peoples and thus had no opportunity to develop immunity from contagious diseases. Smallpox did most of the damage. In the 1630s, it struck in western Siberia and continued on an eastward trajectory past the Yenisey River basin in the 1650s, and deeply into eastern Siberia by the 1690s. As Russians encountered local peoples, diseases spread widely throughout these regions, depleting the population by 50 percent on average. The Yakut and Tungu peoples in central Siberia, for example, sustained mortality rates of 80 percent, while the Yukagir tribes to the east lost 44 percent of its people. Engaging in intercourse, sometimes consensually, but often not, with Siberian women, Russian men also introduced sexually transmitted diseases. Syphilis and gonorrhea frequently led to sterility in women, which depressed fertility rates among societies already in demographic decline. The ravages of disease, combined with Russian technological advantage, explain why tsarist forces conquered Siberia with such small numbers of military troops and Cossacks.

A third region of the early modern world that proved vulnerable to the interaction of disease pathogens lay at the extreme southern border of Africa. In 1713, over fifty years after the VOC carved out a base of operations on the Cape of Good Hope, smallpox came ashore in dirty laundry from a VOC ship. The slaves charged with washing the laundry came in contact with contagious scabs and the virus moved swiftly through the settlement, infecting Europeans and Africans alike. The disease spread beyond Cape Town out into the countryside, affecting large numbers of Khoikhoi. Eventually, the outbreak developed into a pandemic, killing only a few Dutch but as much as 30 percent of the indigenous population. Like other areas of European colonization, the spread of disease played into the hands of Dutch settlers, as the pandemic seriously undermined Khoikhoi social and political organization.

Finally, the same pattern of European arrival into undiscovered territory, quest for control over indigenous resources, and the incidental yet ruinous spread of disease played itself out in Australia, New Zealand, and other islands in the south Pacific. This part of the world came under the influence of European domination relatively late in the early modern period, for Captain James Cook did not begin to reconnoiter the south Pacific until the second half of the 1700s. Following shortly on the heels of British settlement in Australia, pandemic disease broke out in 1789 among the Aborigines. The victims exhibited poxlike boils on their skin, though it is not clear if the culprit was smallpox or chicken pox. Nevertheless, widespread sickness, including pulmonary infections like influenza and tuberculosis, recurred during the nineteenth century. One contemporary estimate placed the total mortality rate at one-third of the Aboriginal population. Tuberculosis and venereal disease formed the most effective killers in New Zealand. The indigenous Majori population followed a number of sexual customs that exposed them to European bacteria. Not only did they practice polygamy, but males also offered their wives to outsiders for sexual hospitality, which British men, far from home, readily accepted. As a result, sexually transmitted diseases disseminated broadly among the Majori. Tuberculosis proved quite deadly and it, along with smallpox and measles, sent the native New Zealand population into steady decline, from as many as 200,000 in 1769 to 42,113 at the end of the nineteenth century.

The spread of Old World pathogens into previously isolated regions of the world formed an important theme in early modern global history. Over the course of the early modern period, millions died as a result of the globalization of disease. Pandemics killed off especially large numbers of indigenous peoples in America, as well as a substantial number in Siberia, South Africa, and the south Pacific. The demographic catastrophes that ensued gave Europeans an unbridled sense of their spiritual and physical superiority and, more tangibly, enabled them to displace peoples more easily and more completely in their colonial enterprises.

Worldwide Dispersal of Plants and Animals

This enormous loss of life makes the long-term demographic trend in the early modern period all the more remarkable: the world's population roughly doubled from 1500 to 1800. The movement of edible plants and animals played an integral part in the strong growth in food production around the world that drove population levels to unparalleled levels. This worldwide dissemination initiated two processes that underlay agricultural production: the introduction of American crops to Africa, Asia, and Europe and the intense cultivation of foodstuffs (from both the Old and New Worlds) in colonial empires around the world.

We can only begin to imagine the thoughts that ran through the minds of Christopher Columbus and his crew in the Caribbean in 1492 as they laid eyes on what in so many ways was a new world to them. He gives us a few hints at his amazement with the flora and fauna in a passage from his journal on October 21:

A thousand different sorts of trees, with their fruit were to be met with, and of a wonderfully delicious odor. It was a great affliction to me to be ignorant of their natures, for I am very certain they are all valuable; specimens of them and of the plants I have preserved. Going round one of these lakes, I saw a snake, which we killed, and I have kept the skin for your Highnesses; upon being discovered he took to the water, whither we followed him, as it was not deep, and dispatched him with our lances; he was seven spans in length; I think there are many more such about here. I discovered also the aloe tree, and am determined to take on board the ship tomorrow, ten quintals of it, as I am told it is valuable.[4]

As a result of Spanish and Portuguese penetration of America, people around the world became familiar with plants and animals they had never before seen. Further, as Europeans penetrated other regions of the world, particularly those that had climates similar to their own, they transplanted, not only American plants but flora from one distant location to another. For example, the Spanish conveyed clover to Mexico and Peru, thistle, oats, ryegrass to California, peach and orange trees to Florida and Georgia, while the English introduced dandelion, henbane, nettles, Adder's tongue, bluegrass, and wormwood to New England. The British also transported clover, knot grass, red sorrel, red-stemmed filaree, and oat grass to Australia and New Zealand. In modern times, 60 percent of Canadian weeds originated in Europe, while almost 40 percent in the United States derive from Europe.

Europeans were most interested in plants that yielded edible produce; thus, explorers brought items like maize (a form of corn) and potatoes back to Europe and merchants introduced these items to Africans and Asians. Americans, in turn, came in contact for the first time with animals indigenous to Europe and Asia, such as horses, cows, and sheep. The early modern period inaugurated a global flow of animals and plants, which greatly influenced the development of world history.

Spanish and Portuguese discovery of plants heretofore unknown to the Old World yielded abundant sources of food. These crops included maize, cassava, white and sweet potatoes, peanuts, squashes, pumpkins, papayas, guavas, avocadoes, beans, pineapples, tomatoes, chili peppers, and cocoa. The most significant, in terms of use as staple crops, were maize, cassava, white and sweet potatoes, and peanuts. They offered an advantage over other crops in that they could be cultivated in climatic zones not always suitable for Old World produce. Maize, for example, could grow successfully in soils that were too dry for rice and too wet for wheat. Similarly, potatoes thrived in a wide variety of soils and in regions of high altitude, producing much more food on a given plot land than cereal crops. The integration of American foods into the global networks of exchange, consequently, represented a tremendous potential in increasing food production in most regions of the world.

Europeans embraced a variety of American crops. Potatoes, maize, and beans made their way into Europe in the 1500s, became adopted quickly, and formed an essential part of many peoples' diets by the 1700s. Beans spread widely across most regions, whereas maize flourished in the south, where hot weather prevailed in the summer. Maize became a dietary staple in the Balkans, Italy, southern France, and Spain. The potato took longer to catch on; it served largely as fodder for livestock, until the Irish adopted it and made it an anchor in their diet in the 1700s. In the nineteenth century, the potato emerged as the national culinary fare of Ireland. The large-scale production of those uniquely American products, tobacco and sugar, found ready markets in Europe.

Europeans also functioned as the primary vectors that brought American crops into Asia and Africa. Maize, sweet potatoes, and peanuts made their entrance to the southeast coast of China in the mid-1500s and into Japan a century later. By the late 1600s, both Japanese and Chinese peasants cultivated these crops in upland regions that were not conducive to rice farming. Maize and sweet potatoes developed into important supplements of the Chinese diet, though livestock were the primary beneficiaries of these products in Japan. The spread of American staple crops into India did not occur until British rule in the nineteenth century, though farmers grew pineapples and guavas in significant amounts as early as the sixteenth century. Fruits have not, as a general rule, served as a dietary staple, so their impact on Indian nutrition was probably negligible. Introduced by the Portuguese and Dutch, American foods filtered into maritime Asia in the 1500s and 1600s. Maize took hold fairly deeply in some areas, notably Timor (Indonesia), but potatoes, cassava, and peanuts did not proliferate until the 1800s. Likewise, these foods also expanded into Ottoman lands in western Asia in the 1500s, though contemporary sources from this area make little mention of American products. Tobacco, enjoyed with coffee (originally from Ethiopia and Yemen), found a ready market for Turkish entrepreneurs who opened coffee shops for male patrons to smoke, drink, and enjoy one another's company.

The dissemination of American crops into Africa also followed in the wake of European overseas incursions. Among American foods, maize and cassava assumed the most important place in African societies, yet beans, tomatoes, sweet potatoes, and peanuts experienced wide cultivation and consumption as well. The slave trade provided the impetus for maize growing along the slaving coasts of west Africa. Producing large quantities of food in the near vicinity of slave ports allowed merchants and slavers to feed their cargo relatively cheaply and without the worry of long-distance transportation costs for provisions. From the coastal areas, maize quickly spread into the central regions of sub-Saharan Africa in the 1500s and 1600s. Farmers adopted cassava much more slowly; they were not widely farmed until the mid-1800s. In modern times, maize and cassava have developed into primary foodstuffs of Africans' diets.

The other side of the worldwide biological exchange in the early modern period was the movement of Old World organisms into a new American environment. The primary, though certainly not exclusively, influx from Eurasia was comprised of sizable animals that served as beasts of burden or sources of protein in Asia and Europe. Curiously enough, almost no domesticated animals inhabited the Americas before the arrival of Europeans. Horses, cows, pigs, goats, sheep, and dogs all came into America from Europe. Andean peoples had trained the llama for carrying materials and riding, while Mesoamericans utilized small dogs and chickens for their purposes, but otherwise domesticated livestock, for any function, was unknown in the pre-Columbian Americas. Scholars have hypothesized that the absence of the wheel in American societies derived in part from the lack of any burden-carrying husbandry. Nevertheless, in general the dissemination of food-producing plants from America into the wider world and the movement of domesticated animals into the New World characterized early modern biological exchange.

As the Spanish and Portuguese took control over large tracts of land in Central and South America, landowners created vast ranches to raise cattle, horses, and sheep above all, but also pigs and goats. The conquest of the vast terrain of North America by British and neo-European settlers did not really get underway until the 1800s. The widespread development of ranching occurred primarily in Central and South America. For the Iberian colonists in these lands, the lack of indigenous draft animals posed a challenge. In short order, then, Europeans imported horses to perform all the tasks they carried out back home in Iberia. Bernal Diaz, the Spanish soldier that chronicled Cortes's conquest of Mexico from 1519 to 1522, remarked on the military advantages the horse afforded the conquistadors. In a campaign against the Tlascalans in central Mexico, Diaz noted that "they were now afraid of our horses and our brave fighting with musket, sword, and crossbow."[5] Horses also enabled Europeans and Americans to travel farther and faster than on foot, and they served as cheap and serviceable pack animals, along with mules and oxen. As the conquest of the Americas got underway in full force, the Spanish and Portuguese also imported cows, pigs, goats, and sheep to provide stable sources of meat. During the sixteenth and for most of the seventeenth centuries, meat had remained a delicacy, available on a regular basis to wealthy elites. In America, by contrast, the extensive raising of beef, veal, and lamb made meat inexpensive and available to most people. As a result, the Spanish and Portuguese were able to feed the large numbers of migrants coming to make their way in the New World in the 1600s and 1700s.

The establishment of ranches portended major changes to the landscape in the Caribbean, Mexico, Brazil, Argentina, New Mexico, and Arizona in the early modern period. The demographic collapse of native peoples enabled Europeans to open up vast lands for pasture. In fact, Spaniards utilized the largest share of lands they took in the Americas for raising livestock. During the 1500s, Spanish America became synonymous with large haciendas used primarily for raising horses and cattle. After one hundred years of colonization, cattle ranchers occupied 70,000 square kilometers as pasture for 1.5 million to 2 million cows, while sheep ranchers held 50,000 square kilometers for 6 million to 8 million head of sheep. All total, including horses and other animals, ranchers in the seventeenth century controlled 125,000 square kilometers, 25 percent of Spanish America, on which they raised seven million to ten million animals.

The Iberian practice of introducing familiar animals into a new colonial environment in order to mass produce them for commercial purposes represented a basic strategy among all Europeans wherever they established control over territory. This pattern played itself out in Dutch colonies in South Africa, Taiwan, and southeast Asia, British settlements in India, Australia, New Zealand, and Hawaii. Europeans brought along their horses, but also bred cattle, horses, and pigs, sometimes in conjunction with raising indigenous herds. In South Africa, for example, Dutch settlers raised horses and pigs that originally came from Europe, alongside African cattle and sheep. The British, on the other hand, finding no large animals suitable for food production in Australia, had to rely on European stocks to initiate cattle and horse farming.

Just as the wholesale production of livestock animals emerged out of early modern biological exchanges, the commercial cultivation of plant crops on plantations also belonged to the global movement of organisms. As part of an emergent ecological regime, large-scale farming enterprises represented the convergence of several biological and economic elements that had lasting effects throughout the world. First, Europeans discovered unique American crops, such as tobacco, and cocoa, that once cultivated were transformed by strong demand into commodities on a world market. The novelty of New World crops and the demand in Old World markets, intensified by the addictive qualities of nicotine and caffeine, integrated American agricultural products into societies around the globe. Second, the American lands utilized by European colonists spanned three climatic zones (temperate, tropical, and subtropical) that were quite favorable for the extensive cultivation of specific Old World crops. The most profitable of these was sugar, which could not be grown at all in Europe; cotton and indigo, more ideally suited for temperate zones in North America, also tapped into ready markets. Consequently, European agriculturalists utilized American soils within favorable climatic zones to grow specific Old World commodity crops: sugar in Brazil and the Caribbean, cotton in North America and Mexico, and indigo in Central and South America.

As Europeans established land-based colonies in other regions of the world, colonial regimes and settlers continued the practice of intensively employing the land for commercial agricultural pursuits. The VOC, for example, took control of Taiwan from 1620 to 1660 and brought in plows, oxen, and Chinese laborers, to transform the landscape for large estates that produced rice and sugar for export to the Safavid Empire and Japan. After the VOC established itself in Indonesia in the early 1600s, colonial authorities adapted this strategy to the particular circumstances there. They promoted monocultural production of the native spices and herbs for which the islands were famous. In this form of agricultural organization, specific regions became dedicated for the large-scale cultivation of a sole crop; thus, they operated in principle like plantations. The British followed a similar policy in Australia, New Zealand, and later in India.

From a comprehensive viewpoint, the worldwide biological exchange played an important part in the commercial production of agriculture for international markets. The spread of American plants and the extensive cultivation of livestock and crops facilitated the spectacular growth in the number of people inhabiting the planet over the course of the early modern period.

Ecological Impact

The substantial growth in agricultural production took a huge toll on ecosystems around the world, as large numbers of settlers opened up new frontier regions and appropriated natural resources to feed and equip the needs of expanding societies. Eager to cash in on these resources, centralized states in Asia and Europe promoted the expansion of these settlements and supported them in pushing aside or subjugating indigenous peoples. Yet as Thomas Malthus pointed out, human populations and food production have an ongoing interactive relationship. Increased production leads to larger populations, which require increased production. With the growth of populations, migrating peoples continually intensified farming and ranching operations, harvested timber at exponential rates, hunted animals at unprecedented levels, and hauled in whales and fish without relent. These activities had two basic effects on ecological systems throughout the world: they drastically transformed landscapes of indigenous societies and seriously reduced the population levels of land and marine mammals.

Deforestation

The most striking topographical effect of early modern frontier expansion was the severe depletion of forests especially, though not exclusively, in Brazil, the Caribbean, North America, Siberia, and China. Deforestation in American lands clearly resulted from European expansion, which itself stemmed in part from the loss of forests in Europe. One of the driving motivations behind exploration and colonization grew out of the need to locate new sources for commodities like wood. In the late middle ages, forests engulfed most land areas across Europe, from the deciduous woodlands that stretched from France to Poland to the coniferous forests that flourished in Switzerland, northern Italy, Scandinavia, and the Baltic. Both coniferous and deciduous forests covered the British Isles.

By the end of the seventeenth century, however, the overcutting of forests without any policy for replanting led to severe deforestation in many parts of Europe. Woods occupied no more than 10 percent of England and Wales, 12 percent of Ireland, and less than 10 percent of Scotland. The Netherlands had no extensive forests remaining, while northern France had approximately 16 percent of its land area with forest cover. Higher, and in some cases much higher, concentrations of woodlands stood in northern Germany and eastern Europe. Even in areas where deforestation had not produced a shortage, the perception of scarcity gripped societies. Scholars have determined that when forest acreage goes below 20 percent of a region's land area, the perception emerges among people that a timber crisis exists. Based on the proportion of forest land across Europe, real forest scarcity plagued some areas, notably the British Isles and the Netherlands, whereas the crisis in other lands was largely one of perception.

Whether imagined or real, the timber shortage preoccupied European political and economic elites throughout the early modern period. The expanding population in Europe necessitated cutting forests to create more acreage for cultivating crops and raising livestock, as well as to provide fuel for more people to cook food and keep warm. Because of the colder northern European climate, wood was especially important as a heating source. In seventeenth-century Germany, well-to-do families consumed 13.8 cords (one cord equals 128 cubic feet of wood) per year, and the average family had to devote between 7.5 and 10 percent of the family income to purchase wood.

At the higher levels of governmental and private financial enterprise, the construction of ships for navies and other marine vessels required an extraordinary amount of timber. Between 1,400 and 2,000 oak, elm, and birch trees went into the construction of one large warship in an age when Spain, Portugal, the Netherlands, England, and France boasted very large navies. Shipbuilding consumed forests in the early modern period. Finally, industrial demand for energy in processing charcoal formed another use for wood, which placed stress on timber supplies. An index of the stress, the price for timber tripled in England during the 1500s, pushing manufacturers to look for new sources for wood and alternative resources of energy. No effective efforts to conserve forests or to replant tree stands got underway in Europe during this period, except for the creation of parks for hunting game by royal and aristocratic families. Therefore, the need for fuelwood and timber gave European elites added reason to support overseas exploration, and growing deforestation made it all the more necessary to acquire new sources of lumber in the early modern world.

Three regions in the American territories experienced the most extensive deforestation: Brazil, several islands in the Caribbean, and the North American Atlantic seaboard. Upon their arrival in 1500, Pedro Cabral and his crew marveled at the profusion of Brazilwood trees along the coast, particularly in the north around what became Recife. Soon Portuguese colonists began referring to the region as Brazil because of the abundance of the tree and its value as an export item. Highly valued for its stunning red interior core, Brazilwood provided stock for high-quality furniture and produced an eye-catching red dye. Quickly Brazilwood became an important cash crop, which provided a strong financial impetus to harvest the trees in large quantities. Portuguese traders did not cut, saw, and transport the trees themselves, rather they traded for the lumber with local Tupi tribes, who prized iron axes, hatchets, and weapons. In short order, Tupi cutters harvested Brazilwood trees at a prodigious rate. During the 1500s, Portuguese merchants imported eight thousand metric tons of

Brazilwood every year, which was equivalent to two million trees in the century. This volume of wood translated into the loss of six thousand square kilometers of forest.

The establishment of sugar and tobacco plantations exacted the greatest damage on Brazil's forests. The Portuguese colony developed into the largest sugar producer in the world, exporting six thousand metric tons annually by the end of the 1500s and 28,500 metric tons by the mid-1600s. This level of production came at the expense of forests, as planters burned over forests, cultivated sugar for fifteen years or so, and then, as soil fertility declined moved into another section of virgin forest. From the mid-sixteenth century to Brazilian independence in 1812, the sugar industry continued to expand and to encroach upon thousands of square kilometers of forest land. Settlers also turned to pursuits other than producing sugar – farming tobacco, mining metals, and ranching livestock – that necessitated cutting forests. Ongoing needs of settlements, such as wood for fuel, lumber for construction, and timber for industry, added to the strain on forest areas. The massive size of the Brazilian forests, one million square miles, made it seem as though forest resources were inexhaustible; thus, very few people perceived a need for any conservation or replanting. Consequently, by the end of Portuguese control over Brazil, colonists had claimed 200,000 square kilometers of forests. The reduction of forest carried significant implications for fauna, as deforestation deprived many forest dwellers of their natural habitat. In addition, colonists hunted jaguars, deer, snakes, and other animals for their hides and shot exotic colored birds for their plumage. The relationship between human settlement and the natural landscape in the colonial era established a permanent legacy for Brazilians, since deforestation over the past two hundred years has driven hundreds of plants and animals to extinction and now threatens to eradicate the rain forest altogether.

Sugar production also transformed the ecological landscapes of a number of islands in the Caribbean. The initial Spanish settlements made little impact on local ecosystems because immigration remained light and colonists did not undertake commercial agricultural enterprises. When disease brought the Arawak peoples to the point of extinction by the mid-1500s, wildlife and wilderness actually advanced in the absence of organized human activity. This state of affairs came to an end around a hundred years later on many islands as the English,

French, and Dutch wrested control away from the faltering Spanish Empire and set up plantations on them. Northern European colonial regimes in the Caribbean created plantations for cultivating cane and processing it into sugar, molasses, and rum. As was the case with the Portuguese endeavor in Brazil, the establishment of large plantations altered the ecosystems of the islands, part of which involved extensive deforestation.

A similar pattern emerged on a group of islands in the Caribbean known as the Antilles: settlers shifted to sugar production, heavy migration of coerced African laborers and free European settlers followed, landowners oversaw the clearing of forests, and the altered habitat impacted plant and animal life. In Barbados, for example, English settlers made the switch to sugar from the 1640s to the 1680s, during which time the migrant population rose from 10,000 to over 80,000. Slaves cleared most of the island's forests, except for woodlots preserved on the estates and for flora in inaccessible highland regions. Few trees remained, compelling planters to import coal from England to boil down the sugar. With the loss of the forests, the birds and land mammals that inhabited the dense growth of trees and underbrush dispersed or perished. Over the long term, deforestation led to serious erosion and hotter temperatures on Barbados.

Similarly, the French established control over Martinique in 1635, and settlers soon thereafter began preparing the land for commercial agriculture. The rain forest in the high inland region survived due to terrain that was inhospitable to humans. Low-lying forests along the coasts, especially in the region near St. Pierre, became the primary area of agricultural operations. Planters turned increasingly to sugar in the 1730s, which required tens of thousands of animals for labor, wood, and coal for processing and livestock for food. During the next one hundred years, three-fourths of the forests and native flora disappeared from Martinique, along with numerous species of turtles, birds, and manatees. Finally, the British took possession of Jamaica in 1655 from the Spanish and turned it into a primary sugar-producing center. The same sequence of land clearing and crop cultivation ensued, though three-fourths of Jamaica lay undeveloped by the late 1700s. One of the reasons that Jamaica retained much more of its biodiversity than the other islands was the powerful economic position of the English planters there. The dominance of their plantations created a disincentive for other planters to migrate to Jamaica to try their hand at making sugar.

English settlements on the North American Atlantic seaboard represented a third theatre of significant deforestation. During the 1600s and 1700s, English migration allowed settlers to embark into the wilderness, to clear acres of forest land, and to establish a homestead on the frontier. In the southern colonies, the creation of tobacco and cotton plantations consumed large plots that ranged from five hundred to one thousand acres per farm. Settlers and their servants cleared forest land through traditional slash and burn techniques, taking over up to ten acres per year. Commercial crops like tobacco and cotton were constant drains on soil fertility, so planters cut open more forests on a regular basis to maintain crop yields.

In addition to growing agricultural cultivation, the commercial markets for wood products reduced forest cover in British North America. The American colonies supplied their mother country, suffering from severe deforestation, with large amounts of timber for shipbuilding, charcoal manufacturing, furniture making, and other domestic needs. Much to the chagrin of the English government, colonials also supplied other countries and other colonial settlements, especially in the Caribbean. Charcoal production consumed about 15,000 acres of forest land every year in the eighteenth century. North America did not experience serious deforestation until the 1800s, when massive immigration, intensive industrialization, and western expansion cut severely into forest cover. The deforestation that did take place in the 1600s and 1700s, however, did diminish biodiversity in cutover regions and push fauna out of their native habitat.

The European conquest of the Americas, therefore, formed a critical point in the history of world biology. A handful of European countries stumbled upon a vast continent replete with a treasure trove of natural resources at a time when forests and arable land were becoming scarce in many areas of Europe. Old World invaders subdued indigenous populations by disease and force, went after valuable timber, metals, minerals, and turned large swaths of forests into farmland. New untapped sources of timber eased shortages in Europe, just as commercial farming and ranching produced a high volume of agricultural commodities for a world market. This episode proved crucial in the transformation of Europe into an industrial juggernaut in the nineteenth century. Biological imperialism in the Americas also permanently altered American landscapes, as thousands of square kilometers of forests vanished, along with the animals who relied on them. The biological exchange facilitated the rise of world population, yet at the expense of biodiversity in America.

Just as Atlantic migrations carried significant ramifications for American ecosystems, the great movement of peoples across Asia also seriously reduced forest cover in western Siberia and throughout frontier regions in China. The major migration streams across the early modern world shared similar characteristics. Three basic similarities in the appropriation of forests also appeared in America and Asia: the need for arable land represented the primary threat to forest cover; in the case of China, a crisis in fuelwood put increasing pressure on woodlands; and the ecological impact of deforestation was severe and permanent. One important difference between American and Asian deforestation materialized as well. New lands brought under cultivation in Siberia and China did not serve international export markets, but sustained local populations that had expanded into frontier areas.

The remarkable Russian conquest of Siberia prompted an extensive migration of peasants into western territories. Encouraged by the central government, peasant migration served the imperial purpose of providing an agricultural basis for Russian military outposts and administrative centers erected to extract sable furs from local peoples. Two distinct topographical regions made up western Siberia, an icy tundra to the north and moist subarctic coniferous (taiga) forests in the south. It was in the taiga, bordering on the northern tundra, which became most hospitable to peasant migration and cultivation. In the second half of the seventeenth century, approximately 34,000 peasants made their way into the Tobolsk region in the vicinity of the Ural Mountains. Another settlement hub lay nearby on the upper Ob River. These settlers cleared the forests using the technique of "burn-beating," which involved cutting and burning over forests and then utilizing the fertile soil, nourished by the ash, for grain cultivation. After the soil began to lose its fertility after ten to fifteen years, the land was converted to rough grazing land for livestock. The settlers moved on to another parcel of forest to cut and burn for crop farming.

Though peasant frontier settlement and cultivation concentrated in the western lands, peasants put down roots in the Yenisey and Krasnoyarsk regions, as well as along the Angara and Ilim Rivers. By 1811, peasant cultivators had established themselves on 120,000 square kilometers. Intensive farming over the course of many generations, down to the present day, wiped out the coniferous forests in these regions and radically changed their ecological structure. With the coming of large numbers of peasant settlers, surviving woodlands came under increasing pressure to supply the fuel needs of communities. The extensive loss of forest cover led to problems with erosion that in time were overcome by planting hay for cattle grazing. During this period, the extensive taiga of western Siberia became a bread basket for the Russian economy.

Like Europe at the outset of the early modern period, China was undergoing a period of rapid growth and dynamic change. Between 1400 and 1800, the population quadrupled, signaling prosperity and expansion, while at the same time placing greater strain on the land. Just as Europeans appropriated new sources of food and fuel in the Americas, the Chinese incorporated spacious frontier lands to the west and south. These territories provided an outlet for population pressure and an untapped supply of land for food production. Europe pursued a path of external colonization beyond the sea, while China followed a strategy of internal colonization across the spaces of Inner Asia. By the end of the early modern period, however, European colonization had contributed to the onset of industrialization, whereas Chinese colonization had not created a stable equilibrium between food supply and population.

The Ming and Qing dynasties made agricultural policy a high priority in their social, economic, and political agendas. This commitment found expression in a variety of initiatives, including establishing tax policies, constructing storage granaries, building dikes and canals, investing in technology, and clearing land to bring more soil under the plow. Lasting well over three hundred years, this ongoing land clearance resulted in widespread destruction of forest cover through slash and burn methods. After villagers eliminated a forest, they reburned the parcel periodically in order to keep wood cover from returning. There is some evidence that villagers kept woods from returning to destroy the habitat of tigers and bandits, both of which represented dangerous threats to local communities. Consequently, the loss of forest cover in many parts of China was permanent. As peasants converted these woodlands into agricultural parcels, they raised the total acreage of farmland in China from 61.7 million in 1400 to over 200 million by 1850.

The introduction of American foods, particularly maize and sweet potatoes, contributed to forest clearing because these crops, unlike rice, could grow in higher elevations, which happened to be covered by trees, shrubs, and underbrush. The highlands of central and southern China, encompassing the Yangzi uplands, Jiangxi, Lingnan, Guizhou, and Hunan provinces, attracted numerous settlers after 1700 to clear forests and to cultivate maize. As Chinese migrants settled in Taiwan in the late seventeenth century, they eliminated forests there for rice production as peasants had done on the mainland. Even in the north in Manchuria, where the Manchu (Qing) emperors prohibited Chinese immigration, the pressures of food production in the eighteenth century induced government officials to overlook peasants who migrated in to cut forests and to cultivate fields.

By the early 1800s, the few unsettled lands that remained in China lay largely in Mongolia and Manchuria. Bringing hundreds of millions of acres under cultivation enabled China to feed its growing population and to provide fuel for domestic consumption. Nevertheless, China's population continued to expand – 320 million in 1800 – thus, Malthus's principles seem to describe the problematic relationship between population and food supply. Despite intense cultivation and extensive deforestation, the growth rate continued to keep up with food production; thus, the nineteenth century witnessed increasing food and fuel scarcity. Along the way, the agricultural dynamo had stripped China of its forest cover, except for some preserved plots and tree plantations. Deforestation in China surpassed the destruction of woods in any other part of the world, leading to extensive erosion and the buildup of silt into waterways. As rains pounded the denuded highlands, the runoff cut deep gashes into hillsides and washed soil into low-lying farmland and canals. Over time, silt buildup distorted the beds of rivers and canals, leading to unpredictable and destructive flooding. Erosion from the highlands and silt buildup in lower altitudes, in a period of scarcity, became a growing preoccupation among Chinese officials and farmers in the 1700s and 1800s.

The striking changes to landscapes around the world and the readily observable ecological consequences of deforestation raise the questions: How did contemporaries understand these changes? And, what did officials try to do about them? The peoples of Europe and China, responsible for the greatest proportion of deforestation, inhabited cultures that treated forests and wilderness areas with a mixture of apprehension and opportunism. In both China and Europe, forests were considered as places occupied by predatory animals, outlaws, and evil spirits. Folk tales in both areas portrayed forests as sites of danger and enchantment; they symbolized the antithesis of civilization where children were seized, spells were cast, and conspiracies were hatched. The dominant belief systems in these two parts of the world, Christianity and Confucianism, also took a rather hostile attitude toward undeveloped land. Christian teaching emphasized human management over the natural world, which encouraged societies to exercise dominion over land and appropriate them for productive use. Confucian thought extolled the sanctity of agriculture and peasant life, promoting the virtue of bringing land, including forests, under cultivation. This does not mean that Christianity and Confucianism either advocated deforestation or fostered ecological irresponsibility. In many cases, such as the Portuguese acquiring as much Brazilwood as possible or Russians burn-beating the taiga of western Siberia, frontier settlers gave little thought to matters outside their own immediate self-interest. Nevertheless, the values that informed European and Chinese cultures placed little restraint on human exploitation of natural resources.

By the 1700s, a growing awareness about ecological degradation caused by deforestation emerged in various parts of the world. Even in the late middle ages, Venetian officials ordered the reforestation of woodlands to counter soil erosion. During the early stages of exploration, Columbus raised concerns that loss of forests in the Caribbean would lead to warmer temperatures and drier conditions as had happened on the Azores. A number of reports from Chinese and British sources frequently decried the barrenness of hillsides where forests had once stood. At the end of the 1500s and throughout the 1600s, a number of European thinkers, such as Francis Bacon and Edmund Halley, had started to draw connections between the state of vegetation and rainfall patterns. They conjectured that the loss of the former led to the reduction of the latter. Observations over drought in British colonial settings in the eighteenth century generated growing concerns with desiccation (drying out of ecosystems). These discussions in European academic circles put pressure on the British and French governments to adopt policies that promoted the preservation of natural habitats and conserved forests in the Caribbean as well as in other colonial settlements. In sixteenth-century China, scholars and government officials recognized the connections between forest clearing, erosion, and flooding. Qing government officers concerned themselves with the ecological effects of land clearance, but for the most part they were not successful in compelling local peasant villages to act against their short-term economic interests.

Even though Europeans and Chinese raised environmental concerns and took a few faltering steps to address them, Japan became the only country that took effective measures to counter the problems of wholesale land clearance. Like many other parts of the world, Japan experienced a prosperous agricultural and commercial economy during the sixteenth and seventeenth centuries. The population almost doubled from 15.4 million people in 1500 to 27.5 million in 1700; with the rising demographic numbers, Japanese farmers doubled the land under cultivation from 3.7 million acres to 7.34 million acres during the same period. This land clearance took place, again as in other areas we have examined, at the expense of overcutting woodlands, leading to serious forest depletion by the second half of the 1600s. Japan's forests stood at the point that wood cover in Europe had reached in 1500 and China in 1800.

Rather than pursuing a strategy of colonizing other lands, externally or internally, the government and people of Japan took a radically different approach. The Tokugawa shogunate (military government) pulled back from active engagement in the regional and world maritime economy and isolated itself from foreign powers and influences. In the 1670s, the shogun Ietsuna started to enact measures to conserve forests and other natural resources, while local leaders placed more stringent controls on the use of village lands. Like their Chinese counterparts, Japanese peasants resorted to new techniques to increase yields in textile and food crops. In addition, the Japanese turned increasingly to nonagricultural sources of protein by expanding the number of fishing and whaling expeditions. The Tokugawa regime also sought to reduce consumption by issuing a wide range of laws that regulated the use of fabrics, managed construction materials, and specified house sizes. Japanese couples kept fertility in check through practicing contraception and abortion, as well as through reducing the frequency of sexual intercourse. Finally, government officials at the central and village level carried out strict measures on the use of forest resources. Consequently, Japan became the only country or region in the world to reverse the pattern of deforestation. Through the cooperation of the central government and local village leaders, that no doubt squeezed people at the mid and lower social levels, Japan's forests made a dramatic come-back by the early 1800s.

Other Landscape Alterations

Deforestation was certainly the most striking transformation of the physical landscape, yet biological encounters in the early modern period brought other wide-ranging changes, too. As was the case with wholesale forest clearance, newly introduced agricultural pursuits resulted in the loss of biodiversity and produced unintended consequences. A brief look at several of the most notable theatres of environmental change will further illustrate the ecological effects of greater global interaction.

Alongside deforestation in western Siberia, Russian peasant settlers wrought basic changes to the grasslands that existed alongside the taiga. The vegetation that inhabited these regions were coarse grasses, including blue grass, fescue, bunchgrass, and shrubs, which the new settlers burned off in order to plant rye, wheat, and other cereal grains for cultivation and consumption. The successful transplantation of cereal crops in western Siberia attracted more peasant settlers so that by the early 1700s one-quarter of the land in the region had become subject to cultivation, a proportion that grew to almost 50 percent by 1800. Farming replaced the diverse grasses of the steppe region with a few cereal crops, and working the fields drove out rodent populations, like the marmot. The ecological impact of cultivation was minimal despite the loss of biodiversity across the region.

Ranching and mining developed into central economic enterprises in Mexico after the Spanish conquest. The coastal lowlands and the central plateau presented a spacious setting for grazing and herding livestock. The promise of great wealth also lured thousands of migrants to mining settlements in northern and northwestern Mexico to try to strike it rich in the silver veins lodged within the earth's crust. Extensive ranching operations emerged in the sixteenth century on estates established throughout central and southern Mexico, yet concentrated in the region north of Mexico City, known as the Valle de Mezquital (Valley of the Mesquite). Before Spaniards moved in, the land supported a diverse array of plant and animal life, with oak and pine forests, grassy savannahs, shrub-covered hills, and fresh water springs. Native peoples farmed the land, using the streams to irrigate their stands of maize, beans, squash, and cotton. Into this varied vista pushed Spanish settlers who took over large land tracts, fenced off estates, and introduced livestock, including cattle, horses, sheep, and a few pigs. Ranchers allowed their livestock to feed on native vegetation in their estates, a consumptive pattern that grew more intense over the course of the sixteenth century. By the end of the 1500s, the consolidation of estates resulted in the conversion of over 60 percent of the land in the region to pasture. Overgrazing by cows, sheep, and horses dramatically altered the landscape, as these animals consumed the grasses, vines, and small shrubs. The failure to allow grasses to recover allowed more aggressive and spiny weeds and prickly bushes, such as cactus, thistle, and mesquite, to take over. Erosion and desiccation followed so that, by the late seventeenth century, the region acquired the appellation "Valley of the Mesquite," where barren soil, arid conditions, and thorny bushes dominated the terrain.

The case in the Valle de Mezquital in the 1500s did not really typify the impact of ranching throughout Mexico. Ranching proceeded alongside Spanish, creole, and mestizo settlers who pushed throughout Mexican lands. Ranchers converted the natural habitats into pastoral monocultures, reminiscent of the pasture lands of Andalusia, the heartland of Spanish livestock farming. As we have seen, the introduction of ranching necessarily reduced biodiversity and altered landscapes. Livestock trampling compacted the soil, leading to erosion, and ranch hands killed off animal predators that threatened the herds. Nevertheless, John Richards, a leading environmental historian, has suggested that the size of herds in relation to habitat, at least in the first half of the seventeenth century, was relatively low: less than one head of sheep, cow, or horse per acre. Environmental conditions turned hot and dry across Mexico, producing drought and famine in the 1600s and 1700s. So perhaps the drier weather patterns placed environmental limits on ranchers or perhaps ranchers learned a lesson from the Valle de Mezquital. Nonetheless, livestock raising did not produce widespread environmental degradation, though it did permanently alter the ecosystem.

Silver mining had a much more deleterious effect on environments in Peru and Mexico. In the latter case, silver miners opened 453 mines, spanning the whole range of the country from Chihuahua in the north to Tegucigalpa in the south. In addition, prospectors panned for gold, as well as for silver, in upland streams across Mexico. To produce silver in a purified form, laborers first had to extract the ore from within a shaft, usually deep beneath the earth's surface, and then smelt it in a blast furnace or mix it with mercury in a lengthy and arduous process. Production required laborers, horses, cattle, all sorts of industrial equipment, and loads of mercury, imported from Europe. These mining operations exacted a heavy toll on local communities, though effects of mercury pollution went far beyond regional environments. After use, mercury was dumped into waterways or directly into the ground, or evaporated into the atmosphere. During the early modern period, over sixty-five thousand metric tons were shipped into Mexico, and ultimately all of it came to reside in the air, streams, soils, and peoples of the region. Richards has concluded that "it is likely that mercury pollution from the silver mines of Mexico and Peru constituted the single largest source of pollution in the entire early modern world."[6] Since the ingestion of mercury creates severe health problems, even death, in humans, wildlife, and vegetation, this industrial pollution carried important consequences. And, since every year in the early modern period 150 metric tons of mercury flowed into wind patterns that circled the world, silver mining in Mexico and Peru had global ecological implications.

Depletion of Mammals and Fish

The population takeoff in the early modern period, combined with the global movement of peoples, led to a serious depletion of land and marine mammals, as well as fish, in most parts of the world. Commerce in hides, as we saw with the relentless pursuit of sables in Siberia and beavers in North America, accounted for the wholesale hunting of many mammals. Deer in North America, big cats in South America, China, and Africa, otters in Asia and South America, as well as other land mammals with prized hides, increasingly found themselves in the sights of hunter's muskets. Further, a culture of hunting big game animals for sport emerged in parts of Africa, Asia, and the Americas, giving rise to the stalking and shooting of lions, tigers, elephants, and other mammals for the thrill of the kill. The most substantial threat, however, were frontier societies, as settlers cut deeply into the natural habitat of wildlife and killed off predators who threatened humans and livestock. Marine mammals and fish suffered significant depletions usually for very different reasons, namely because they served as cheap sources of food and fuel for expanding populations. The vast reduction of large mammals thus formed an integral part of the biological encounters in early modern interactions around the world. A look at several notable examples will illustrate the new dangers that human expansion posed for large land and marine mammals, as well as some fish populations.

In various parts of China, a number of stories circulated out of local communities in the 1600s and 1700s concerned with the comings and goings of tigers. For thousands of years, the forests of eastern and southeastern Asia had provided a home to tens of thousands of tigers, leopards, and other big carnivorous cats that preyed on game such as deer and boar. These large animals were forest predators that required over twenty square kilometers of woodland cover per cat to sustain themselves. Preferring game as their quarry, tigers and other predatory cats did not generally attack humans unless their cubs were threatened, other food sources proved inaccessible, or loss of habitat brought the animals into close contact with humans. So the frequency of reports about tigers suggests that, as the Chinese migrants were pushing into frontier areas and clearing forests on a wide scale, they were coming into contact with tigers. Many accounts, dating in the 1600s, related terrifying episodes of a tiger, or in some cases several tigers, entering a village to seek prey in the form of livestock or humans. Observations about tigers, later in the 1700s, tended to also include comments about the absence of large predatory animals.

Thus, while this evidence is sketchy and unsystematic, it points to the loss of wildlife that is consistent with the loss of natural habitat in the early modern period. Studies in Thailand and Indonesia have shown that a similar loss of forest cover led to severe depletion of tigers, even to the point of extinction. The comprehensive forest clearing that took place in early modern China destroyed the normal habitat of large land mammals, like tigers, pushed them into marginal lands, deprived them of food sources, brought them into greater competition with one another, and ultimately reduced their numbers substantially.

As Dutch settlers expanded beyond Cape Town in South Africa in the second half of the seventeenth century, they played the central role in the dramatic decline of all sorts off large land mammals. Unlike the case in China and in other areas, the loss of wildlife in South Africa had little to do with land clearance but had everything to do with hunting. The region, as the continent, contained a great range of land mammals, some dangerous, some valuable, and some inconsequential to humans: elephants, big cats, rhinoceroses, monkeys, baboons, zebras, giraffes, antelopes, boars, warthogs, hippopotamuses, cape buffaloes, hyenas, jackals, and ostriches. Traveling from a region virtually empty of large animals, European visitors marveled at the exoticism of these creatures. Some animals were clear threats to humans and their livestock, which grew in abundance as a result of the settlers' extensive ranching operations. Consequently, settlers and Khoikhoi servants relentlessly pursued elephants, predatory cats, hyenas, jackals, and rhinoceroses. Hunters also coveted the hides, body parts, and/or meat from game animals, hippopotamuses, cats, and ostriches. The Dutch, however, sought out South African animals far beyond colonial needs, since big-game hunting became a very pleasurable sporting activity among colonists. For a variety of reasons, then, Dutch settlers took up killing South African wildlife with great enthusiasm and with little restraint. By the end of the 1700s, these large animals retreated beyond the frontier of colonial settlement, and the land occupied by the colonists became devoid of large land animals.

Due to both extensive land clearance and unrelenting hunting, Brazil suffered intensive mammal depletion in the early modern period. As we saw earlier in this chapter, the Portuguese, through enslaved African labor, cleared hundreds of thousands of square kilometers in forests to prepare the terrain for sugar plantations. In so doing, the planters destroyed the habitats of many different animals, including big cats, deer, boar, monkeys, and otters. A lively export trade in the hides of exotic animals, reptiles as well as mammals, and in the plumage of brilliantly colored birds like the macaw and toucan presented a secondary threat to Brazilian wildlife. Portuguese merchants acquired and exported the skins of jaguars, deer, otters, agoutis, pacas, snakes, alligators, tapirs, and seals. By the end of Portuguese rule in 1822, the flora and fauna in the vast Atlantic forest had undergone an extensive transformation that greatly diminished the biological variety and ecological complexity of Brazil.

The loss of wildlife extended beyond mammals and other animals on land to maritime creatures that provided food and fuel to expanding world populations. Coastal societies have hunted whales probably since neolithic times, when the gigantic mammals surfaced close to shorelines during their migratory cycles. Peoples along the coasts of North and South America, northwestern Asia, Japan, the south Pacific, southern Africa, and northern Europe utilized the blubber for oil, the bones for a variety of technical applications, and the meat for food. Given the limited maritime technology, whale hunting was a small-scale operation, occurring near the shoreline and harvesting only the slowest and weakest members of the gam. With the advent of new shipbuilding and navigational technology in the fifteenth and sixteenth centuries, however, enormous treasures from the deep became accessible to mariners. Consequently, commercial whaling and fishing far out in the Atlantic, Pacific, Indian, and Arctic Oceans emerged to tap into long-distance markets.

The north Atlantic and Arctic Oceans, ranging from the northeastern coast of Canada to areas around Greenland, constituted an extremely fertile whaling region for northern European operators. Between the sixteenth and late eighteenth centuries, a host of whaling companies from different countries competed, sometimes fiercely, for exclusive access to the best locations. Several of the richest spots included the waters around Iceland, off the coast of Newfoundland and Labrador, surrounding Greenland, and on all sides of the Svalbard islands north of Norway. Large, yet slow swimming mammals, the bowhead and right whales inhabited these frigid currents in abundance. At the start of the sixteenth century, perhaps as many as 36,000 bowheads made this region their home. The oil that could be wrung from the blubber of the bowhead and right whales found a strong market in Europe and an adult whale could produce between 70 and 140 barrels of oil. Thus, whaling was an extremely profitable enterprise; certainly only the richest of rewards could have enticed men into the bitterly cold waters and coastlines of the north Atlantic and Arctic Oceans.

In order to take better advantage of these opportunities, whaling companies developed more substantial whaling galleons and more sophisticated techniques over the course of the early modern period. Depending on the vessel and the location, a crew could ensnare, slay, and dissect a whale either out at sea or, after killing it, tow the mammal to the shoreline where teams of men processed it. If out at sea, the galleon contained large storage vessels for the oil, meat, bones, and other redeemable body parts until the ship returned to port. The technology and division of labor created a highly efficient operation that enabled companies to harvest and process a high volume of whales, as well as gather in a large number of walruses and seals. Whalers from the Basque region of southwestern France sent annual expeditions to Labrador where on average they took in between 240 and 360 whales per year, totaling somewhere between 21,600 and 32,400 over most of the sixteenth century. Dutch, German, English, Danish, Russian, and French companies vied for bowhead whales in the Arctic near Greenland and off the coast of the Svalbard islands. Establishing the largest enterprises and employing occasional force, Dutch companies reaped the greatest success. They and the German firms sent out 176 expeditions per year at the end of the seventeenth century, taking in an enormous quantity of whales. It is estimated that all European whalers harvested between 150,000 and 200,000 bowhead whales during this period, and by the mid-nineteenth century, they and the Atlantic walrus teetered on the edge of extinction.

As whale herds in the north Atlantic and Arctic faced severe depletion at the end of the 1700s, whaling companies turned their sights to other regions of the world. The much warmer, southern currents of the Pacific Ocean offered a great bounty in right, cachalot, and sperm whales. Driven by the continuing demand for whale oil, British organizations appeared in the Pacific in 1776 and were joined later in the 1800s by crews from France, the United States, Japan, and Prussia. In particular, the waters around the islands of Oceania, off both coasts of Japan, and the area between New Zealand and New South Wales in Australia proved the most fertile for harvesting whales. The industry in the south Pacific reached its peak rather quickly, in the 1850s, and fell off sharply in the second half of the 1800s due to the discovery of fossil fuel oil in Pennsylvania.

One beneficiary in the exhaustion of northern whale herds was the Atlantic cod, which could enjoy a much more bounteous supply of plankton and small crustaceans, the primary diet of the massive maritime mammals. Cod in abundant schools inhabited the waters of the north Atlantic; they schooled in particularly large numbers off the coasts of New England and Canada. As these territories became more heavily populated with northern European immigrants in the seventeenth and eighteenth centuries, cod emerged as a cheap and vital source of protein in North America and as a profitable export commodity to Europe. By the end of the 1600s, British and French fishing companies had established extensive operations. English fishermen, for example, hauled in over twelve metric tons of cod in 1677, a sum matched by their French counterparts. Fueled by increasing population levels, cod harvests increased significantly during the eighteenth century. In the 1770s, the English catch had more than doubled its take from the previous century. During the period from 1580 to 1750, the total fish harvest by the entire fishing industry reached around 200,000 metric tons per year. Despite these voluminous numbers, the net effect on the general cod population across the north Atlantic appears negligible, though local stocks, especially those most accessible from the shore, did undergo serious depletion. When yields dropped in a certain area, fishermen simply moved to more fertile locations, enabling the depleted regions to recover.

The Limits of the Frontier

The global expansion of peoples into frontier territories carried enormous consequences for the relationship between human societies and natural ecosystems. The spread of Eurasian and African pathogens into new environments gave Europeans a biological advantage over indigenous peoples in America, Siberia, South Africa, Australia, New Zealand, and Oceania. Devastated by disease, native societies in these lands faced exploitation and subjugation by outside invaders. In many areas (namely all but Mexico and Peru), settlers from agriculturally based societies displaced neolithic peoples who subsisted on small-scale farming, hunting, fishing, and gathering. The distribution of new American crops – potatoes, maize, cassava, and peanuts – around the world, along with the introduction of Eurasian livestock to Central and South America, contributed to an unprecedented population growth, doubling by the end of the early modern period.

Ecosystems in these frontier zones, as well as those in China and southeast Asia, which also experienced heavy immigration, underwent substantial transformations. Settlers cleared forests to open more land for cultivation and appropriated forest products to export for regional or world markets. Extensive deforestation led to widespread loss of biodiversity, fostered soil erosion, and, in some cases, created serious silt buildup in waterways, causing flooding. If land clearance often proved harmful to the landscape, it represented an unmitigated catastrophe for wildlife. Forest animals came under tremendous stress as a result of agriculture's steady advance, leading to serious decline in many species. Settlers, commercial hunters, and trappers made matters worse for big cats, elephants, sables, deer, beavers, otters, and other animals by pursuing them without restraint. Agriculture did not stop at the shoreline, but extended out into the global sea lanes, as fishermen and whalers farmed the oceans and coastlines, harvesting massive amounts of whales, walruses, seals, and fish.

The exceptional food production of the early modern period was a great boon to human populations. By the end of the eighteenth century, a growing number of people around the world began to express concerns about the loss of biodiversity and advocate programs of land and wildlife conservation, a discourse that ultimately gave way to modern environmentalism. Writing at the same time, Thomas Malthus raised doubts about whether humans could outproduce their ability to reproduce. Perhaps industrialization of agriculture in the modern world has proved him wrong, though at the end of the early modern period it had become clear to many that the frontier and its resources were no longer inexhaustible.

Works Consulted

Crosby, Alfred W. *The Columbian Exchange: Biological and Cultural Consequences of 1492.* Westport, Conn.: Greenwood Press, 1972.

———. *Ecological Imperialism: The Biological Expansion of Europe, 900–1900.* Cambridge: Cambridge University Press, 1986.

Dean, Warren. *With Broadax and Firebrand: The Destruction of the Brazilian Atlantic Forest.* Berkeley: University of California Press, 1995.

Díaz, Bernal. *The Conquest of New Spain*, J. M. Cohen ed. London: Penguin, 1963.

Grove, Richard H. *Ecology, Climate and Empire: Colonialism and Global Environmental History, 1400–1940*. Cambridge: White Horse Press, 1997.

———. *Green Imperialism: Colonial Expansion, Tropical Island Edens, and the Origins of Environmentalism, 1600–1860*. Cambridge: Cambridge University Press, 1995.

Kurlansky, Mark. *Cod: A Biography of the Fish That Changed the World*. London: Penguin, 1997.

Marks, Robert B. *Tigers, Rice, Silk, and Silt: Environment and Economy in Late Imperial South China*. Cambridge: Cambridge University Press, 1998.

McNeill, William H. *Plagues and Peoples*. Garden City, N.Y.: Anchor Press, 1976.

Perdue, Peter. *Exhausting the Earth: State and Peasant in Hunan, 1500–1850*. Cambridge, Mass.: Council on East Asian Studies, Harvard University Press, 1987.

Price, A. Grenfell. *The Western Invasions of the Pacific and its Continents: A Study of Moving Frontiers and Changing Landscapes, 1513–1958*. Oxford: Clarendon Press, 1963.

Richards, John F. *The Unending Frontier: An Environmental History of the Early Modern World*. Berkeley: University of California Press, 2003.

Thomas, Benjamin. *The Atlantic World: Europeans, Africans, Indians, and their Shared History, 1400–1900*. Cambridge: Cambridge University Press, 2009.

Thornton, John. *Africa and Africans in the Making of the Atlantic World, 1400–1800*. 2nd ed. Cambridge: Cambridge University Press, 1998.

Watts, Sheldon. *Epidemics and History: Disease, Power, and Imperialism*. New Haven, Conn.: Yale University Press, 1997.

Wear, Andrew. "Medicine in Early Modern Europe, 1500–1700," in Lawrence I. Conrad, Michael Neve, Vivian Nutton, Roy Porter, and Andrew Wear eds. *The Western Medical Tradition, 800 BC to AD 1800*. Cambridge: Cambridge University Press, 1995, 215–369.

Williams, Michael. *Deforesting the Earth: From Prehistory to Global Crisis*. Chicago: University of Chicago Press, 2003.

6

The Transmission of Religion and Culture

In September 1579, Akbar, the great Mughal emperor, requested that two Jesuit missionaries from the Portuguese station in Goa come to his capital in Fatehpur Sikri (northern India) to explain to him and his court the mysteries of the Christian religion. Professing an ecumenical belief known simply as the "Divine Faith," Akbar promoted religious toleration and enjoyed theological debate, a rarity in the early modern world. The Jesuits dispatched three (instead of two) of their most learned priests, Rudolph Acquaviva, Francis Henriques, and Anthony Monserrate. They resided at the Mughal court for almost three years, during which time they participated in many religious conversations with Akbar and held theological disputations with Muslims and Hindus. In and around the Mughal court, the Christian missionaries, Muslim mullahs, Hindu gurus, and others debated issues such as whether Jesus was the Son of God, whether Muhammad was God's greatest prophet, and whether Krishna was a divine incarnation.

In one exchange, Akbar observed that the Qu'ran claimed that Jesus foretold Muhammad's arrival when Christ promised a "Holy Spirit which the Father shall send in my name [to] teach you all things." To this way of thinking, Muhammad was a holy figure who came to fulfill Christ's mission. But the Jesuit Monserrate answered sharply that "Christ made no definite mention of Muhammad by name in the Gospel, but that he [Christ] spoke in general terms of many false prophets who were to come."[1] According to this line of interpretation,

Muhammad was a false prophet and imposter. Akbar never converted, leaving the Jesuits bitterly disappointed.

This episode reveals the intriguing cultural connections made possible by the widespread movement of peoples in the early modern period. The proliferation of travel created new matrices of global interaction in which preachers carried religious teachings into distant lands, travelers described foreign societies for audiences back home, and intellectuals introduced science and technologies into unfamiliar domains. As ideas, stories, and customs from distinct parts of the globe circulated across oceans and continents, societies appropriated these forms of knowledge in various ways according to local needs and perceptions. Chinese astronomers, for example, adopted many European mathematical calculations, but rejected the "barbarous" notion that the earth is spherical. On the mission field, leaders in the Sudan embraced Islam, but adapted it to indigenous traditions that honored local holy sites and sacred figures wholly at odds with orthodox Islam.

Because of their extensive interaction with one another, societies across the world underwent analogous patterns of change. We have already examined parallels in state and empire building, commercial activity, food production, and environmental degradation. The development of ideas and perceptions – religious, scientific, aesthetic, folkloric – also followed a similar trajectory, as Islam and Christianity became global faiths, foreign travelers described ethnic groups and their customs, and societies made use of technologies from distant lands. As a result of the circulation of intellectual and cultural merchandise, universal forms of knowledge emerged in many parts of the world by the end of the 1700s.

The Spread of Universal Religious Systems: Christianity and Islam

In this age of global interaction, influential religious movements bubbled up in diverse regions of the world. In the Punjab region of the Mughal Empire, Guru Nanak (1469–1539) broke with the formalized structure of Hinduism and attracted millions to a faith that developed into Sikhism. In Ming and Qing China, Confucian scholars, attracted to certain Buddhist concepts, advanced a neo-Confucianism that was both humanistic and otherworldly. In Safavid Iran, apocalyptic

expectations, along with political coercion, fueled widespread conversion to Shi'a Islam. In other Muslim lands, Sufi mystics, regarded
as holy men, introduced assorted spiritual devotions that gave Islam
new dimensions. In Romanov Russia, traditionalists known as Old
Believers split with the Orthodox Church over liturgical innovations,
creating ecclesiastical strife and violence. And in Europe, the Reformation unleashed momentous religious energies that spawned spiritual
renewal and bloody wars.

Religious systems also expanded into new territories in the early modern period: Buddhism flowed into Mongolia and Manchuria, Sikhism
blossomed in northwest India, Shi'ism stretched across all of Iran
and southern Iraq, neo-Confucianism followed Chinese conquerors
into Turkestan and Tibet. Yet the two religions that extended their
reach across oceans and continents, thus warranting attention as the
most global systems of belief, were Christianity and Islam. Christian
missionaries and colonizers converted thousands of Americans and
enslaved Africans, enabling Christianity to play a dominating role in
societies from Argentina to Canada. Priests and preachers also planted
Christian communities across western and South Africa and along the
coasts and islands of the Indian Ocean from India to Japan. With the
same goal in mind, Sufi missionaries and Muslim merchants carried
the Prophet's message into sub-Saharan regions of Africa, southeast
Asia, India, and China.

Islamicization: The First Wave
Islam extended its reach across lands and among peoples, verifying
its status as a universal religion in the early modern world. Islamic
advances drew from the remarkable episodes of Muslim expansion
in its long history from the 600s to the 1300s. During this period,
merchant and missionary enterprises, as well as military conquests,
enabled Islam to become a major force in Eurasia. Muslim merchants
traveled extensively across the commercial centers in the Middle East,
central and southeast Asia, and along the port cities of the Indian
Ocean. Many trading partners in India, Afghanistan, the Sudan, the
Swahili coastline, and China found it advantageous to convert in order
to forge a sense of trust and common identity in economic exchanges.
Accompanying the merchants, missionaries and Sufis (mystical holy
men) proselytized and preached in these diverse areas. The diffusion

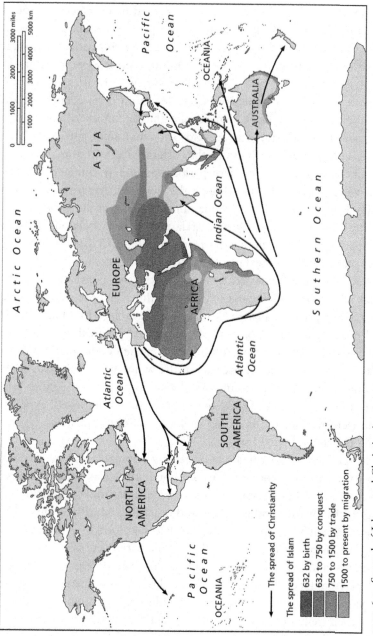

MAP 6.1. Spread of Islam and Christianity, 1500–1800

of the Muslim faith in Eurasia also benefited from the conversion of nomadic Turkish, Mongol, and Timurid peoples in central Asia who spread the faith. At the outset of the early modern period, then, Islam had already established itself as an important presence across Eurasia.

As in preceding periods, diffusion into new territories and consolidation in already claimed ones resulted from empire building and through missionary work that accompanied commercial enterprises. The rise of the Safavid, Mughal, and Ottoman Empires provided Islam imperial backing from India to the eastern Mediterranean. Ottoman expansion in the early modern period was largely confined to states that were already Muslim, though the sultan Suleyman took control of Hungary, Serbia, Transylvania, and Romania in the 1500s. These territories, however, experienced relatively few conversions to Islam because of the large numbers of orthodox and Catholic Christians, who retained the support of their institutional churches.

Iran and India underwent the most extensive Islamicization, as a result of empire building in early modern times. In both states, emperors actively promoted Islam by patronizing scholars, building schools, and erecting mosques. Safavid shahs claimed political legitimacy on the basis of their devotion to Shi'ism. Yet the development of Islam in these empires differed because of the willingness of Safavid shahs and their religious allies to impose Shi'ism forcefully throughout Iran. Over the course of the 1500s and 1600s, Safavids harassed, expelled, and even massacred Sunnis, as well as Christians and Jews, so that Shi'a Islam dominated Iran.

Mughal emperors ruled over a densely populated empire in which the overwhelming majority of the population was Hindu. Consequently, the Mughal state in its early history took a conciliatory approach toward Hindus, Sikhs, and other non-Muslim groups. This pluralistic environment fostered a much less uniform Muslim approach to religious practice and belief than in the core areas of the Ottoman domains and in Safavid Iran. Orthodox Sunni religious scholars (ulama) competed with a variety of different spiritualist sects, led by Sufi mystics, who incorporated Hindu rituals, saints, and shrines into their religious exercises. These spiritualist masters, willing to accommodate a wide range of observances, scored significant successes in Gujarat and Bengal. The Mughal inclination to religious coexistence came to an end with the reign of Shah Jahan (1628–1658) and

Aurangezeb (1658–1707). Shah Jahan turned back many of Akbar's tolerant policies, while Aurangezeb, a zealous Muslim, imposed the head tax (jizya) on non-Muslims, destroyed Hindu temples, attacked Sikhs, and passed a number of legal measures in keeping with Islamic moral codes. When he died in 1707, Muslims stood bitterly divided from their Hindu neighbors.

The most common means for the transmission of Islam in the early modern period occurred through joint commercial and missionary activity. The integration of southeast Asia into the commercial economy of the Indian Ocean in the 1400s brought Islam to the maritime region. Coinciding with the rise of commerce in the region, Muslim expansion reached its apex from the early 1400s to the mid-1600s. The circulation of merchants from Arabia connected the Indonesian islands and Malay peninsula to the heart of the Muslim world in Mecca and Medina. Merchants established trade diasporas that opened many areas to preachers and divines who accompanied merchant operations. These missionary figures were usually Sufi masters who traveled with merchants to provide spiritual guidance. The lucrative commercial connections induced indigenous rulers and economic elites to adopt Islam, and these leaders sanctioned the preaching and proselytizing of Sufis. Merchants also intermarried into local elite families, and often their new wives, in accordance with Islamic law, converted. In accordance with Islamic law, the children from these unions grew up as Muslims, married, and reproduced another generation of Muslims. When a critical mass of people turned to Islam, towns constructed mosques for worship and schools for instruction. By these means, Islam penetrated deeply into maritime southeast Asia.

By the time of the Portuguese arrival in the early 1500s, sizable Muslim communities had begun to form in Borneo, Magindanao (in the Philippines), Melaka, Johor, and Patani (on the Malay peninsula), and in many locations across the Indonesian archipelago, including Aceh, Banten, Mataram, south Sulawesi, Sumbawa, and Ternate. With the Spanish conquest of the Philippines in the 1560s and 1570s, both Christianization and Islamicization were expanding simultaneously in maritime southeast Asia. The antipathy between Islam and Christianity, as well as commercial competition, bred bitter conflicts pitting the Iberian kingdoms against local Muslim elites and their Arab and later Ottoman allies. European efforts to control the trade and production of spices produced a backlash among many indigenous communities that united against European encroachment, facilitating the spread of Islam across the islands. With the rise of the VOC in southeast Asia in the mid-1600s, religious tensions receded since the Dutch company had little interest in promoting Christianization. Nevertheless, Islam remained a permanent fixture in many southeast Asian societies.

The incursion of Islam into the African Sudan followed the southeast Asian pattern. Just south of the Sahara, the Sudanic belt was a grassy plain that stretched across the continent from the Atlantic Ocean to the Red Sea. Muslim forays into this region entered first at the western and eastern ends via mercantile connections with Berber and Arab peoples in north Africa. Berbers, who made their way into the western Sudan, introduced Islam in the 700s. Sizable empires, first the Ghana, then the Mali, then the Songhay, dominated the region from the tenth through the sixteenth centuries.

Islam continued to make gains in the Sudan and sub-Saharan regions during the early modern period. In the eastern region, a centralized state, the Dār Fūr Sultanate came to power in the mid-1600s, which sponsored Islamic teachers, preachers, and missionaries. Sultans presented themselves as "Commanders of the Faithful," so Islam acquired an official status in the eastern Sudan. Political authorities in Dār Fūr descended from Arabic-speaking Muslims from Egypt who had migrated south for the purpose of trade. Arab migrations also facilitated the advance of Islam into Somalia and Mauritania. In the western Sudan, Songhay emperors ruled as devout Muslims throughout the 1400s and 1500s. As in the east, ruling and merchant elites followed Islam, while commoners clung more doggedly to traditional folk customs. Consequently, Islam closely intermingled with pagan rituals and practices, producing a highly syncretistic version of Muslim observance in the Sudan and the Sahara until jihadist reform movements arose in the 1700s.

In both southeast Asia and Africa, Sufi missionaries made up the most effective instruments of initial and ongoing Islamicization. Originating in Persia in the tenth and eleventh centuries, Sufism combined Islamic doctrine with a diverse number of mystical and philosophical traditions to promote spiritual union with God. Muhammad al-Ghazali (1058–1111), a Persian theologian and mystic, attracted a large following. Sufism never espoused a specific doctrine but incorporated eclectic beliefs and observances within the general framework of Islam. Distinct schools and brotherhoods, both Shia and Sunni, developed over the centuries. Revered as wise and holy men, Sufi missionaries in southeast Asia and Africa caught the attention of native peoples and drew many of them as disciples who soaked up the teachings of their masters and then disseminated the religious message in the course of their daily coming and going. Because of their eclecticism, Sufis, not unlike Jesuit missionaries, adapted many indigenous religious customs, shrines, and sacred figures and incorporated them within the practice of Islam. In Indonesia and India, Sufis adopted the practices of Hindu and Buddhist cults, including the veneration of spirits, saints, and ancestors, while laying considerably less stress on the official practice and doctrines of Islam. In many cases, societies in Africa and southeast Asia were not converted to Islam in this period, as much as they simply appended some of its teachings to their own religious culture. Therefore, the Muslim tradition in the regions penetrated by Sufi missionaries was accommodating and syncretistic.

Christianization: The First Wave

The global spread of Christianity in the early modern period grew out of deep-seated religious struggles in Europe during the 1500s and 1600s. Known as the Reformation, these powerful reform movements created a permanent rupture in western Christendom. A groundswell of reform-minded clerics and intellectuals called attention to corruption and carnality in the Roman Catholic Church at the end of the middle ages. Critics, like Erasmus of Rotterdam (1466/1469–1536) and Thomas More of England (1478–1535) disparaged the worldliness of popes and prelates, the ignorance and immorality of clergy, and the general malaise in pastoral ministry. During this turmoil, several figures, such as Martin Luther (1483–1546) and John Calvin (1509–1564), challenged basic theological positions of the Church, maintaining that only the Bible (not ecclesiastical pronouncements) constituted the basis for religious doctrine and only faith in Christ (not good works) led to salvation. Collectively called Protestants, a number of distinct denominations appeared in the 1500s – Lutherans, Calvinists, Anabaptists, the Church of England – that were all opposed to the Catholic Church (and one another). Authorities within the Catholic Church, beginning in the late 1500s, managed to renew the pastoral corps, regain a spiritual focus, and mount an effective campaign against Protestants. The religious struggles gave way to a series of wars across Europe until the mid-1600s.

These profound religious changes in Europe exuded a forceful missionary impulse. The essential aim of Protestant preachers focused on convincing people that Catholicism was rife with false teachings and superstitious rituals, requiring believers to turn to a more Bible-oriented faith. As Catholic leaders sought to revitalize their church and to counter Protestantism, clerics also attempted to educate people about the fundamentals of their faith and to instill a more heartfelt devotion among Catholics.

Reformation Europe, therefore, constituted a mission field. This missionary drive took on a militant character in Spain and Portugal because of the lengthy armed conflict against Muslim territories. Christian knights had engaged Muslim forces in Iberia and the Middle East for over four hundred years in a quest to re-Christianize all of Spain and to retake the Holy Land. One goal of Portuguese explorers in their trek around the coasts of Africa was to unite with Prester John, a legendary Christian king, to deal a death blow against Muslim powers in the east. Many religious authorities understood the discovery and exploration of new lands as a divine mandate to take the Christian faith, boldly and forcefully, into the wider world.

The Catholic Church proved more successful than Protestant groups in missionary endeavors. Spain and Portugal, staunchly Catholic powers, made missions a high priority, whereas the chief Protestant countries that launched colonial enterprises, England and the Netherlands, undertook missions largely under the auspices of private companies. With an overriding concern for profit, company officers gave less precedence to spreading the word of God. And, by virtue of the considerably larger numbers of priests and nuns in religious orders – Protestants rejected such clerical associations – the Catholic Church marshaled far more personnel in foreign missions than did Protestant denominations. Franciscans, Dominicans, Augustinians, Jesuits, and Ursuline nuns poured out in significant numbers to Africa, America, and Asia.

The scope, scale, and strategy of missionary activity corresponded closely to the basic structure of colonial regimes. As the Spanish and Portuguese proceeded to conquer and settle large regions in the Americas, priests from religious orders, especially Franciscans, Dominicans,

Augustinians, and later Jesuits, followed in the wake of conquest. In the second half of the 1500s and in the 1600s, religious women joined the enterprise by running schools, especially for native girls in the Americas. Efforts at evangelization followed closely on the heels of military subjugation, so many natives remained wary of a gospel that came from the hands of conquerors. For their part, many priests, such as Bartolomé de las Casas (1474–1566), spoke out against the atrocities of conquistadors and attempted to shield Americans from rapacious predation. Missionaries achieved the greatest success in Mexico, the southern lands of North America, and the narrow coastal band along the Andes Mountains. At midcentury, 800 to 900 friars roamed about Mexico and 350 more traversed Peru. The first convent of nuns in America was established in Mexico in 1540, though religious women did not make an appearance in Brazil until after the 1650s.

An abrupt shift in American missions occurred in the 1570s with the consolidation of royal authority in the Spanish and Portuguese colonies. When they came under firmer political control, authorities attempted to replicate Iberian institutions in the Americas, including church organizations. Dioceses became more clearly delineated, and bishops, along with parish priests and inquisitors, migrated to the New World in increasing numbers, supplanting the friars and their work of evangelization. Ecclesiastical organization became more reminiscent of the Catholic Church in Europe, consequently priestly labor centered around the pastoral needs of the colonists and away from converting indigenous peoples. Because of disease, there were also far fewer native American souls to save.

A missionary enterprise that fell outside, and eventually into conflict with, the American colonial empires was Jesuit Reductions in Paraguay and Uruguay. In the second half of the 1500s, Jesuits voyaged to the Americas independent from any colonial authority and any local ecclesiastical jurisdiction. To create an atmosphere more conducive to Christianization, Jesuits set up separate communities among the Guarani people (i.e., Reductions), which were safe from colonialists, slave raiders, and old habits. The Reductions became a huge success, quite popular among the Guarani because of the protection from outside forces and the intermingling of indigenous rituals and music in worship. The Jesuit fathers garnered much respect and fame among South American natives for allying with them against slave hunters.

The Reductions, however, came to a tragic end in the mid-1700s, when a colonial treaty between Spain and Portugal stipulated their removal. When the fathers and the Guarani refused, Spanish and Portuguese forces wiped them out in 1754.

French Jesuits, along with two other religious orders (Recollects and Capuchins), assumed responsibility for Catholic missions in the spacious territories of North America claimed by France. New France was primarily an empire for trade with natives and for resource extraction, so the empire was far less densely settled by European migrants than Mexico, Peru, or Brazil. In the same way, missions in New France contained far fewer missionaries, and their outposts were widely scattered. Recollects arrived in New France in 1615, followed by Jesuits ten years later. French missionaries concentrated their work in the Great Lakes region and along the St. Lawrence River. Headquartered in Quebec, the Jesuits gained a monopoly over operations by 1632; they achieved their greatest success among the Hurons in the region around the St. Lawrence River. Recollects, Jesuits, and Ursuline nuns continued to conduct missions across New France until the end of the 1700s when the British brought an end to the French empire in North America. Under the direction of Marie de l'Incarnation (1599–1672), Ursulines established orphanages and schools among Algonquin, Huron, and Iroquois nations.

The Catholic missionary experience in Africa and Asia contrasted sharply with the broad attempts at evangelization in the western hemisphere. In the Americas, priests and nuns moved about extensively, their movements limited primarily by colonial boundaries. Africa and Asia, with their dense populations and strong states, did not lend themselves to aggressive missionary activity. In most areas, missionaries attached themselves to the fortified factories the Portuguese set up along the African and Asian coasts of the Indian Ocean. The ecclesiastical center of the Portuguese Asian empire lay in Goa, where an archbishop resided and the inquisition took up residence. The Jesuits ran a robust mission from Goa, where they established an indigenous clergy and reached out to areas across south Asia. Nevertheless, the missionary influence of clerics in most Portuguese settlements was fairly limited. The Kongo, the Philippines, Japan, and to a lesser extent eastern Indonesia and Vietnam, were exceptions to the general

Africa-Asian pattern, as missionaries carried out extensive operations in these territories.

The Portuguese struck a close alliance with the Kongolese monarch Nzinga a Nkuwu, who converted in 1491 and allowed missionaries into the Kongo. His son, Nzinga Mvemba (r. 1509–1542) became a devoted Christian and was christened Afonso I. During his rule, Portuguese missionaries recorded large numbers of baptisms. From there Portuguese adventurers, looking for slaves, and missionaries, looking for souls, moved into Ndongo in the 1520 and 1530s. Ultimately the slaving and soul-saving enterprises came into conflict, as the Kongolese and Ndongolese resisted the insatiable Portuguese demand for slaves. Nevertheless, Catholic Christianity remained influential in the region, blending with indigenous religious customs.

From a long-term perspective, the most successful theatre of Christianization in all of Asia lay in the Philippines. Unlike the restricted use of priests in Portuguese factories, the Spanish sent large numbers of missionaries to evangelize the Philippines as part of its conquest of the islands. Colonization commenced in 1565, and by 1594, 267 priests were at work, preaching, building schools, and combating local religious practices. The strategy brought exceptional results, as the Philippines actually became thoroughly Christianized by 1650 with over half a million converts by the end of the 1600s. Since the Spanish retained control of the islands until the late 1800s, Christianity has remained an important force in Filipino society until the present day. From the Philippines, missionaries made significant headway in northern Sulawesi (in eastern Indonesia), the Moluccas, and Vietnam from the late 1500s to the mid-1600s.

Large-scale Christian evangelization also took place in Japan beginning in the mid-sixteenth century, but this campaign in the end provoked a political backlash that led to de-Christianization. The Jesuit Francis Xavier, who had labored in Indonesia, introduced Christianity to Japan in 1549, several years after Portuguese merchants had established contact there. Xavier organized a mission from the capital in Kyoto and from there Jesuits preached and taught, claiming 150,000 converts by 1582 and 222,000 by the early 1600s. The territorial lord (daimyo) Oda Nobunaga (1534–1582) supported Jesuit missionary efforts, though he never converted to Christianity. The rather rapid success of the Jesuits induced their director in Japan, Gaspar Coelho, to play politics with the feudal lords (daimyo). In 1587, the powerful daimyo Toyotomi Hideoshi became alarmed about the military influence of Japanese Christians and he began restricting the practice of Christianity. Between 1614 and 1639, shoguns rode a wave of anti–foreign sentiment to repress Christianity systematically. These measures resulted in the massacres of thousands of Christians, the expulsion of all priests, and the virtual extirpation of Christianity from Japan.

The missionary effort in China represented a unique situation. On the one hand, priests did attempt large-scale evangelization, yet on the other hand, Chinese intellectual culture and governmental policy greatly circumscribed their efforts. The Jesuit Matteo Ricci first attracted the attention of Confucian scholars in the 1580s with his knowledge of their classic texts, his facility with the Chinese language, and his scientific and mathematical expertise. Ricci made the case to these influential elites that Christianity harmonized with ancient Chinese philosophy, an argument that neither Confucian scholars nor all of his own Jesuit brethren completely accepted. Nevertheless, Ricci's learning and skill gave Christianity an allure to Chinese elites. Over the course of the 1500s and 1600s, Jesuits, as well as Dominicans and Franciscans, labored in the Chinese mission field. By the end of the seventeenth century, the Chinese church boasted 120 priests and perhaps as many as 500,000 lay Christians. This number is far less impressive, however, when one considers that the population of China at the time approached 200 million. The downfall of the Chinese mission in the 1700s resulted from intense disagreement over the extent to which Confucian customs could be accommodated by the Catholic Church. Christianity lingered as a marginal religion in Chinese society.

Protestant missionaries accompanied English and Dutch empire builders and settlers, though their activity among indigenous peoples was less extensive, and consequently less effective, than their Catholic rivals. Widely successful Protestant missions did not emerge until the nineteenth and twentieth centuries. Most pastors who went overseas in the early modern period took the religious needs of colonists as their primary responsibility. In the Calvinist tradition, Dutch Reformed pastors worked in the service of the Dutch East and West India Companies in Batavia (Indonesia), New Amsterdam (New York), South

Africa (Cape Town), and other commercial outposts. Dutch missionaries conducted evangelization campaigns in Taiwan and Brazil and also enjoyed some success in Ceylon and Indonesia. In these areas, the presence of Catholic missionaries in nearby areas functioned as a motivating force for the Reformed Church. In Taiwan and Brazil, however, the Dutch effort ended in disappointment. In 1666, the Qing dynasty ousted the VOC from Taiwan, and in 1654 Portugal retook Recife, chief city of the Pernambuco region of Brazil.

Ministers from the Church of England followed English settlers into North America, India, and the West Indies in the 1600s. Like the Dutch, English missionaries focused their work primarily on colonists, though a number of Puritan ministers launched missions. In 1701, the church chartered the "Society for the Propagation of the Gospel in Foreign Parts" to beef up its overseas missionary effort. The most involved English evangelizing endeavor occurred in New England by Puritan ministers in the second half of the 1600s. A handful of these pastors undertook the effort to learn native languages, interact with local tribes, and preach to them. The most effective missionary was John Eliot, dubbed "the apostle to the Indians," who worked among Algonquin tribes in and around the Massachusetts Bay colony from the 1630s to the 1680s. He translated the Bible into Algonquin and created separate villages of Christian converts, known as "praying communities." Converted natives in these communities had to abide by Protestant Christian rules of conduct, learn English, and deport themselves as Europeans in dress and manner.

By 1674, four thousand "praying Indians" lived in a dozen or so segregated villages. King Philip's War (1675–1676), a bloody conflict between English settlers and Algonquin tribes dealt the "praying communities" a serious blow, from which they never fully recovered. After this conflict, English churches curbed their proselytizing work among Algonquin and other native societies, though ministers did continue to carry out missions in English-held territories. In the early 1700s, a revivalist movement in the northeast known as the Great Awakening spawned renewed efforts at Christianizing native peoples.

An essential component of early modern empire building, missionaries carried Christianity into cultures whose basic assumptions about religion and morality were far removed from European ones. Thus, indigenous peoples interpreted Christian teachings from their own cultural framework. Even those who seemed responsive to Christianity, submitted to baptism, and participated in Christian religious practices, embraced this faith at varying levels and in diverse ways. The earliest missionaries in the Spanish Empire baptized millions of Mexicans in the 1520s and 1530s. Most of these neophytes probably had little understanding of the Christian concept of baptism or about any other doctrines.

The majority of converts in America, Africa, and Asia continued to observe their customary religious practices, along with their new Christian obligations. In Africa, converts incorporated Christian saints into the panoply of spirit mediums who intervened in daily affairs and recognized Christian teachings as forms of divine revelation that complemented indigenous ones. At the other end of the spectrum, some individuals embraced Christianity deeply and made a radical break from their inherited religious culture. For example, Kateri Tekakwitha (1656–1680), a young Mohawk woman, became a devoted Christian, enduring hardship from fellow Mohawks and taking a vow of chastity. Likewise, Xu Guangqi (1562–1633), Li Zhizao (1553–1630), and Yang Tingyun (1557–1627) were Confucian scholars who converted, and their devotion earned them the title "pillars of the church" in China. Conversion to Christianity, therefore, comprised a very wide assortment of experiences.

Christian missionaries embarked on several basic strategies to bridge the chasm between European religious assumptions and indigenous ones around the world. One tactic, utilized by Franciscans and Dominicans in Spanish America, operated on what might be called a gradualist understanding about conversion. In Mexico, Peru, New Mexico, and Arizona, missionaries displayed little preoccupation about what natives actually comprehended about Christianity when urging them to undergo baptism. Franciscans, like Pedro de Gante and Bernardino de Sahagún, used songs, dances, theatrical performances, and visual aids to try to persuade Americans that God and Christian saints possessed more power than their deities, who were, in the missionary view, demons and devils. The central premise behind this approach regarded conversion as a prolonged process that needed constant direction from priests. The gradualist understanding allowed for a blending of Christian and local belief systems, though over time, as converts became increasingly acculturated to Christianity, native beliefs and practices faded away.

A similar strategy, employed by Jesuits, in China, Japan, India, as well as in North and South America, accommodated a wide range of non-Christian social customs and religious practices. In China, Ricci dressed as a Confucian scholar and argued that Christianity represented a return to the classical purity of Confucianism in order to entice an influential element among Chinese elites. Jesuits also permitted Chinese Christians to participate in Confucian rites that venerated their ancestors. Robert de Nobili (1577–1656), missionary to India in the 1600s, followed Ricci's example by stressing commonalities between Hinduism and Christianity and adorning himself as a Brahmin monk. In North America, Jesuits adopted the lifestyles of native peoples, learned their languages, and traveled with them wherever they went. One Jesuit explained, "a Missionary does not fear to make himself a Savage, so to speak, with them, in order to make them Christians... We must... follow them to their homes and adapt ourselves to their ways, however ridiculous they may appear, in order to draw them to ours."[2] The relativistic stance adopted by Jesuits, though controversial among Catholics, enabled them to penetrate societies around the world more deeply than any other Christian missionary group.

Concerned above all with protecting the purity of the Christian faith as it crossed cultural borders, an opposite strategy practiced by Protestant missionaries and Recollects in North America required that indigenous peoples adopt European cultural attributes before they could become Christians. This approach offered little or no compromise with indigenous customs and presumed that authentic Christianity was inextricably interconnected with European values. Puritans in New England, for example, insisted that native Americans take up European style of dress, learn the English language, settle down on a homestead, embrace European sexual mores, and forsake their former lifestyles. In essence, native peoples had to become Europeans before they could become Christians.

The early modern age formed an important phase in Islamic and Christian expansion throughout major regions of the world. The patterns of development in both universal religions were remarkably parallel, as Islam and Christianity profited from empire building and long-distance commerce and achieved their greatest successes when missionaries adapted their religious systems to indigenous cultures.

Orthodoxy vs. Accommodation: The Second Wave

The interweaving of Islam and Christianity with local religious customs and concepts created internal struggles within both religions. Orthodox critics appeared who regarded the mixing of beliefs and practices as dangerous idolatry or blasphemy that compromised religious truth. Orthodox movements emerged in both religions that attempted to root out all of the accretions introduced by Sufi and Jesuit missionaries. These campaigns functioned as a second wave of Islamicization and Christianization in the early modern world.

The blending of Islam with native saints, shrines, and spirits came under fire at the end of the 1700s, as powerful reform movements rocked Muslim societies. A widespread perception of political and religious corruption gripped many clerics in the 1700s, as the once powerful core states, Ottoman, Safavid, and Mughal, had deteriorated significantly. Many religious leaders concluded that their societies needed to return to the fundamentals of their faith and eliminate the extraneous practices touted by earlier generations of missionaries. Out of these criticisms grew a militant emphasis on Muslim identity, rooted firmly in the image of Muhammad as moral exemplar. Revivalist movements placed emphasis on unswerving obedience to shari'a law and the hadith (traditions about the sayings and deeds of Muhammad), as well as the eradication of all syncretistic practices. The most intense sites of Muslim renewal were Arabia, west Africa and the Sudan, India, and western China.

Home to the holy cities of Mecca and Medina, Arabia emerged as a primary center of Islamic reform in the 1700s. Many ulama there had grown alarmed at the practice of venerating Sufis throughout the Muslim world at their tombs or at shrines where pilgrims came to seek miracles. Many stories of miracles and supernatural intercessions circulated about the Sufis and their shrines. The decline of Muslim imperial fortunes seemed to some as a mark of God's displeasure with superstition and idolatry. For ulama, like Muhammad Ibn al-Wahhab (1703–1792), Muslims had to return to the unvarnished purity of the Prophet's teachings. Al-Wahhab drew heavily from the writings of a fourteenth-century legal scholar, Taqi al-Din Taymiya (d. 1328), who had undergone persecution for his severe condemnations of popular shrines in Cairo and Damascus.

Ibn Taymiya belonged to the conservative Hanbali legal tradition that eschewed the accumulation of legal opinions and religious sources in favor of the sole authority of the Qu'ran. Beginning in the 1740s, al-Wahhab preached and taught in Arabia, denouncing the shrines of Sufi saints, pushing a strict morality, and laying great stress on transcendent monotheism. His unbending stance brought controversy, as he labeled Sufi brotherhoods pagan and polytheistic. For al-Wahhab, there could be no compromise with the austere morality of the Prophet or with the exercise of shari'a law. If heretical Muslims refused to turn from their idolatrous practices, al-Wahhab advocated jihad against them.

Had it not been for a fortuitous encounter with an ambitious tribal chief, Muhammad Ibn Saud (d. 1765), al-Wahhab's career would have resembled that of the many other obscure reformist ulama of the regions. Ibn Saud, for whom the present-day country of Saudia Arabia is named, found common cause with al-Wahhab. The religious reformer threw his support behind the chieftain and in return, this strict brand of Islam held sway in any conquered lands. The Saudi dynasty waged a long campaign against a number of local tribes and against the Ottoman Turks, which controlled Mecca and Medina. By 1816, the Saudis had made all of Arabia their domain, but a few years later the Turks retook the western slice of the peninsula that contained the holy cities. Al-Wahhab's followers destroyed dozens of Sufi shrines, radically reformed Islam, and waged jihad on Muslims who clung to the old ways. Wherever the Saudis ruled, the Wahhabi strand of Islam enjoyed the dynasty's full support, including all of Arabia after the disintegration of the Ottoman Empire in 1923.

Just as itinerant merchants and missionaries had carried Islam to many parts of the world in previous centuries, Wahhabism also made its way into various Muslim lands, most notably into Africa through traveling Arab reformers. In the western Sudan, the collapse of the Songhay Empire at the end of the 1500s led to political fragmentation. In place of the empire, independent, urban-centered states, called the Hausa states emerged as dominant powers. The economic basis of the region remained trade, as cities dominated the cultural landscape. The syncretistic strains of Islam that had won influence in this region mixed easily with the eclectic, urban, commercial culture and accommodated itself to the secularism of Hausa rulers.

At odds with the Hausa states, pastoral peoples in the countryside had adopted the reformist message of local and Arab ulama influenced by Wahhabism. These rural dwellers belonged to the Fulani ethnic group that had migrated into the western Sudan and Sahara in the 1400s. Aggrieved by the harsh rule, the secular outlook, and the immoderate lifestyle of the Hausa kingdoms, the Fulani found the strict morals and the religious militancy advocated by the reformist ulama appealing. The Fulani of western Sudan united behind Uthman Don Fodio (1756–1817) to conduct jihads in the region against the Hausa states and united the region under a caliphate at Sokoto (1809–1903). Across western Sudan, Fulani leaders restored shari'a law, reduced the role of women in society, required them to dress in an orthodox manner, and enforced a strict moral regime. Thus, like Arabia, western Africa became home to states heavily influenced by Islamic reformers in the 1700s.

Powerful currents of renewal also surfaced in India in the seventeenth and eighteenth centuries. In opposition to the tolerant, ecumenist policies of Akbar, influential ulama demanded the imposition of the shari'a and stressed the utter incompatibility between Islam and all other religious systems. The foremost proponent of the centrality of the shari'a was Shaykh Ahmad Sirhindi (1564–1624) who fought all forms of syncretism for Muslims, including sacrificing animals, worshipping saints, and participating in Hindu festivals. The strict Islamist program found its strongest state sponsorship during the reign of the devout Muslim emperor Aurangezeb in the second half of the 1600s. The ambitious expansion of Aurangezeb into Bengal (northeastern India) and the Deccan (southern India) caused a backlash from Hindu warlords who formed breakaway states after the death of the emperor in the early eighteenth century.

The central figure behind Islamic revival in India was the ulama, Shah Wali Allah (1703–1762) and then his son Shah Abd al-Aziz (1746–1824). Influenced by Sirhindi, Wali Allah also studied in Mecca and Medina and introduced a program of moral and social reform to his madrasa (religious school) in northern India. Like Wahhab, Wali Allah condemned Hindu and Sikh rituals that had crept into Islam, and criticized rulers for their moral laxity. Unlike Wahhab, Wali Allah worked to cleanse what he believed were superstitious observances in the Sufi brotherhoods, rather than doing away with the associations altogether. Islamic reformism in India, as in Arabia and Africa, was thoroughly committed to Sunni orthodoxy and thus necessarily abhorred Shi'ism. Consequently the renewal movement stirred bitter animosity with Shi'ite enclaves in south Asia. During the 1800s, Wali Allah's successors created a madrasa at Deoband, just north of Delhi, which developed into a locus of fundamentalist Islam and a rallying point against both religious pluralism and British imperialism.

Finally, Islamic revivalism, mixed with mystical Sufism, extended its reach into central Asia at the end of the 1700s, leading to political upheaval in several western provinces in China. The Chinese government had openly encouraged Muslim immigration from central Asia for commercial reasons; by the early modern period millions lived in the western regions of Xinjiang, Yunnan, and Gansu. Referred to as the Hui people, Muslims struggled to balance the observances required by their faith with prevalent customs in Chinese culture. Orthodox Islam obliged Muslims to learn at least some Arabic to gain access to religious texts, prohibited consumption of pork (a primary Chinese meat staple), and prescribed a manner of dress and deportment. The Qing government, however, put pressure on the Hui to reject the foreign habits and to conform to Chinese cultural forms.

In this environment, Islamic reformism merged with a peculiar branch of Sufi mysticism, known as the New Teaching, to rebel against Qing authority in order to establish an independent Muslim state. One of the key figures in the introduction of reformist elements into Chinese Islam was Ma Mingxin (d. 1781), a Sufi mystic who studied in Arabia, the center of Wahhabism, for sixteen years. After his return to northwest China in 1744, Mingxin worked to moderate Sufi syncretism, such as venerating saints, and introduced other reforms. Some of these innovations alienated Muslims who followed other Sufi traditions, leading to ongoing violence between Islamic groups. Putting down rebellions in Xinjiang, Qing authorities apprehended Mingxin and beheaded him for subversion. His execution fomented major rebellions against the Qing into the 1800s, which the central government crushed with severity.

The campaign against syncretism in the Muslim world marked a distinctive phase in the development of Islamicization. Sufi brotherhoods planted the Muslim faith throughout Asia, the Indian Ocean, and northern and eastern Africa. Large empires, including Ottoman,

Mughal, Safavid, and Songhay, consolidated these gains, and emperors patronized religious scholarship, education, and worship. In most regions, the worship of shrines, the veneration of sacred sites, and the continuation of local religious observances became incorporated within Islamic practice. Ulamas in the 1600s and 1700s sparked a diffuse movement to remove all these extraneous elements from Islam. By the beginning of the 1800s, orthodoxy was well on the road to triumph over accommodation in Islamic societies.

The quest to translate abstract religious concepts into real-life human societies in ways that were both authentic and comprehensible also plagued Catholic missions. In response to Protestant criticisms, the Catholic Church beginning in the mid-1500s launched a major campaign of reform. Part of this effort concentrated on eliminating pagan practices and folk customs, such as worshipping nature spirits and practicing magic. Church authorities during the Catholic Reformation made it a priority for bishops and other clerics to visit communities under their jurisdiction to correct errors and to punish the stubbornly wayward.

The obsession with Catholic orthodoxy also extended to mission fields in America, Asia, and Africa. The first generation of Catholic missionaries anchored their religious message in the beliefs and observances of indigenous peoples. Portuguese missionaries told Kongolese natives that the crucifix possessed supernatural powers; Jesuits in North America posed as shamans that could exercise power over local magicians; Franciscans in Mexico superimposed the cult of the Virgin of Guadalupe onto devotion to the goddess Tontantzin; Jesuits in China cast Christianity as a classical form of Confucianism. In addition to the deliberate attempts at religious mixing, a number of Christian theological concepts, such as sin, atonement, and penance, did not clearly translate, at least immediately, into cultures outside of Europe. Protestant missionaries did not as a general rule purposefully use a syncretistic strategy. Undergoing a bitter conflict with Catholics in Europe over nonbiblical traditions, Protestants proved much less accepting of non-Christian practices. Thus, syncretism in the spread of Christianity into the wider world was a singularly Catholic issue.

By the late 1500s, ecclesiastical authorities began to take measures to impose orthodoxy in the mission field. The Council of Trent, ending in 1563, energetically affirmed the Catholic Church's commitment to doctrinal uniformity. At about the same time, church institutions – bishops, parishes, inquisitions – were becoming standardized in the Iberian empires. Clerics in the Americas, Africa, and Asia witnessed all sorts of peculiar combinations of Christianity and traditional rites. In the Kongo, a young female religious figure, Dona Bertrice, claiming to have a vision of St. Anthony, led a movement to fuse Christian and African beliefs. She adopted basic Christian tenets, but Africanized them, maintaining that the Kongo was the Holy Land, Christ came from the Kongo, and the early apostles were African. Much to the dismay of Catholic priests, Dona Bertrice also sanctioned the local practice of polygamy. Authorities in the Kongo seized her and burned her at the stake in 1706, though her Antonian movement, so called because of her devotion to St. Anthony, lived on in sub-Saharan Africa. Priests in Peru complained that natives and mestizos venerated mummified ancestors, erected sacred totems, and patronized spirits at trees, wells, and mountains. The Catholic Church considered all such practices as idolatry.

In time, ecclesiastical officers set in motion the customary disciplinary measures: inquisitors to persuade and punish offenders, parish priests to teach and preach converts, and nuns to instruct children. Authorities also took extraordinary actions. Pedro de Villagómez, the archbishop of Lima, instigated a campaign against idolatry in 1640 that continued in sporadic outbursts until 1750. Creole "idolatry inspectors" went into villages looking for evidence of idolatry, destroying shrines, confiscating properties, and disrupting observances tainted with native rituals, figures, or expressions. Priests also held up celebrated Catholic saints, as well as local pious figures, for role models of the Christian life and as intercessors in times of trouble. Nevertheless, traditional cults in America, Asia, and Africa, proved quite resilient to ongoing attempts at Christianization and remained part of indigenous cultures down to the present day.

The tension between syncretism and orthodoxy in overseas missionary endeavors also ignited smoldering resentments among influential forces within the Catholic Church. Tolerant of folk rituals in China, India and South America, the Jesuit order embodied all the accommodation that Franciscans and Dominicans steadfastly opposed. The need to coordinate missionary efforts led Pope Gregory XV to establish the Sacred Congregation for the Propagation of the Faith (*Congregatio*

Propaganda Fide) in 1622. The Congregation organized evangelization in non-Catholic territories and standardized Catholic practices among indigenous peoples. The most sensational problems that came before the Congregation and ultimately the papacy were controversies involving Confucian rites in China and Hindu customs in India. These episodes clearly illustrated the conflicts over syncretism in the spread of Catholic Christianity.

The Chinese court had allowed the Jesuits to operate in China from the late 1500s and, for the most part, they enjoyed a favorable relationship with Chinese elites. The Jesuits periodically encountered hostility from Confucian mandarins or provincial officials. Despite infrequent episodes of aggression, Jesuits benefited from good relations with the imperial court. Jesuit expertise in scientific fields endeared the missionaries to emperors. The missionaries also cultivated an affinity with Confucians who ran the imperial bureaucracy. Because of their belief in the compatibility between Confucianism and Christianity, Jesuits allowed Chinese converts to continue to observe Confucian rites. These included attending Confucian temples, celebrating Confucian festivals, venerating ancestors at shrines, and making devotional offerings to the emperor.

Fiercely hostile to Jesuit accommodation, Dominicans in Asia roundly condemned the Confucian rites as religious rituals at odds with Christian teaching. Beyond the conceptual disagreements, a fierce rivalry between the Jesuit and Dominican orders fueled the acrimony. During the second half of the 1600s, both sides attacked the other party and sent numerous petitions to Rome, though no definite judgment appeared until the early 1700s.

At the same time, a similar dispute was taking place in the Jesuit mission in India. Until the early 1600s, the missionaries in south Asia had largely confined themselves to the coastal cities where the Portuguese had set up fortified trading posts. In 1606, the Italian Jesuit Roberto de Nobili started to evangelize in the interior of southern India, the religious culture of which was dominated by Hinduism. De Nobili attempted to bridge the cultural divide by learning Sanskrit and local languages, mastering Hindu texts, and deporting himself as a Brahmin religious figure. Brahmins made up the highest caste in Indian society. Separating himself from other Jesuits (whom Brahmins despised), he incorporated Hindu customs into his ministry and prohibited mixing between converts and priests from different castes. This meant, for example, priests segregated lower-caste Christians from converts from higher castes. These practices became known as the Malabar rites in Catholic circles. As de Nobili gained a following, critics, including Portuguese Jesuits, assailed the blending of Hindu culture within Christianity just as Dominicans complained about Jesuit strategy in China. Resentments simmered among missionaries until 1703, when French Capuchins lodged a grievance against the Jesuits and their methods.

As these disputes in Asia widened in the early 1700s, the papacy began to close the door on accommodation in the mission field. Clement XI dispatched Charles Maillard de Tournon in 1703 to India and then China to bring clarity to the boundaries of orthodoxy in non-Christian societies. De Tournon condemned the Malabar rites and prohibited missionaries from tolerating them. Three years later, de Tournon stood boldly before the Kangxi emperor in China and reiterated papal condemnations of the Confucian rites. Clerics appealed, negotiated, and disputed these cases until 1742, when Benedict XIV upheld previous judgments in a definitive fashion. In the Americas and Asia, after over two hundred years of missionary work, church authorities rejected what they believed were the accommodation of native rituals and religious customs.

Thus, after the first wave of Christianization into the wider world, church leaders sought to rid Christian communities of the syncretistic elements that had grown into them and to end accommodation as a strategy of evangelization. The results were quite mixed. In the Americas, converts continued to blend folk culture and religion into a Christian identity. For example, Magdalena Callao, a celebrated healer in seventeenth-century Cañete, Peru, sought spiritual power from a natural holy site and used Andean materials in her therapeutic practices, but also invoked the Virgin Mary. Native religious leaders persisted in shamanistic prophecies, claims, and predictions, though they had converted to Christianity. In Africa, Christians continued to practice polygamy, sacrifice animals, and honor the spirits of their ancestors. There were countless other examples that all together demonstrate the widely diverse ways men and women created their own syncretistic religious identities, in spite of the efforts by church authorities to eliminate them.

The conflict between syncretism and orthodoxy formed an unavoidable phase in the development of Islam and Christianity as they spread into new lands and new cultures. Since religious systems evolve over time and push into different spaces, their missionaries have to root their message in the mental framework of peoples who possess very different premises about the supernatural. To do otherwise rendered their faith alien, incomprehensible, and irrelevant. Consequently, Sufis, Jesuits, and other proselytizers in the initial missionary thrust recognized sacred indigenous sites and incorporated local rituals. Then in due course, after the newly sprouted religious communities grew into a conspicuous presence with a regular set of observances, customs, and institutions, the divergence from orthodoxy became interpreted by some as problematic. Fearing the erosion of the authentic religious truth, reformers pushed for a return to standard doctrines and practices. These struggles, also common in other religious traditions, mark the globalization of belief and practice in an age of intense cross-cultural interaction.

Constructions of Knowledge

Ethnography

Acquiring knowledge about the broader world became an essential element in the expansion of early modern states. Hundreds of travelers writing for patrons or audiences in their homelands described a wide range of subjects from ethnic groups and their customs to plants and animals in their natural habitat. Travel accounts, descriptions, and chronicles of faraway lands and peoples formed a major literary genre. Scholars today find these sources valuable because they provide ethnographic content, which means that the works described peoples and their society, concentrating on their customs, from a foreign observer's point of view. Consequently, these sources enable us to comprehend how travelers from one society classified and categorized people in other cultures. In short, ethnographic texts suggest how people in this age of expansion constructed knowledge of the world in order to make sense of it.

Characterized by expansion and intensified travel, the early modern period gave rise to ethnographic writing. Travelers in previous centuries, such as Marco Polo from Venice, Ibn Battuta from Morocco, and Sima Qian from China, left written descriptions of other peoples and cultures, but they borrowed much of their material from written sources or hearsay. In contrast, early modern writers placed much more emphasis on their direct presence among the "other" peoples. We should not take ethnographic descriptions at face value, however, because writers embedded their cultural prejudices in their observations. For example, Han Chinese pictorial accounts of the Miao (Hmong) people in Guizhou province (southwest China) carried the generic title *Illustrations of the Southern Barbarians* (*Miao man tu*). Likewise, Jonathan Twist, a Dutch governor of Melaka, titled a chapter in his *General Description of the Indies* (*Generale beschrijvinge van Indien*), "Of the Heathens and their God-worship." Clearly these texts tell us as much about the worldview of the authors as they do about the Miao or Malay societies.

Europeans produced far and away the most accounts of foreign societies, though ethnographies appeared by writers in Qing China, Tokugawa Japan, and the Ottoman Empire. Hundreds of European writers, including Pierre Belon, Cristobal de Acosta, Johan Huygen van Linschoten, and Carl Linnaeus, classified peoples, described their religious beliefs, marital practices, political organizations, and popular festivities, sometimes intricately illustrated with woodcuts. Naturalists voyaged on long expeditions, mapping the flora and fauna of the world, an enterprise that eventually contributed to Charles Darwin's theory of natural selection. The pulp fiction motif also appeared in the more sober-minded descriptions of plants, animals, and customs. Accounts by Baltazer Springer and Antonio Galvano contain stories with mermaids, dog-headed people with tails, women with pig faces, and men with overly large genitalia. Asians generated ethnographies on a far lower scale than Europeans. Nevertheless the presence of these texts in such diverse regions as China, Japan, and Anatolia indicate that ethnography represented a global early modern phenomenon. Thus, the impulse to depict, illustrate, classify, and categorize foreign societies was almost universal, though Europeans demonstrated the most profound enthusiasm for it.

Ethnography in Asia and Europe bore a number of thematic similarities, though the production and format of the genre differed significantly. Chinese, Japanese, and Ottoman ethnographies usually derived from imperial sources of patronage, whereas a variety of patrons or audiences sponsored European works. In 1751, the Qianlong emperor ordered the creation of an illustrated manuscript depicting ethnic groups across China and foreign lands, including Europe. This work, *The Illustration of Tributary Peoples*, drew from earlier ethnographic material, such as gazetteers (this is the commonly used term for official Chinese publications, usually about local conditions, personages, and events) and albums of non-Chinese peoples in the Qing empire. Produced under the auspices of frontier administrators, the gazetteers and albums classified scores of different ethnic groups, their customs, physical appearance, and dress. The most well-preserved albums were known as Miao albums, because they portrayed Miao ethnicities in Guizhou, Yunnan, and other southwestern territories. The purpose behind the Qing enterprise aimed at providing cultural information about peoples brought recently into the empire in order to govern them more effectively.

With similar imperial goals, the Tokugawa dynasty of Japan commissioned illustrated depictions of the Ainu people on the island of Hokkaido in the 1700s. In 1720, the scholar and politician Arai Hakuseki (1656–1720) published the *Ezo-shi* based on his direct contact with the Ainu. Hakuseki's work ignited a firestorm of curiosity, for thereafter a flourishing Ainu motif, known as *Ainu-e*, ensued, which persisted into the 1800s. Like the Qing materials, the *Ainu-e* recounted and embellished the exotic mores and practices of this subjugated ethnic group.

Various Ottoman ethnographers also benefited from imperial patronage, though its general purpose seemed simply to satisfy the curiosity of sultans and their court rather than to facilitate political control. Scholars have not yet uncovered the extent to which Ottoman ethnography developed, but scattered evidence points to an array of artistic material that represented foreign groups. A renowned Turkish artist, Levni (Abdulcelil Çelebi, d. 1732), illustrated a number of works that described European diplomats, common folk engaging in many different activities, as well as palace scenes in the early 1700s. Levni borrowed from earlier Turkish, Arabic, and Safavid albums, intimating a vibrant cross-cultural artistic and ethnographic sharing in the region. In addition, European patrons contracted with Turkish artisans for illustrated editions of Middle Eastern subjects, circulating Ottoman ethnography in the west.

Other Turkish ethnographers wrote of their own accord. Mustafa Ali (1541–1600), an intellectual and government official, produced an account of Cairo in 1599 (*The Conditions of Cairo*) based on his experiences there. In the work, Ali described and rendered judgment on the habits of soldiers, the duties of civil servants, the customs of women, as well as a host of Egyptian conventions. The most voluminous travel account in the Muslim world came from the pen of Evliya Çelebi (1611–1682), who traveled extensively across Asia, Africa, and Europe. The *Book of Travels*, which consisted of ten books, recounted Çelebi's voyages, as well as the people and lands he encountered between 1640 and 1680. A well-educated, upper-class Turk, Çelebi referred to himself as "the world traveler" and mixed fictive tales along with perceptive observations. Since he was a devout Sunni Muslim, he expressed horror at Shi'ite religious customs he witnessed in Iran. Similarly, he regarded Europeans as "Franks," a common Muslim epithet for western Christians that recalled images of bloody, barbarian crusaders. Passing through Kalmyk societies in central Asia, Çelebi gave an account of a feast whose main dish was human flesh. When Çelebi declined an invitation to join, his host explained, "We eat his flesh so that his soul will enter one of us. Thus, he does not die, but goes together with us.... But if you want to know what it tastes like, just kiss a woman and see how sweet it is."[3] While sources for exploring Ottoman ethnography remain meager, it is clear that Turks were traveling widely and relating their encounters to others back home.

European ethnography arose from a very wide variety of disparate sources and formed a considerable decentralized body of writing and illustrating. Colonial powers required governors in the field to report on conditions and peoples they encountered or ruled, but European ethnography did not take the shape of an imperial-sanctioned gazetteer or album. Rulers occasionally commissioned a chronicler to write works that contained substantial ethnographic material. Philip II of Spain (who also ruled Portugal after 1580) appointed the Portuguese historian Diogo do Couto (1542/3–1616) to write an account of the Portuguese in Asia in 1595. Nevertheless, most European ethnographers drafted their descriptions, chronicles, or travel accounts for a variety of audiences. To mention just a few examples, the Spanish priest, Bartolomé de las Casas wrote *The History of the Indies* in the 1500s to bring attention to the cruelty of conquistadors in Mexico;

Sir Walter Raleigh (1554?–1618) and Richard Hakluyt (1552–1616) drafted *The Discoverie of Guiana* (1591) and *The principall Navigations, Voiages and Discoveries of the English nation* (1589), respectively, to promote English colonization in the Americas; and Louis-Antoine de Bougainville (1729–1811) composed *Voyage around the World* (1771) to describe the beauty of the Pacific Islands.

Even though the production and format of Asian and European ethnographic works differed significantly, themes in the texts and the pictures shared remarkable characteristics. In a fundamental sense, a common venture engaged all Eurasian ethnographers: to comprehend "the other" (i.e., all the unfamiliar and strange peoples, social customs, and philosophical ideas in a period of global expansion). All writers conveyed a mixture of fascination and revulsion with foreign societies as early modern ethnography both demonized the unfamiliar and glamorized the exotic.

In the initial periods of expansion, explorers and chroniclers gave most attention to customs and practices of indigenous peoples that marked them as uncivilized. An account of the Daya Gelao people near the southern coast of China described their custom of breaking off the two front teeth of a bride so that she would not harm the bridegroom's family. A 1608 description of the Miao in Hunan province remarked that "They are also called Zihong. Their delight in killing is extremely keen. Whey they get an enemy they chew his raw flesh. When a man dies he is buried only after his wife remarries."[4] On the other side of the world, Amerigo Vespucci in the early 1500s observed that tribes in Brazil, "marry as many wives as they please . . . they cruelly kill one another . . . for they eat one another . . . I knew a man whom I also spoke to who was reputed to have eaten more than three hundred human bodies."[5] The accounts that flowed out of frontier regions in Asia, Africa, and America from travelers made the bloodthirsty, sexually depraved cannibal a stock image of many frontier peoples.

Over time prevailing stereotypes of savagery gave way to romanticized perceptions about societies regarded as primitive. Gazetteers and albums devoted to societies in southwestern China illustrated the rustic simplicity and domesticity of common folk. Writers and artists represented indigenous men and women tending their fields, hunting tigers, dancing around a pole, sacrificing animals, and pursuing marriage partners, as well as many other down-to-earth activities. European voyages of discovery in the 1700s produced representations of indigenous peoples as naturally virtuous and innocent, which replaced the dominant images of the sexually perverted cannibal. Buoyed by the discoveries of James Cook in the 1760s, British, French, and Dutch explorers cast about in the south Pacific, which included Australia, New Zealand, Hawaii, Fiji, and Tahiti. Writers and painters depicted indigenous peoples from these lands as embodying a primitive nobility uncorrupted by civilization. Artistic representations presented native women as physically appealing and sexual, often partially or fully naked, intermingling with men, who appeared as handsome, classic figures. The Pacific islands and the American frontier acquired the fictional aura of lush, sensual utopias, where simple people lived easily and happily without toil and conflict. The construction of the noble savage evolved into a major literary and artistic component of the Romantic movement at the end of the 1700s.

Long-term trends in ethnographic characterizations also reflected important political and cultural developments in the metropole, or home society. The Qing rulers' overarching objective in all their frontier regions, including Xinjiang, Turkestan, Guizhou, and Yunnan, sought to acculturate recently subjugated groups into their new state. The ethnography of Miao societies exhibits this longstanding effort to make them Chinese. Consequently, depictions of various communities functioned as a gauge of how well they were advancing to that goal. With regard to the Songjia ethnic group, a gazetteer in 1673 put the matter explicitly, "Now they have moreover changed completely and become Chinese and do not revert [to their old ways]."[6] With other peoples, writers commented regularly either on how tame they had become or how barbarous they remained. By the end of the 1700s, reports optimistically asserted that frontier peoples, with all their exotic customs, had nevertheless been absorbed into the Middle Kingdom under the benevolent rule of the emperor.

A similar dynamic occurred in European ethnography about Asia that paralleled important cultural and political shifts in the west. In the 1500s and 1600s, the splendor of illustrious Asian courts struck awe into European visitors, and writers described the remarkable political authority of Asian emperors and kings. Francis Henriques, a Jesuit, described Akbar's celebrated imperial city of Fatehpur Sikri, "it well shows his great power and the riches he has, so that even those who have seen many good things are unfailingly struck with wonder."[7] Admiration for the cultural trappings of imperial power blended with European condemnations of "oriental despotism." Catholic writers, outraged at the persecution of Christians, presented Japanese society as blindly devoted to ruler and society. Attitudes toward Islamic states carried an additional layer of alienness due to centuries of long hostility between Muslims and Christians. Dutch, French, and English travelers and commentators regularly condemned Islamic law as tyrannical and cruel. Stories circulated about Turkish atrocities against Christians, the ruthless barbarity of Turkish forces, and the bondage of women under male Turkish control. Europeans came to regard Asiatic regimes as despotic states ruled by royal power, unchecked by noble dynasties, legislative institutions, or political parties.

In the second half of the 1700s, an important change occurred in western ethnography, as a result of a preoccupation with race. European theorists, in trying to make sense of the world and assert western supremacy in an age of encounter, divided humanity into basic racial categories. Building on previous theories, Carl Linnaeus posited in 1740 that humanity was comprised of four basic races, divided by skin color. In this widely accepted schema, Asians were yellow. From there, it only took a small theoretical step for George Buffon in 1749 to correlate pigmentation with the degree of a civilization's achievement. From the European perspective, all non-white peoples, including "the yellow race" were inferior to Caucasians. This racist outlook mirrored a growing frustration with the Chinese refusal to open itself to western influence, trade, and religion. As the eighteenth century drew to a close, westerners wrote derisively about Asian culture, considering it backward, reactionary, and narrow-minded.

Cartography and Astronomy

The increased contact between peoples from different cultures co-incided with a revival in intellectual and scientific inquiry in several parts of the world. In Europe, astronomers and mathematicians, such as Nicholas Copernicus (1473–1543), Galileo Galilei (1564–1642), and Isaac Newton (1642–1727), forged a new conception of the cosmos and introduced a scientific approach to considerations of natural phenomena. In North America, intellectuals as diverse as the Puritan Increase Mather (1639–1723) and the skeptic Benjamin Franklin

(1706–1790) wrote about science and conducted scientific experiments. In China, literati in the fashion of Wang Lun (1456–1496) and Li Shizhen (1518–1593) undertook a program for "investigating things and extending knowledge" that produced learning in a wide array of subjects, including pharmacology, medicine, and botany. In the early Ottoman Empire, over three hundred schools (madrasas) passed along the scientific achievements of the medieval Islamic world to students. The versatile scholar Taqi al-Din (1526–1585) wrote on a wide range of subjects and constructed an observatory in Istanbul in 1577. Renewed interest in mathematics, medicine, and astronomy took hold in Japan and Korea as well. As a result of cross-cultural contact, the distinct innovations in specific regions circulated globally, enabling scholars to appropriate bodies of knowledge as they saw fit.

Two fields of inquiry that invited cross-cultural borrowing were cartography (map making) and astronomy. Maps not only represented contemporary geographical knowledge, but they also symbolized perceptions of the world. For example, Matteo Ricci's 1584 world map, *Complete Map of the Earth's Mountains and Seas*, placed China at the center of the world to make it more appealing to his Chinese hosts. On a practical level, this period of exploration and empire building necessitated accurate maps; consequently, cartography attracted attention from scholars and ruling dynasties across the world. Just as cartographers were charting the contours of the globe, astronomers were mapping the heavens. Stars, comets, planets, and celestial space had enchanted thinkers since the dawn of civilization, in part because most people believed that astronomical phenomena instigated or foretold earthly events, a branch of study known as astrology. The need for precise calendars to date important religious occurrences, plan the agricultural season, and stage auspicious political ceremonies compelled ruling elites to patronize astronomers and oversee their work. Since astronomy incorporated complex mathematical calculations, sustained observations, and inherent conceptions of the universe, the study of celestial movements stood in the forefront of scientific advances in early modern science.

Several episodes of cross-cultural borrowing in the fields of cartography and astronomy illustrate the diffusion of ideas and their adaptation in various parts of the world. One instance reveals the confluence of cartographic traditions in east Asia. In 1402, a team of Korean cartographers led by Yi Hoe constructed the first world map in east Asia. Known as the *Kangnido*, the map depicted Asia, emphasizing Korea, China, and India, but also included Europe and Africa. Yi drew upon Chinese, Persian, Japanese, and Islamic maps to create a synthetic picture of the known world. Copied and modified repeatedly in the early modern period, *Kangnido* maps found their way into Japan, China, and other areas. The entrance into Japan probably resulted from a Japanese invasion of Korea at the end of the 1500s in which the invaders looted items of value. After the maps filtered into China, they exerted influence on cartographic perspectives in the Middle Kingdom, just as the Chinese maps that circulated into Korea reshaped later versions of the *Kangnido*. For example, a 1775 map (Yŏji Chŏndo) displayed Chinese, European, and *Kangnido* influences by giving more accurate proportions to Korea, China, and Africa, and giving more detail to Europe.

Another point of intellectual adaptation occurred in the Ottoman Empire during its golden age in the 1500s and 1600s. Beginning in the fifteenth century, Ottoman intellectuals cultivated learning in the corpus of science from medieval Muslim scholarship in Persia and Arab lands. Thus, Ottomans maintained an active engagement with centers of learning in the Islamic world. The Ottoman astronomer Taqi al-Din, for example, relied heavily on astronomical observations and calculations from Ulugh Beg (1393/4–1449), a Timurid astronomer and ruler in Samarkand.

At the same time, many Turkish scholars took in aspects of European science, despite intermittent but prolonged warfare between Ottomans and the Christian west. The geopolitical and religious antagonism did not inhibit Ottoman scholars from adopting western ideas that they found useful. Trade, travel, and migration, especially by Jews fleeing European persecution, enabled Turks to gain access to an extensive western literature in medicine, anatomy, cartography, and astronomy. In the field of cartography, Piri Reis (1470–1554) created a world map, known as the *Atlantic Map*, in 1513 by making use of Arab, Chinese, and Iberian maps. Though only a fragment of his map has survived, Reis detailed African, American, and European coastlines along the Atlantic Ocean. Reis also produced a navigational treatise, *The Book on Seafaring*, that incorporated material from Portuguese and

Spanish sources. One hundred years later, the empire's most renowned geographer, Katib Çelebi (1609–1657), relied on Islamic maps, and geographies, as well as the *Atlas Minor* of the Flemish cartographer Gerardus Mercator (1512–1594). Other Turkish cartographers translated maps by Mercator and Joan Blaue (1596–1673), who served as the official map maker for the Dutch East India Company.

A third cross-cultural intellectual exchange resulted from the Jesuit missionary presence in China in the late 1500s to the mid-1700s. Jesuit priests recognized at once that the Chinese court placed a very high priority on discerning significant astronomical events. According to Chinese political theory, the emperor ruled the Middle Kingdom at the pleasure of Heaven, so events in the heavens signified approval or disfavor of an imperial regime. Emperors, then, became heavily invested in ensuring that the important political and social rituals in a given year take place at favorable points on the astronomical calendar. The Chinese Board of Astronomy served the Son of Heaven by forecasting the most fortuitous days for imperial rituals.

The missionaries sought to gain the confidence of influential Confucian scholars and the respect of the emperor by demonstrating the benefits of recent advances in European astronomy. Heliocentric theory, first advanced in Europe by Nicolas Copernicus (1473–1543) and supported by extensive mathematical calculations, gave Jesuit astronomers an advantage. Adam Schall von Bell (1591–1666) and Giacomo Rho (1593–1636) were able to predict astronomical events, such as eclipses, with greater precision and provide a more accurate calendar than their Chinese counterparts. Some Chinese astronomers opposed the foreign innovations and some officials distrusted the priests' ulterior religious motives. Yet others urged the emperor to adapt western science for Chinese uses. Xu Guangqi (1562–1633), a Christian convert, argued that incorporating European mathematics and measuring techniques allowed Chinese astronomers to form a comprehensive scientific structure. Similarly, the Jesuit Matteo Ricci and the Confucian scholar Zou Yuanbian (1551–1624) asserted that western learning derived ultimately from ancient Chinese philosophy. Despite periodic political struggles at the imperial court, Jesuits enjoyed the support of Ming and Qing emperors. The Shunzhi emperor (1638–1661) appointed Schall as director of the Board of Astronomy in 1645, a post held by a Jesuit until 1775. In the field of astronomy, Confucian scholars appropriated significant elements of western learning and brought them into the Chinese intellectual and scientific tradition.

The Chinese were much less receptive to European advances in cartography. Because of their navigational experiences in the 1400s and 1500s, European mariners and map makers revolutionized the understanding of world geography. Building on the cartographic work of Amerigo Vespucci and Sebastian Munster, Abraham Ortelius created the first modern-looking world map in 1570, the *Theatrum Orbis Terrarum* (Theater of the World's Lands). Ortelius's map was the first to incorporate the world's oceans and major land masses into a coherent spherical framework. Cartography in China had also attained a significant degree of nuance and complexity by the mid-sixteenth century, incorporating square grids and sophisticated measurements. In the early 1300s, Zhu Siben produced an influential territorial map of China based on geographic knowledge of Eurasia gleaned from Mongol expansion. This map became the basis of a widely circulated altas known as the *Guang Yutu* (Enlarged Territorial Atlas) in 1555.

The Chinese view of the world stood at odds with the western cartographic tradition that attempted to project an integrated conception of global space. Chinese intellectuals believed the world was flat, with the Middle Kingdom located at the cultural center surrounded by tributary and barbarian lands. Shortly after his arrival in 1582, Matteo Ricci created a world map that he modified from Ortelius, which, out of deference to his hosts, placed China at the center of the globe. Ricci's map, with its comprehension of all the continents and oceans, generated a large amount of interest among intellectual elites. Later other Jesuits, including Niccolo Langobardi, Manuel Dias, and Francesco Sanbiasi, produced newer versions of the Ortelius-Ricci model. While the Jesuit maps stirred interest, they also garnered criticism from Chinese cartographers who rejected the spatial attention given to barbarian lands. As a result, these maps had little long-term influence on Chinese cartography, and the *Guang Yutu* maps remained the most authoritative until the 1800s.

The Kangxi emperor did, however, make use of Jesuit cartographic skill, commissioning them to undertake various mapping projects, and in 1708 he directed them to create an extensive imperial map, which took almost ten years for dozens of Jesuits, divided into working groups to complete. As the Qing expanded into Xinjiang and Tibet later in the 1700s, the emperor dispatched Jesuit survey teams to these territories in order to include them in subsequent editions of the atlas. This Kangxi-Jesuit imperial atlas combined European cartographic technology with Chinese geographic scholarship, since Jesuits and their Chinese and Manchu technicians consulted many local maps. Place names and topographic designations appeared in Chinese styles. Nevertheless, few cartographers outside the imperial palace had access to the Kangxi-Jesuit atlas, so this European–Chinese hybrid actually exerted little influence across the empire.

Jesuit missionaries not only served as conveyors of western learning to China but also functioned as advocates of Chinese culture to consumers in Europe. These dual roles made the Jesuits important mediators of cross-cultural exchange from one end of Eurasia to the other. Consequently, Chinese thought and its application became a prevalent theme in the European Enlightenment of the 1700s. Centered in France, Enlightenment figures advocated the use of rational thought to refashion aspects of society that they identified as illogical, superstitious, and inhumane. The Catholic Church in particular and Christianity in general embodied for many of these intellectuals the height of tyranny and superstition. For these thinkers, the Chinese philosophical tradition appeared as the most potent antidote to Christianity. The emphasis on mutual respect, family honor, political benevolence, and the collective welfare of the community exemplified a rational approach to religion that could supplant Christianity. Voltaire championed Confucian morality, Francois Quesnay praised Confucian agrarianism, and Christian Wolff extolled Confucian philosophy.

Devotees of the Enlightenment formed images of China that fit their own needs. Beyond Jesuit missionaries, most intellectuals did not bother to learn Chinese, and they cherry-picked information that suited their purposes. Thus, just as Chinese elites appropriated facets of western learning for their own needs, Europeans also constructed images of China that primarily served their aspirations at home.

Religious and Intellectual Interconnections

The transmission of religion, culture, and technology accompanied the interaction of peoples around the world in the early modern period.

Growing out of religious reformations in western Europe and western Asia, Christianity and Islam skipped across mountains, plains, and oceans to create worldwide religious bodies. The formation of global Islamic and Christian communities was not a one-directional process in which missionaries simply implanted their faiths among vacuous and compliant societies. Rather indigenous peoples engaged Christianity and Islam with their own cultural frameworks, molding these universal faiths into religious systems they could comprehend and act on. As a result, those who embraced Islam and Christianity created an assortment of syncretistic practices and beliefs that in time came to be identified as idolatry by religious authorities. The global spread of religious belief, then, established links yet also fostered cultural conflicts between disparate regions of the world.

Societies also gained much greater awareness about other peoples and forms of thought from around the world. European ethnographers constructed images of exotic peoples, oriental despots, bloodthirsty cannibals, and noble savages in Asia, Africa, America, and Oceania. Qing gazetteers depicted the barbarian frontier folk in southwestern regions of the empire and, over time, signified how Miao and other peoples were becoming increasingly Chinese. Ottoman travelers also described alien societies to audiences back home. As foreigner travelers introduced new forms of knowledge, illustrated clearly in the fields of cartography and astronomy, intellectuals adapted and domesticated the elements that suited local needs. Asian and European scientists borrowed from one another and, in so doing, pushed science and technology into modernity.

Works Consulted

Axtell, James. *The Invasion Within: The Contest of Cultures in Colonial North America*. Oxford: Oxford University Press, 1985.

Bentley, Jerry H., and Ziegler, Herbert F. *Traditions and Encounters: A Global Perspective on the Past*, vol. 2 *From 1500 to the Present*. 2nd ed. New York: McGraw Hill, 2003.

Ch'en, Kenneth. "Matteo Ricci's Contribution to, and Influence on, Geographical Knowledge in China," *Journal of the American Oriental Society* 59(1939), 325–359.

Cogley, Richard W. *John Eliot's Mission to the Indians before King Philip's War*. Cambridge, Mass.: Harvard University Press, 1999.

Correia-Afonso, John ed. *Letters from the Mughal Court: The First Jesuit Mission to Akbar (1580–1583).* St. Louis, Mo.: Institute of Jesuit Sources, 1981.

Cussen, Celia. "The Search for Idols and Saints in Colonial Peru," *Hispanic American Historical Review* 85(2005), 417–448.

Dankoff, Robert. *An Ottoman Mentality: The World of Evliya Çelebi.* Boston: Brill, 2004.

Deal, David M., and Hostetler, Laura. *The Art of Ethnography: A Chinese "Miao Album."* Seattle: University of Washington Press, 2006.

Elman, Benjamin A. *On Their Own Terms: Science in China, 1550–1900.* Cambridge, Mass.: Harvard University Press, 2005.

French, Katherine L., and Poska, Allyson M. *Women and Gender in the Western Past,* vol. 2 *Since 1500.* Boston: Houghton Mifflin, 2007.

Gladney, Dru G. "Islam in China: Transnationalism or Transgression," in Touraj Atabaki and Sanjyot Mehendale eds. *Central Asia and the Caucasus: Transnationalism and Diaspora.* New York: Routledge, 2004, 184–213.

Goffman, Daniel. *The Ottoman Empire and Early Modern Europe.* Cambridge: Cambridge University Press, 2002.

Greer, Allan, and Bilinkoff, Jodi eds. *Colonial Saints: Discovering the Holy in the Americas, 1500–1800.* New York: Routledge, 2003.

Gunn, Geoffrey C. *First Globalization: The Eurasian Exchange, 1500–1800.* Lanham, Md.: Rowman and Littlefield Publishers, 2003.

Halperin, Charles J. "Russia in the Mongol Empire in Comparative Perspective," *Harvard Journal of Asiatic Studies* 43(1983), 240–255.

Hostetler, Laura. *Qing Colonial Enterprise: Ethnography and Cartography in Early Modern China.* Chicago: University of Chicago Press, 2001.

Hsia, R. Po-Chia. *The World of Catholic Renewal, 1540–1770.* Cambridge: Cambridge University Press, 1998.

İhsanoğlu, Ekmeleddin. *Science, Technology and Learning in the Ottoman Empire.* Burlington, Vt.: Ashgate Publishing Company, 2004.

Inalcik, Halil. *The Ottoman Empire: The Classical Age 1300–1600.* New York: Praeger Publishers, 1973.

Israeli, R. "Islamicization and Sinicization in Chinese Islam," in Nehemia Levtzion ed. *Conversion to Islam.* New York: Holmes & Meier, 1979, 159–176.

Lapidus, Ira M. *A History of Islamic Societies.* 2nd ed. Cambridge: Cambridge University Press, 2002.

Ledyard, Gari. "Cartography in Korea," in J. B. Harley and David Woodward eds. *Cartography in the Traditional East and Southeast Asian Societies.* vol. 2, bk. 2 *The History of Cartography.* Chicago: University of Chicago Press, 1987, 235–345.

Levtzion, N. "Patterns of Islamicization in West Africa," in Nehemia Levtzion ed. *Conversion to Islam.* New York: Holmes & Meier, 1979, 207–216.

Levtzion, Nehemia, and Voll, John O. eds. *Eighteenth Century Renewal and Reform in Islam*. Syracuse, N.Y.: Syracuse University Press, 1987.

Mancall, Peter C. ed. *Travel Narratives from the Age of Discovery: An Anthology*. Oxford: Oxford University Press, 2006.

Marco, Barbara De. "Conversion Practices on the New Mexico Frontier," in James Muldoon ed. *The Spiritual Conversion of the Americas*. Gainesville: University Press of Florida, 2004, 36–56.

Meeuwse, Mark. "Dutch Calvinism and Native Americans: A Comparative Study of the Motivations for Protestant Conversion among the Tupis in Northeastern Brazil (1630–1654) and the Mohawks in Central New York (1690–1710)," in James Muldoon ed. *The Spiritual Conversion of the Americas*. Gainesville: University of Florida Press, 2004, 118–141.

Mills, Kenneth. "The Limits of Religious Coercion in Mid-colonial Peru," in John F. Schwaller ed. *The Church in Colonial Latin America*. Wilmington, Del.: Scholarly Resources, 2000, 147–182.

Monserrate, Antonio. *The Commentary of Father Monserrate, S. J., on His Journey to the Court of Akbar*, J. S. Hoyland and S. N. Bannerjee eds. London, Bombay: Oxford University Press, 1922.

Morgan, David. "Persian Perceptions of Mongols and Europeans," in Stuart B. Schwartz ed. *Implicit Understandings: Observing, Reporting, and Reflecting on the Encounters between Europeans and Other Peoples in the Early Modern Era*. Cambridge: Cambridge University Press, 1994, 201–217.

Muldoon, James. "Introduction," in James Muldoon ed. *The Spiritual Conversion of the Americas*. Gainesville: University Press of Florida, 2004, 1–16.

Mungello, D. E. *The Great Encounter of China and the West, 1500–1800*. 2nd ed. Lanham, Md.: Rowman & Littlefield Publishers, 2005.

Nelson, Howard. "Chinese Maps: An Exhibition at the British Library," *China Quarterly* 58(1974), 357–362.

O'Fahey, R. S. "Islam, State, and Society in Dār Fur," in Nehemia Levtzion ed. *Conversion to Islam*. New York: Holmes & Meier, 1979, 189–206.

Newby, L. J. "'The Pure and True Religion' in China," *Third World Quarterly* 10(1988), 923–947.

Outram, Dorinda. *The Enlightenment*. Cambridge: Cambridge University Press, 1995.

Parker, Geoffrey. *The Military Revolution: Military Innovation and the Rise of the West, 1500–1800*. Cambridge: Cambridge University Press, 1988.

Rawlings, Helen. *Church, Religion and Society in Early Modern Spain*. New York: Palgrave, 2002.

Reid, Anthony. "Early Southeast Asian Categorizations of Europeans," in Stuart B. Schwartz ed. *Implicit Understandings: Observing, Reporting, and Reflecting on the Encounters between Europeans and Other Peoples in the Early Modern Era*. Cambridge: Cambridge University Press, 1994, 268–294.

————. *Southeast Asia in the Age of Commerce 1450–1680*, vol. 2 *Expansion and Crisis*. New Haven, Conn.: Yale University Press, 1988.

Richards, John F. *The Mughal Empire*. Cambridge: Cambridge University Press, 1995.

Ricklefs, M. C. "Six Centuries of Islamicization in Java," in Nehemia Levtzion ed. *Conversion to Islam*. New York: Holmes & Meier, 1979, 100–128.

Subrahmanyam, Sanjay. "Forcing the Doors of Heathendom: Ethnography, Violence, and the Dutch East India Company," in Charles H. Parker and Jerry H. Bentley eds. *Between the Middle Ages and Modernity: Individual and Community in the Early Modern World*. Lanham, Md.: Rowman and Littlefield Publishers, 2007, 131–154.

————. *From the Tagus to the Ganges: Explorations in Connected History*. New Delhi: Oxford University Press, 2005.

Sweetman, David. *Women Leaders in African History*. London: Heinemann, 1984.

Tietze, Andreas. *Mustafa Ali's Description of Cairo of 1599*. Vienna: Verlag Österreichischen Akademie der Wissenschaften, 1975.

Tracy, James D. *Europe's Reformations, 1450–1650*. Lanham, Md.: Rowman & Littlefield Publishers, 1999.

Vaughan, Alden T. "Introduction: Indian-European Encounters in New England, an Annotated Contextual Overview," in Alden T. Vaughan ed. *New England Encounters: Indians and Euroamericans, ca. 1600–1850*. Boston: Northeastern University Press, 1999, 3–40.

Vlahakis, George N., Malaquis, Isabel Maria, Brooks, Nathan M., et al. *Imperialism and Science: Social Impact and Interaction*. Santa Barbara, Calif.: ABC-CLIO, 2006.

Yee, Cordell D. K. "Traditional Chinese Cartography and the Myth of Westernization," in J. B. Harley and David Woodward eds. *Cartography in the Traditional East and Southeast Asian Societies*. vol. 2, bk. 2 *The History of Cartography*. Chicago: University of Chicago Press, 1987, 170–202.

Conclusion

Converging Destinies

At the end of the sixteenth century, contemporaries from around the globe expressed an unshakeable unease at what they feared were uncertain directions in world affairs. In Anatolia, the Turkish intellectual Mustafa Ali felt compelled to write a world history (*The Essence of History*) to make sense of all the war and social turmoil that engulfed the Ottoman Empire. Ali feared that the heyday of the empire was long past and dark days lay ahead. At roughly the same time in Madrid, Philip II of Spain lamented military losses and political rebellion exclaiming, "if this is not the end of the whole world, I think we must be very close to it." And on the eastern edge of Eurasia in Huguang province (south central China), the governmental official Zhang Tao fretted about the corrosive social effects of commercialism. He grumbled, "As the prospect of wealth fueled avarice, the moral order that had held society together gave way . . . Each exploited the other and everyone publicized himself." Given that the Ottoman, Spanish, and Chinese empires lasted into the modern age, these dire observations appear exaggerated from our vantage point in the twenty-first century. Yet there were many people in America, Asia, Africa, and Europe who believed the world was coming to an end. So, for those on the ground in the sixteenth century, the world was changing in unexpected and worrisome ways.[1]

These deep-seated anxieties grew in part out of the large-scale processes of interaction that brought substantial change to societies around the world. We have examined these interactions: empire building, long-distance trade, migration, biological exchange, and cultural diffusion. They were set in motion by the simultaneous expansion of centralized states across Eurasia in the 1400s and 1500s, as societies recovered from domination by the Mongols and decimation by the plague. Over the course of this period, Ming emperors embarked on the conquest of inner Asia; Romanov tsars began a push throughout Siberia; Ottoman, Safavid, and Mughal rulers consolidated large empires from India to Tunisia; and a cluster of European states initiated expansion into the Americas, Africa, and Asia. The simultaneous movement of so many extensive empires was remarkable, even unique, in world history. This pattern of empire building integrated global space for the first time in human history, driving people, animals, goods, and pathogens across continents.

These global interactions made a significant impact on societies around the world by the end of the early modern period. In 1800, the world was radically different from what it had been in 1400. In Africa, traditional centers of political and economic power had disintegrated and the traffic in slaves had exacted a heavy toll on many societies. In America, Europeans and creoles had supplanted and subjugated millions of American and African peoples in creating new societies and new nations. Ongoing engagement with the wider world propelled western European countries on a course of remarkable power and influence that enabled them to dominate the globe in the 1800s and 1900s. Regimes throughout all of Asia underwent a rise-and-fall trajectory over the course of the early modern age. After expanding imperial power and flourishing economically for most of the period, fundamental changes brought about by greater global integration left all Asian regions much weaker by the 1800s. The anxieties of Mustafa Ali, Philip II, and Zhang Tao at the end of the 1500s point to an awareness of the conjunctures that were reshaping their societies and that transformed the world by the beginning of the nineteenth century.

Africa: Moving Toward Integration and Incorporation

How did the regions of Africa fare, as a result of early modern interactions? In the large northern sector that encompassed the Sudanic Belt and the Mediterranean, several distinct geopolitical features stood out at the beginning of the nineteenth century. The large Songhay Empire had fragmented into smaller political units after a Moroccan army marched across the Sahara and routed Songhay forces in 1591. The Hausa city-states, especially Kano and Katsina, continued to thrive through their traditional commercial links to the Mediterranean and through the new ones to the Atlantic. The Hausa states, however, did not retain their independence into the 1800s. Revivalist Muslim clerics roused the pastoral Fulani people of the western Sudan, which spawned jihads against regimes deemed corrupt and unorthodox. Small states, empires on the west coast, such as the Oyo Empire, and the Hausa cities fell to Fulani warriors and became absorbed into the Caliphate of Sokoto that governed most of the Sudan throughout the nineteenth century. The eastern portion of the Sudan, Darfur, Chad, the Sinnar kingdom, but not Ethiopia, underwent heavy Arabization, as the growing merchant class of the region, with its expanded trading connections to the Middle East, became deeply influenced by Arab culture and orthodox Islam.

The contraction of the Ottoman Empire in the eighteenth century allowed the territories of north Africa a great deal of local autonomy. Dynastic rulers presided over Algeria, Tunisia, Libya, and Egypt under the nominal auspices of the Ottomans, except for Morocco, which had successfully resisted Turkish control in the sixteenth century. These states, in partnership with local corsairs (pirates), took advantage of the absence of any significant naval power in the Atlantic by raiding and robbing European and U.S. merchant ships in the region. The trans-Saharan trade continued to tie the north African territories to the Sudan.

The elongated western coast of Africa experienced the full impact of the early modern Atlantic economy and European colonization of America. In the northern region from the western Sudan to the Gulf of Guinea, new states connected to Atlantic commerce, especially the slave trade, rose to prominence. The African states of Oyo, Asante, and Dahomey developed into powerful and prosperous commercial centers that shipped kola nuts, slaves, and gold north across the Sahara and a much larger volume of slaves, as well as gold, to the European entrepôts on the Atlantic coast. The Oyo Empire swallowed up Dahomey in the late seventeenth century, so by 1800 the Oyo and Asante Empires stood as the paramount states in the region. The Oyo, however, did not endure for long, as the Fulani forces that engulfed the Sudan brought down the Oyo in the early 1800s.

The sub-Saharan western coast and central region of Africa were also pulled into the Atlantic orbit. By the end of the seventeenth century, the once powerful kingdoms of Kongo and Ndongo had ceased to exist in any significant way. The Portuguese appetite for slaves to feed sugar plantations brought disruption and turmoil that pitted states against one another, with one side usually allied with the Portuguese or Dutch. The kingdom of Loango, however, avoided the fate of the Kongolese and Ndongolese, profiting immensely from its association with Portuguese and Dutch merchants. By 1800, Loango emerged as the most significant kingdom on the west coast, south of the Sahara.

Rounding out Africa, the eastern coast witnessed the rise of an important empire on the Zimbabwe Plateau and a strong state along the northwestern coast of Lake Victoria. On the Zimbabwe Plateau, the Rozwi Empire dominated the southeastern corner of the continent, and along with the Mutapa kingdom, expelled the Portuguese from the region at the end of the seventeenth century. Based on the widespread cultivation of bananas and the starchy vegetable, plantain, Bugundan kings constructed a stable and strong state on the coast of Lake Victoria. The Swahili cities that had once been such prominent centers of commerce remained stagnant by the end of the nineteenth century, while small tribal societies competed for access to commercial routes connected to the Indian Ocean networks.

In sum, Africa at the close of the early modern period had become more connected to global economic networks and more incorporated into universal religious systems. The northern half of the continent experienced intense Islamization and moderate Arabization as a result of jihadist campaigns and trading connections to the Middle East. The Atlantic commercial economy, centered around the slave trade, drew in the western coast and some central regions, giving rise to new states and destroying others. The loss of millions to enslavement in America and Asia distorted gender roles in local societies and fostered violence between territories. Interior kingdoms prospered from connections to maritime commerce in the Indian and Atlantic Oceans. European settlements remained small and confined to the western coastline; they stayed that way until the period of intense imperialism in the late nineteenth century. The only two sizable European holdings in Africa in 1800 were a Portuguese settlement in Angola and a Dutch colony in Cape Town that England took over in 1806.

America: New Multiethnic Societies

In contrast to Africa's growing, gradual interconnections to global commercial networks and universal religious systems, America underwent sweeping transformations in the early modern period. Peoples from three continents – America, Europe, and Africa – converged, forging entirely new multiethnic and multicultural societies in a hemisphere previously unknown to those who lived outside of it.

Owing to the impact of these interactions, America was radically different in 1800 from what it had been in 1492. Colonized by the Iberian countries, Central and South America formed a distinct cultural zone bound together by the blending of Iberian, American, and African traditions. The common political denominator in 1800 that tied these diverse regions together continued to be Spain and Portugal. Spanish colonial authorities lay claim to, if not effectively controlled, all of Central America, most of South America, the southern regions of North America from Texas to California in the west, and Louisiana to portions of Florida in the east. In addition, Spain asserted authority to areas in the Great Plains of North America, Cuba, the Dominican Republic, and other islands in the Caribbean. For its part, Portugal maintained jurisdiction over Brazil. The rambling Spanish Empire fell under the centralized rule of two viceroys, one in Lima and one in Mexico City, who governed on behalf of the Spanish monarchy. Brazil possessed a similar political organization.

Widespread sexual interaction between Americans, Europeans, Africans, and their descendants produced multiethnic societies in which the range of pigmentation reflected the spectrum of power and status. Peninsulares, or the Spanish in America, wielded all political authority, much to the chagrin of European creoles, who despite their economic prosperity, possessed little formal political power. Mixed race peoples, such as mestizos, mullatos, and zambos, fell considerably lower on the social scale, while indigenous Americans and enslaved Africans ranked at the bottom of society. Slavery remained an institution in Central and South America until the first half of the nineteenth century, when most countries began abolishing it. Cuba and Brazil were the last American countries to manumit all slaves; they did so in 1880 and 1888, respectively.

By 1800, Spain and Portugal were spent powers in Europe, having undergone sustained economic and political decline during the 1600s. This weakness, along with the revolutionary ideal of political liberty that was gaining traction among creoles in the early nineteenth century, signaled the waning days of Iberian empires in America and the beginning of independent nation building. Between 1810 and 1822, the peoples of Central and South America established their independence from Spain and Portugal.

The historical trajectory of the Caribbean closely followed the fortunes of the slave trade and plantation economies in the early modern period. In 1800, Spanish, English, French, and Dutch planters still were running sugar-producing plantations under the protection and support of colonial regimes. Slavery persisted in many islands long after the abolition of the Atlantic trade in the first two decades of the 1800s, just as colonial operations persisted well into the twentieth century. The lone exception was the republic of Haiti, created in 1795 from the French colony of St. Domingue. A combined force of slaves and free persons of color, led by Toussaint L'Ouverture, overthrew the French regime and founded the second oldest independent republic in the western hemisphere after the United States.

In North America, one of the most significant alterations was the presence of a new neo-European state, the United States of America. Fixed by the 1783 Treaty of Paris, the borders of the new nation ranged from the Great Lakes in the north, to the Mississippi River in the west, to the thirty-first parallel that separated the United States from Spanish Florida in the south. Right from the start the young government under its first president, George Washington, made plans to expand settlement into lands occupied by native nations and tribes. The birth of the United States in fact marked a new and intensive phase in the regression and retrenchment of native peoples in North America. Twenty years of war had destroyed native villages and properties, at a time when some U.S. officials were calling for the removal of all natives from the country's territorial boundaries. A long pattern of conflict, negotiation, warfare, renegotiation, and forced removal pushed native peoples farther west and into marginal areas in

Oklahoma and the Dakotas. The United States, however, was charting a course of expansion, industrialization, and nation building at the start of the nineteenth century.

Rigid attitudes about race by European creoles who dominated North American societies, combined with the labor needs of southern planters, thwarted attempts to abolish slavery throughout the United States at its constitutional convention in 1789. By 1804, all the northern states, focused on industry and trade, banned slavery, but the southern agricultural states of Maryland, Georgia, South Carolina, North Carolina, and Virginia continued to allow the practice. It took over seventy years after the adoption of the constitution and a bloody civil war to bring slavery in North America to an end.

The cumulative effects of global interactions in America were transformative. Indeed, of all regions in the world, American societies underwent the most widespread change and became home to new societies composed of European, African, and indigenous peoples.

Asia: The Rise and Decline of Empires

Many regions across Asia profited immensely from the increased tempo of cultural engagement for nearly all of the early modern period. The most striking feature across the world's largest land mass, comprising almost 30 percent of the earth's total land area, was the rise of enormous centralized empires. Empire builders in China, Russia, India, Anatolia, and Iran took advantage of revived commercial activity and population growth to consolidate political control over new territories and new peoples. By the end of the early modern period, however, the large states of Asia (aside from Russia) had either disappeared (Safavid), gone into serious decline (Mughal, Ottoman), or showed unmistakable signs of regression (China). Despite the weakening of these imperial regimes, certain byproducts of empire building survived the period: the expansion of orthodox Islam, enlarged trade associations, and pronounced ethnic assimilation.

By 1800, almost all Asian regimes had fallen into a state of political and economic stagnation that enabled European powers to gain greater leverage from their colonial stations. The degree of decline varied significantly from China, which still boasted one of the world's most productive economies, to Iran, which had disintegrated into warring territorial kingdoms. Similarly, the factors that contributed to degeneration stemmed from circumstances particular to each state. Despite these caveats, a wide-ranging inertia bred by the striking success of imperial societies from the 1400s through the 1600s contributed to a general crisis at the end of the 1700s.

China in 1800 remained an economic powerhouse and imperial giant. Nonetheless, telltale signs of decay had become evident to foreign observers. The economy supplied an extraordinarily high level of demand, which ensnared producers in traditional processes of production rather than allowing them to experiment with technologies that ultimately could bring much greater yields. Agriculture and industry persisted as labor-intensive operations because labor was cheap. As a result, producers lacked incentives to invest in mechanization, and the empire offered farmers no additional land to bring under cultivation. Chinese foreign policy had grown tentative, so imperial expansion had ground to a standstill. Finally, in the early 1700s, English merchants identified a product they could exchange with Chinese brokers in lieu of silver: opium. Demand for the addictive narcotic, which was smoked, grew precipitously over the course of the 1700s, from 200 chests a year in 1729 to 10,000 a year in the early 1800s. The sale of opium enabled the British to overcome the imbalance in the value of trade goods that had favored the Chinese since the 1500s. European powers took advantage of Chinese stagnation and subjected the Middle Kingdom to the humiliation of western imperialism in the nineteenth century.

India experienced a remarkably rapid descent in the eighteenth century, chiefly due to imperial overreach by the emperor Aurangezeb in the early 1700s. Extending the borders of Mughal domains into the Deccan region of southern India strained the royal treasury, provoked rebellions from overtaxed peasants, and stoked the resentments of small Hindu rulers (Marathas). Subsequent emperors could not sustain these borders, so they granted a great deal of autonomy to the Marathas. Then in the 1720s, various Maratha princes started rolling back Mughal expansion, pushing imperial control back to the northern region around Delhi. External invasions from Afghanistan and Iran hastened the disintegration of the state.

Even though the Mughal Empire came to pieces in the early 1700s, the Indian economy proved resilient until the last quarter of the century. Like the situation in China, a large population provided a cheap labor force, which produced a high volume of agricultural and industrial products, including a variety of cotton and other textiles, steel, pottery, and opium. Textile producers lost a significant domestic market with the fragmentation of the central state. As the English East India Company embarked on a policy of territorial conquest in the 1750s, company officials used the tax revenue it extracted from local areas to pay for goods it exported to Europe and China. British troops in the pay of the company conquered Bengal, the industrial core of India, in 1757 and placed it at the disposal of company needs. By the end of the 1700s, large regions of India had succumbed to British pressure, while the economy of the subcontinent grew raw products for European manufacturers. India became a British colony in the mid-nineteenth century until winning independence in 1948.

The Ottoman state went into an extended slide in the 1700s, manifested by losses on the battlefield that chipped away at the edges of empire. In the 1770s, Russian troops defeated Turkish Janissaries on several occasions, clipping Ottoman territory around the Black Sea and Caucasus Mountains. Subsequently, Ottoman regions in the Balkans, north Africa, and all of Arabia began to slip away as well. While the empire was shrinking at the fringes, a stubborn refusal to adopt new technologies by conservative ulama played a role in weakening economic production. As a result, Ottomans lost ground to competitors from Europe who produced items of equivalent quality at higher volumes and for lower prices. English, Dutch, and French mercantile companies also gained more control over trade routes and bypassed Ottoman territories. Ottoman elites with significant buying power continued to acquire fine textiles and clothing, but they purchased them from France and Italy rather than from Turkish manufacturers. In addition, important changes in the state structure bled the empire of revenue and governmental efficiency. The Janissary corps underwent substantial reductions with the loss of effective Turkish control over the Balkans. Without renewed waves of recruits committed to serve the sultan and his state, longstanding Janissaries began to look after their own interests. Sultans had to rely increasingly on Turkish landholders to carry out the functions of the state; these officials worked primarily to carve out privileges and revenues for their family dynasties. The Ottoman Empire retained staying power as a geopolitical force in eastern Europe and the Middle East throughout the 1800s, although it did so from an increasingly economic, military, and political disadvantage.

Because of its Siberian conquest in the 1600s, Russia came onto the geopolitical scene as an important power in Europe by 1800. The tsars, Peter the Great (1672–1725) and Catherine the Great (1762–1796), had successfully subdued the Boyar nobility, constructed a strong centralized state, and expanded south and east at the expense of the Ottoman Empire and Poland. Russia staked a claim to the northern region of the Black Sea, pushing the Ottomans out of the Crimea. A short time later, Catherine's forces gained control of Polish and Lithuanian territories and participated in the partition of Poland with France and Austria in the 1790s. The weakness of the Ottomans and the Baltic states also facilitated Russian imperial expansion. Acquisitions in northeastern Europe pulled Russia into the orbit of European power struggles in the nineteenth century, prompting Napoleon's invasion in 1812.

The growth of state and empire, however, masked the weak productive capacity of the economy. Russian agriculture and industry was essentially stuck in the middle ages with feudal landlords ruling over millions of serfs, few urban centers, and minimal mechanization. Other more dynamic agricultural models, such as capitalistic organization in Europe or state regulation in China, eluded Russia until the second half of the 1800s. Russia required large numbers of cultivators to produce food, which restricted mechanized production of industrial goods. A lack of capital available for investment also greatly limited industrial innovation. Consequently, Russia was drawn into geopolitical affairs without the productive capacity to compete effectively.

Maritime Asia and Oceania came under growing European dominance at the end of the early modern period. All European powers in Asian waters had competed for access to trade goods and sought to manipulate commercial routes by conquering strategic sites on the coastlines. From its headquarters in Batavia (Jakarta), the Dutch brought more territory in Indonesia under colonial control in the 1740s and in the nineteenth century, the Dutch exercised hegemony over the entire archipelago. At the same time, the English East India Company expanded its reach from Bengal across large portions of India. By 1800, British interests were becoming the dominant ones in south

Asia. Spain, which had colonized the Philippines in the late 1500s, held onto the islands until the late 1800s.

By the end of the eighteenth century, British, French, and Dutch officials were exploring and making contact with peoples across Oceania. James Cook traveled around Australia, New Zealand, Tahiti, Hawaii, and other islands from 1768 to 1779. He published an account of his voyages, which generated fervent interest in England and on the European continent. Thereafter, British and French merchants opened exchanges in Oceania and set up outposts on island groups in the western Pacific. On the heels of Cook's reconnaissance of Australia, the British government set up a settler colony in 1788 composed mainly of convicted criminals. For fifty years, Australia served as a large penal colony within the burgeoning British Empire.

Japan was only one of a very few locations in maritime Asia that managed to chart a course independent of western influence. The Tokugawa shogunate in the 1600s had expelled all foreigners, violently eradicated all vestiges of Christianity, and stipulated a policy of isolation. Tokugawa officials did not rigorously enforce this rule, since Dutch, English, and Chinese merchants were granted limited access to Japanese commerce at a constructed island in Nagasaki Bay. Though Japanese merchants were prohibited from traveling outside the country, authorities routinely overlooked those who did. A period of peace, internal stability, and moderate commercial success characterized Japanese society at the beginning of the nineteenth century.

At the dawn of the modern era, most regions in Asia were heading in a very different direction from their bearing during most of the early modern period. The rise of centralized empires, commercial prosperity, and cultural optimism gave way to political weakness, economic vulnerability, and social insularity. Dominance from the 1400s to the 1700s cultivated an ethos for imperial rule, military operations, and economic production that grew stale by 1800 and obstructed innovation and adaptation.

Europe: From the Middle Ages to Modernity

Europe's early modern trajectory represented the direct antithesis to the Asian arc of rise and fall. In 1400, western Eurasia formed a cultural backwater of feuding princes and squabbling churchmen, yet in

1800 a handful of nation-states stood on the brink of world domination. The processes of interaction that integrated world societies as never before enabled merchant elites and political states to accumulate enormous wealth, develop strong states at home and durable empires abroad, dispatch settlers to America and South Africa, and establish long-distance commercial operations. These achievements positioned European states to embark on a course of unbridled imperialism in the 1800s and 1900s.

Worldwide movements and exchanges contributed to rising European ascendancy by the early nineteenth century, though growth was quite uneven across the continent. Those states that were able to participate in the rise of the Atlantic economy and overseas colonial ventures gained considerable economic advantages. By 1800 England had surpassed its Iberian, French, and Dutch rivals and formed, along with France, the richest and strongest nation on the continent. France had profited from it merchant empires and had constructed a highly centralized state under Louis XIV, which was a dominating force on the continent. The English East India companies propelled the English on their way to empire in India and Asia, while the French under Napoleon (1799–1815) readied themselves for an imperial spread across Europe. Though Napoleon's empire was short-lived, France remained a continental power until World War I. Squeezed by France on the continent and England on the high seas, the Netherlands and Belgium (independent after 1830) persisted as viable economic engines, if no longer as significant geopolitically.

Spain, Portugal, and the Italian states had moved to the periphery among the constellation of European countries. Owing to its long involvement in wars on the continent and overseas, Spain had completely overextended itself by the mid-seventeenth century. Most of the American wealth that came into Spanish ports passed right on through the country to financial institutions in northern Europe. Spain did not develop an industrial or financial infrastructure, so when Peruvian and Mexican silver dried up, Spanish officials had little to show for it. By 1800, Spain was losing its grip on its Central and South American colonies. Portugal had suffered because of rivalry with Spain on the continent and with other colonial powers in Asia and America. Portugal actually was absorbed into the Spanish Hapsburg monarchy from 1580 to 1640. As the driving focus of the European commercial economy shifted from the Mediterranean to the Atlantic, the Italian city-states lost their position as the premier entrepôt for Asian goods. Northern Italy also turned into a primary battleground between the Valois monarchy of France and the Hapsburgs in the first half of the 1500s as both dynasties sought to incorporate the rich lands and cities into their realms.

Although cut off from the Atlantic and Mediterranean, Prussia and Austria constituted the strongest states in central Europe. The ancestral lands of the Hapsburgs, Austria continued to be an important factor in the region due to its historic place in the Holy Roman Empire. Austria annexed Hungary at the end of the 1600s and continued to hold its own despite persistent wars with other emergent powers in the region, Prussia, Russia, and the Ottoman Empire. Prussia rose to great prominence in the 1600s and 1700s due to the formidable military state created by the Hohenzollern monarchs. Despite Prussia's limited land area, Frederick William the Great Elector (r. 1713–1740) and Frederick the Great (r. 1740–1788) constructed a highly efficient bureaucracy and highly disciplined army that incorporated the nobles into service or military roles. Prussian merchants actively participated in trade with Russian, Swedish, and Baltic counterparts in commercial networks in the Baltic Sea. Consequently, Prussia took possession of rich territories, including the bustling manufacturing region of Silesia in the 1740s. Prussian chancellors built on these gains in the 1800s to form the core region of a unified Germany in 1871.

In addition to powerful states, another significant feature in Europe at the beginning of the 1800s was the industrialization that was getting underway in England. The impulse for mechanized production originated in the textile crafts in England from the 1750s to 1800, where demand was high, raw materials were plentiful, labor was available, and capital was accessible. Once mechanization in this industry gained momentum, it led to the discovery of steam power, generated mass production in other industries, and inspired the development of railway and motorized naval transportation. From 1800 to 1850, industrialization spread to other parts of Europe, first in Belgium and France, and to the United States. By 1900, most regions of Europe were, if not fully industrialized, at least headed in that direction.

Several factors contributed to the onset of industrialization that arose from early modern processes of interaction. American and

African wealth flowed into Europe from the 1500s through the 1700s. In addition to precious metals, materials for industrial applications, like natural oil products, wood, coal, and iron, as well as raw products for manufacture, such as cotton, sugar, and indigo, fueled European factories. Just as American products provided the material basis for industrialization, enslaved Africans and coerced Americans supplied most of the labor for the extraction of these resources. Another important element in the inception of European industrialization was the financial capital accumulated from the Atlantic economy and the American colonies. Profits from the slave trade; from sugar, cotton, and tobacco production; and from the mining of metals, created vast sums of wealth for European states and commercial organizations. This meant that enormous amounts of money were available for the capital investment that was necessary for starting up a factory, building a railroad, or developing technological research. Early modern commercial operations also facilitated the growth and maturation of financial institutions to lend capital and extend credit.

Thus, Europe on the eve of the modern age had undergone tremendous changes that transformed small, decentralized kingdoms into powerful states, some of which had maritime empires in America, Asia, and Africa. The possibilities for profit propelled Europeans overseas and the cultural exchanges greatly influenced societies at home. These interactions closely intertwined the destiny of Europe with societies around the world.

Global Interdependence and Competition

The global sweep of people into new places brought extensive changes to every region of the world over the course of the early modern period. Access to new international networks of trade and the diffusion of orthodox Islam created new states and empires in the Sudan and along western Africa. Millions of enslaved Africans dispersed their native traditions and cultures to America and Asia due to the global demand for labor. America and Oceania were completely transformed by the dissemination of foreign pathogens and the acquisitive ambitions of European peoples. Indigenes, migrants, and colonists constructed new societies and new cultures that have left a permanent legacy in the modern world. Large empires rose in Asia engulfing most of the continental land mass and promoting intense commercial prosperity in maritime regions. Success, however, led to stagnation and decline as these empires relied on traditional agricultural and military technologies to deal with population pressures and external threats to imperial regimes. Europe remarkably became a world power, driven by aggressive political and commercial elites in the quest for land, trade, and Christian converts. Global interaction thus inaugurated a new chapter in history that brought isolated regions of the world together into integrated networks of interdependence and competition.

Works Consulted

Brook, Timothy. *The Confusions of Pleasure: Commerce and Culture in Ming China*. Berkeley: University of California Press, 1998.

Campbell, I. C. *A History of the Pacific Islands*. Berkeley: University of California Press, 1989.

Ehret, Christopher. *The Civilizations of Africa: A History to 1800*. Charlottesville: The University Press of Virginia, 2002.

Fernandez-Armesto, Felipe. *The World: A History*, vol. 2. Upper Saddle River, N.J.: Pearson Prentice-Hall, 2007.

Fleischer, Cornell. *Bureaucrat and Intellectual in the Ottoman Empire: The Historian Mustafa Âli (1541–1600)*. Princeton, N.J.: Princeton University Press, 1986.

Goffman, Daniel. *The Ottoman Empire and Early Modern Europe*. Cambridge: Cambridge University Press, 2002.

Johansen, Bruce E. *The Native Peoples of North America: A History*, 2 vols. Westport, Conn.: Praeger, 2005.

Mungello, D. E. *The Great Encounter of China and the West, 1500–1800*, 2nd ed. Lanham, Md.: Rowman & Littlefield Publishers, 2005.

Nash, Gary B. *Red, White, and Black: The Peoples of Early America*. 3rd ed. Englewood Cliffs, NJ: Prentice Hall Publishers, 1992.

Reid, Anthony. *Southeast Asia in the Age of Commerce 1450–1680*, vol. 2 *Expansion and Crisis*. New Haven, Conn.: Yale University Press, 1988.

Richards, John F. *The Mughal Empire*. Cambridge: Cambridge University Press, 1995.

Parker, Geoffrey. "The Place of Tudor England in the Messianic Vision of Philip II," *Transactions of the Royal Historical Society* 12(2002), 167–222.

Shillington, Kevin. *History of Africa*, 2nd ed. New York: Palgrave Macmillan, 1995.

Subrhamanyam, Sanjay. "Connected Histories: Notes Towards a Reconfiguration of Early Modern Eurasia," *Modern Asian Studies* 31(1997), 735–762.

———. "On World Historians in the Sixteenth Century," *Representations* 91 (2005), 26–57.

Tierney, Brian, and Painter, Sidney. *Western Europe in the Middle Ages 300–1475*. 6th ed. Boston: McGraw Hill, 1999.

Trigger, Bruce E., and Swagerty, William R. "Entertaining Strangers: North America in the Sixteenth Century," in Bruce G. Trigger and Wilcomb E. Washburn eds. *The Cambridge History of the Native Peoples of the Americas*, vol. 1, pt. 1 *North America*. Cambridge: Cambridge University Press, 1996, 325–398.

Notes

1. European States and Overseas Empires

1. M. N. Pearson, *The New Cambridge History of India*, vol. 1, *The Portuguese in India* (Cambridge: Cambridge University Press, 1987), 20.

2. Asian States and Territorial Empires

1. Matteo Ricci, "A Discourse of the Kingdom of China," in Peter C. Mancall, ed. *Travel Narratives from the Age of Discovery: An Anthology* (Oxford: Oxford University Press, 2006), 180.

3. International Markets and Global Exchange Networks

1. Charles Johnson, *A General History of the Robberies and Murders of the Most Notorious Pirates* (1724) quoted in Hans Turley, *Rum, Sodomy, and the Lash: Piracy, Sexuality, and Masculine Identity* (New York: New York University Press, 1999), 1.

4. The Movement of Peoples and Diffusion of Cultures

1. <www.cilt.org.uk/key/trends2005/trends2005_community.pdf>; David Eltis, "Introduction: Migration and Agency in Global History," in David Eltis ed., *Coerced and Free Migration: Global Perspectives* (Stanford, Calif.: Stanford University Press, 2002), 3.
2. Gary B. Nash, *Red, White, and Black: The Peoples of Early North America*, 3rd ed. (New York: Prentice-Hall, 1992), 39.
3. George Sanderlin ed. and trans., *Bartolomé de las Casas: A Selection of His Writings* (New York: Alfred A. Knopf, 1971), 100.

4. Matthew 2:1–2 in *De Nyew Testament: The New Testament in Gullah Sea Island Creole with Marginal Text of the King James Version* (New York: American Bible Society, 2005), 4.

5. The Formation of New Demographic and Ecological Structures

1. Thomas Robert Malthus, *An Essay on the Principle of Population*, Philip Appleman ed., 2nd ed. (New York: W. W. Norton & Company, 2004), 19.
2. Malthus, *Principle of Population*, 43.
3. Quoted in Sheldon Watts, *Epidemics and History: Disease, Power, and Imperialism* (New Haven, Conn.: Yale University Press, 1997), 93.
4. John Cummins ed., *The Voyages of Christopher Columbus: Columbus' Own Journal of Discovery Restored and Translated* (New York: St. Martin's Press, 1992), 104–105.
5. Bernal Días, *The Conquest of New Spain*, J. M. Cohen ed. (London: Penguin, 1963), 149.
6. John F. Richards, *The Unending Frontier: An Environmental History of the Early Modern World* (Berkeley: University of California Press, 2003), 369.

6. The Transmission of Religion and Culture

1. Antonio Monserrate, *The Commentary of Father Monserrate, S. J., on His Journey to the Court of Akbar*, J. S. Hoyland and S. N. Bannerjee eds. (London, Bombay: Oxford University Press, 1922), 131.
2. Quoted from James Axtell, *The Invasion Within: The Contest of Cultures in Colonial North America* (Oxford: Oxford University Press, 1985), 80.
3. Quoted in Robert Dankoff, *An Ottoman Mentality: The World of Evliya Çelebi* (Boston: Brill, 2004), 59.
4. Laura Hostetler, *Qing Colonial Enterprise: Ethnography and Cartography in Early Modern China* (Chicago: University of Chicago Press, 2001), 150.
5. Amerigo Vespucci, *Mundus Novus* (1504) in *Travel Narratives from the Age of Discovery: An Anthology*, Peter C. Mancall ed. (Oxford: Oxford University Press, 2006), 220.
6. Hostetler, *Qing Enterprise*, 155.
7. John Correia-Afonso ed., *Letters from the Mughal Court: The First Jesuit Mission to Akbar (1580–1583)*, (St. Louis, Mo.: Institute of Jesuit Sources, 1981), 22.

Conclusion: Converging Destinies

1. Cornell Fleischer, *Bureaucrat and Intellectual in the Ottoman Empire: The Historian Mustafa Âli (1541–1600)* (Princeton, N.J.: Princeton University

Press, 1986), 243; Geoffrey Parker, "The Place of Tudor England in the Messianic Vision of Philip II of Spain," *Transactions of the Royal Historical Society* 12 (2002), 180; Timothy Brook, *The Confusions of Pleasure: Commerce and Culture in Ming China* (Berkeley: University of California Press, 1998), 1–3.

Index

CPSIA information can be obtained
at www.ICGtesting.com
Printed in the USA
LVOW03s0012180817
545394LV00003B/164/P